STUDIES IN IMPERIALISM

general editor John M. MacKenzie

When the 'Studies in Imperialism' series was founded more than twenty-five years ago, emphasis was laid upon the conviction that 'imperialism as a cultural phenomenon had as significant an effect on the dominant as on the subordinate societies'. With more than ninety books published, this remains the prime concern of the series. Cross-disciplinary work has indeed appeared covering the full spectrum of cultural phenomena, as well as examining aspects of gender and sex, frontiers and law, science and the environment, language and literature, migration and patriotic societies, and much else. Moreover, the series has always wished to present comparative work on European and American imperialism, and particularly welcomes the submission of books in these areas. The fascination with imperialism, in all its aspects, shows no sign of abating, and this series will continue to lead the way in encouraging the widest possible range of studies in the field. 'Studies in Imperialism' is fully organic in its development, always seeking to be at the cutting edge, responding to the latest interests of scholars and the needs of this ever-expanding area of scholarship.

Empire of scholars

D1706354

Manchester University Press

Empire of scholars

UNIVERSITIES, NETWORKS AND THE BRITISH ACADEMIC WORLD 1850–1939

Tamson Pietsch

MANCHESTER UNIVERSITY PRESS

The right of Tamson Pietsch to be identified as the author of this work has been asserted by her in accordance with the Copyright, Designs and Patents Act 1988.

Published by Manchester University Press
Altrincham Street, Manchester M1 7JA, UK
www.manchesteruniversitypress.co.uk

British Library Cataloguing-in-Publication Data is available

Library of Congress Cataloging-in-Publication Data is available

ISBN 978 0 7190 9930 4 *paperback*

First published by Manchester University Press in hardback 2013

This paperback edition first published 2015

The publisher has no responsibility for the persistence or accuracy of URLs for any external or third-party internet websites referred to in this book, and does not guarantee that any content on such websites is, or will remain, accurate or appropriate.

Printed by Lightning Source

CONTENTS

GENERAL EDITOR'S INTRODUCTION

Empires invariably promote the dispersal of institutions based on metropolitan precedents. This was certainly true of the British Empire, which distributed a whole range of such bodies, often founded on European models (but soon diverging from them) around the world. These may be divided into the religious and the secular, although at times (as in the educational and medical fields) the two could be intertwined. Among the secular can be found botanic gardens, libraries, museums, schools, various intellectual societies, both literary and scientific, zoos, and eventually colleges and universities. Some of these, particularly in India, have their origins in the late eighteenth and early nineteenth centuries, but the later Victorian era was the classic time of great expansion for such institutions. Tertiary colleges had appeared in Canada and Australia by the 1850s; a few students were attending the South African College at the Cape in the same era; and universities were founded in India in the aftermath of the 1857 Revolt, but in the last decades of the century their spread around British colonies was rapid, particularly in areas of extensive white settlement.

This book is the first to chart the development of universities in the British Empire, usefully starting with the foundations of tertiary education in the period between the beginning of the nineteenth century and 1880. As with so many of the other bodies mentioned above, the creation of universities became an essential marker of colonial 'development', a means whereby colonies could assert their own maturing identities, expand their elites, and form the cadres that would be employed in and facilitate the emergence of the political, religious, intellectual and educational institutions within their borders. As Pietsch points out, however, it would be wrong to see these processes purely in terms of the relationship between the centre and the peripheries of empire, as part of a process of unidirectional dispersal of ideas, institutional forms and personnel. It was a good deal more complex than that. As she notes, we should also observe inter-colonial influences, a complex web of intermeshing connections which brought the local and the global together, ultimately producing reverse flows and influences, as well as wider relationships within the Anglophone world, notably with the United States.

The reader will find here explorations of the manner in which personal networks could be vital in these processes, the ways in which appointments were made, and through them the formation of the characteristics of the various colonial institutions. But we should be aware that it had been essentially a British 'white' (and usually male) world. Before 1914, at the very least, women and other races were invariably excluded. The twentieth century was to be well advanced before these wider forms of global inclusion began to feature within a truly interactive Anglophone academia. The beginnings of change would indeed only come about under the influence of the world wars of that century. From the First World War onwards, we hear of the various means by which the more mature American universities began to influence first Canada and later other colonies. The book particularly examines the manner in which the scientific disciplines were influenced by these cross-currents, as well as the remarkable emergence of notable figures from colonial backgrounds who became key figures in Britain, not least influencing developments before and after the Second World War, for example in atomic physics. As these processes accelerated, the old model of imperial influence and exchanges began to decline. Colonial universities increasingly became part of a global network of institutions throughout the Anglophone world and beyond. Nevertheless, as this book suggests, we should be wary of the notion of 'globalisation' until relatively recent times. It was only then that colonial universities participated in, and sometimes led, the full opening out of university education both to women and to indigenous peoples. It was only in the era of the (now defunct) Inter-University Council for Higher Education Overseas, established in 1946 (a body on which I served at one part in my career) that universities in the non-settler territories were fully acknowledged along with those in the 'old' dominions.

This notable book is based upon research conducted in Australia, Canada, New Zealand, South Africa and the United Kingdom. It makes a striking contribution not only to the history of tertiary education and universities in many parts of the world, but also to studies of what has been called 'imperial careering' (in this case of academics), of the emergence and increasing specialisation of scientific disciplines, of the creation of wider Anglophone networks, and of the development of wider access to the tertiary educational sector. Useful appendices list foundation dates of colleges and universities across the British Empire and also chart those institutions which had affiliated status with the University of Oxford. There is every indication that the interest in the historic development of the university sector across the globe, as well as its myriad intellectual and institutional connections, is currently growing. This book constitutes a key landmark in such studies.

John M. MacKenzie

PREFACE AND ACKNOWLEDGEMENTS

In many ways this book began more than fifteen years ago at the University of Adelaide, where I frequently spent undergraduate seminars gazing at the fading photographs of past history professors hanging on the wall. George Cockburn Henderson, Keith Hancock, G. V. Portus, and Hugh Stretton all stared down at me, and written after all their names were the letters *M.A. (Oxon)*. I cannot have been anything but dimly aware of this at the time, and neither do I remember being especially conscious of the uniform image of the white, male scholar they presented. However, when some years later their path to Oxford was one that I too followed, I began to wonder.

Initially I wanted to write about ideas. I wanted to know what they meant to people, where they came from, and how they got made, particularly in the context of the British Empire. But aware of my own unlikely passage to Oxford, and with the Adelaide professors still staring down at me, it seemed impossible to do this without thinking about the people who made knowledge, and the institutional structures and contexts that made them. I realised that before I could write about ideas I needed to know a lot more about the worlds that produced them – and academia seemed an obvious place to begin.

This study focuses on the elite world of universities in the United Kingdom and the settler colonies, and on the white, middle-class men who inhabited them. As instruments of culture and expertise, these were institutions that helped extend colonial rule, and the knowledge produced by those who worked in them was dependent upon a host of situated relationships with local agents and actors whose participation has since been erased. My focus, however, is not on these expanding and expansionist aspects of universities but rather on their internal practices, structures and organisation. Not all readers will be sympathetic to this endeavour, but I hope this book will encourage them to think in new ways about the history of subjects and institutions they know well.

This book is therefore about the origins of my own academic career. It is my attempt to understand the system of which I am part, the traces it has left upon me, and the disparities that continue to characterise it. It is thus doubly important that I acknowledge those who have helped me in the course of its development. I am grateful to the Rhodes Trust, the University of Oxford History Faculty, the Menzies

Centre for Australian Studies, the University of Sydney, Corpus Christi College (Oxford) and, most recently, Brunel University in London, for funding various iterations of this project and for the confidence such funding inspires. Above all I am indebted to Oxford's New College. For eight years it granted me friendship and a home, and it was during my time there as the Sir Christopher Cox Junior Fellow that most of this book was written. I would be remiss if I did not extend particular thanks to Michael Burden, Caroline Thomas, Jane Shaw, Ruth Harris, and Laura Marcus for many a restorative glass of wine and walk around the garden, as well as to the crowd of regular diners who spent countless evenings with me discussing Other Things. Aspects of this project were developed in my doctoral research, and I thank Jose Harris and John Darwin for guiding me through that process and for their wisdom since. At Corpus, Jay Sexton and John Watts were the best of colleagues, and together with Andrew Thompson, Saul Dubow, Martin Conway, Janet Wilson, Julia Horne, Geoffrey Sherington, Roy McLeod and Frank Bongiorno, they helped knock some of the edges off me and my arguments. During my time at Oxford I was fortunate to be part of a group of young scholars working in the Department of History. I particularly thank Rob Fletcher, Ben Mountford, Ali Raza, Ian Desai and Gerard McCann for keeping the faith with the Transnational and Global History seminar, and Robert Priest, Erika Hanna and Frances Flanagan for continuing to talk to me about cultural history.

Numerous librarians and archivists have assisted me in the course of my research. I wish especially to acknowledge the staff at Rhodes House, the Bodleian Library, Archives New Zealand, the National Archives, the British Library and Adelaide, Birmingham, Cape Town, McGill, Melbourne, Queen's, Sydney, and Toronto universities for their many kindnesses. I am grateful to Rebecca Hodes for her research assistance in the Cape Town archives, to Micha Lazarus for his editorial work, and to the publishers of *History of Education* and the Institute of Historical Research for permission to incorporate work that has already been published elsewhere. Especial thanks go to Elleke Boehmer, Saul Dubow, Frances Flanagan, Joyce Goodman, Ruth Harris, Julia Horne, Matthew Houlbrook, Ben Mountford, Wilf Prest, Robert Priest, Deryck Schreuder, Geoffrey Sherington, and to my anonymous readers. Having better things to do, you generously gave your time to reading parts of this manuscript when it was less than respectable, and your comments have improved it immeasurably. For its shortcomings, I remain responsible.

Finally I'm grateful to my parents and to Tim and Ann for helping me towards that seminar room in Adelaide, and to Vesna, Maria, Charles, John and Lynne for opening up the world beyond it. Many others, now dispersed, have kept me company along the way. Amos, Annie, Deidre, Doug, Hannah, Heidi, Julia, Kirstie, Kylie, Nick, Renae and Sam – it's been a long time, but through it all you have baked cakes, sent postcards and drunk wine with me, and this makes me very happy. Sam and Nathan – thanks for being the best of brothers, and for bringing Ainsley, Sarah and Annabel into my life. And last, to Liora, Joyce, Frances, David, Eloise, Jen and Rahul – we have discussed all manner of things (not least endless iterations of the question of home and away) in all manner of places and at all times of the day and night. I hope we always will.

NOTE ON TERMINOLOGY

In keeping with recent contributions to the scholarship on imperial history, I see empire not as a territory of conquest but as something defined by its various practices of control.[1] In this sense the British academic world was very much part of the empire that John Darwin has called 'the Britannic experiment'; a circulating world of people, goods and ideas, which helped maintain ties between the Dominions and Britain.[2] The universities founded in the settler colonies were very much 'colonial' institutions. They were products of a proud 'colonial nationalism' that lasted beyond the achievement of 'Dominion' status, in which large numbers of those who lived in Canada, Australia, New Zealand and (to a lesser extent) South Africa, identified both with Britain and with the colony in which they were born or lived. Universities fostered these ties: they extended dominion over the soil and over its original inhabitants by sanctioning what counted as knowledge and by providing much of the expertise needed to map and regulate and heal; and they extended dominion within the people, by shaping culture and identity. But there were other parts of the empire, which are also commonly referred to as 'colonies' – in Africa, India and South East Asia – where universities were established by British officials and more explicitly associated with the imposition of rule and the institution of foreign language and culture. The term 'colonial university' also brings with it these connotations, and it is to avoid this conflation that I frequently use the term 'settler university' and 'settler scholar'. In doing so I wish to signal that these were institutions made by colonial settlers, who saw themselves as independent and autochthonous members of a wider British community. At times I also speak of 'colonial knowledge', a term which has been the subject of lively scholarly interest, and one that is usually taken to refer to the forms of knowledge (including administrative practices, as well as classificatory processes and more traditional forms of inquiry such as history) used to maintain imperial authority. Most of the debate centres on the role played by the colonised in the production of such knowledge, but my emphasis here is looser and more in line with that employed by Saul Dubow. While acknowledging its political function and role as an instrument of power, he suggests that what he calls 'colonial local knowledge' was also 'bound up with conceptions of self-empowerment and in demonstrating one's worth to peers and betters'.[3]

This knowledge bore the marks of the environments in which it was made; environments that included the perspectives of distance, the innovations born of isolation, and the necessity of developing applied understanding in independent and growing settler communities. These were soft as well as hard forms of knowledge; forms of knowledge that, like the specimens sent to Kew Gardens in an earlier era, were of great value to modern scholarship, but that, unlike those specimens, were lodged in people and their skills and experience.

Notes

1 Jane Burbank and Frederick Cooper, *Empires in World History: Power and the Politics of Difference* (Princeton, NJ: Princeton University Press, 2010), 3–4, 122.
2 John Darwin, *The Empire Project: The Rise and Fall of the British World-System, 1830–1970* (Cambridge: Cambridge University Press, 2009), 144–79.
3 Phillip B. Wagoner, 'Precolonial Intellectuals the the Production of Colonial Knowledge,' *Comparative Studies in Society and History*, 45, no. 4 (2003): 783; Saul Dubow, *A Commonwealth of Knowledge: Science, Sensibility, and White South Africa, 1820–2000* (Oxford: Oxford University Press, 2006), 14.

ABBREVIATIONS

AAC	Academic Assistance Council
AAS	Australian Academy of Science
ACU	Association of Commonwealth Universities
AIF	Australian Imperial Force
ANZ	Archives New Zealand
BCSO	British Central Scientific Office
BEF	British Expeditionary Force
BIR	Board of Invention and Research
BL	British Library
BLSC	Bodleian Libraries Special Collections
CSIR	Council for Scientific and Industrial Research
DSIR	Department of Scientific and Industrial Research
FRS	Fellow of the Royal Society
IMB	Imperial Munitions Board
IES	Indian Education Service
LSE	London School of Economics
MUA	McGill University Archives
NAUK	National Archives UK
NPL	National Physical Laboratory
NRC	National Research Council
QUA	Queen's University Archives
SMLA	Science Museum Library Archives
SPSL	Society for the Protection of Science and Learning
UAA	University of Adelaide Archives
UBA	University of Birmingham Archives
UCTA	University of Cape Town Archives
ULA	University of London Archives
UMA	University of Melbourne Archives
UK	United Kingdom
US	United States
USA	University of Sydney Archives
UTA	University of Toronto Archives
YMCA	Young Men's Christian Association

INTRODUCTION

On the morning of Tuesday 2 July 1912, Henry Darnley Naylor made his way through London's Bloomsbury Square to join the opening session of the first Congress of the Universities of the British Empire, about to begin at the University of London. Attending on behalf of the University of Adelaide, along with 158 other delegates and at least 180 nominated representatives from across Britain and the empire, he listened to the Earl of Rosebery, chancellor of the University of London and former Liberal Prime Minister, deliver the opening address. 'From Oxford to Sydney,' Rosebery began,

> from St. Andrews to Saskatchewan, and from Dublin to the Cape, we are all joining hands to-day and singing as it were in imagination 'Auld Lang Syne'. At a meeting which represents every part and region of this world-wide empire (applause) I would ask you, gentlemen, is not this after all the best kind of empire, the best kind of imperial feeling, a form of imperialism to which the Least Englander could not object – that of co-operation in high and noble tasks, with the common sympathy, affection and energy which would characterize the members of an immense family[?](Hear, hear.)[1]

The proceedings of the meeting suggest that Naylor and his fellow delegates shared these sentiments. Describing themselves as 'fellow-workers in the same prolific field, co-partners in the same high cause', at the 1912 Congress they asserted their membership of an academic community that reached out beyond the borders of the British Isles.[2]

Framed in the gendered and gentlemanly, racial and familial discourses fundamental to the imperial cultures of the era, the 1912 Congress appears to tell a familiar story.[3] It seems typical of the conventions and conferences of the Edwardian period, in which representatives from the settler colonies came to London to assert their independence while also professing their imperial loyalty.[4] The colonial delegates who attended it are recognisable as agents of cultural imperialism: they helped extend British dominion over indigenous lands and peoples, asserting their metropolitan 'expertise' in the colonies and fashioning loyal imperial subjects in the classroom.[5] Perhaps they were even the émigré second sons and third-class men that writers from J. A. Hobson to Donald Fleming and Richard Symonds suggest filled colonial universities.[6] Naylor himself initially appears to typify this cliché of the colonial academic. An Oxbridge graduate who had

distinguished himself in manly pursuits such as football and moun-
taineering, he accepted a post for 'health reasons' at Ormond College
in the University of Melbourne immediately after leaving Cambridge.[7]
Taking up a Chair in Adelaide in 1906, he taught classics to colonials
for the rest of his academic career.

Yet this characterisation does injustice to the complex lives of men
like Naylor. A Walker prizeman with a first-class degree, in Australia he
advocated reform of the classical curriculum, served as an enthusiastic
Workers' Education lecturer, supported women's issues, championed
the League of Nations, and rejoiced at what he saw as the 'marked
disappearance of class distinction' in the colonies.[8] Neither was Naylor
cut off in Adelaide from British scholarship. He had made a trip back to
England in 1906 and his visit in 1912 was part of a twelve-month stay
in Europe and the United Kingdom. In the course of this year he met
not only with his old Cambridge classmates, but also with his close
friend the Australian-born Oxford classicist Gilbert Murray, and with
former Adelaide colleagues, W. H. Bragg at Leeds and Horace Lamb at
Manchester.[9] A third trip followed in 1921, and in 1927 Naylor again
returned, this time to enter politics and work for the League of Nations
Union. During his career at Adelaide he had contributed regularly to the
London-based *Classical Review* and the *Classical Quarterly*, served as
vice-president of the British Classical Association and published three
books through the University of Cambridge Press. His obituary appeared both in the Adelaide newspapers and in *The Times* of London.[10]

How are we to understand the academic world that Naylor inhabited? He undeniably operated at the juncture of culture and empire,
but his mobility and his continued participation in the world of British
scholarship suggest that, although working in a colonial university, he
hardly sat at the margins of British academia. When Rosebery spoke at
the 1912 Congress, he drew a relationship between academic practice,
sociability and the spaces of empire that demands consideration. This
book takes seriously the aspirations and articulations of Naylor and
his fellow delegates, and investigates the contours of the academic
world in which they lived.

Disconnected histories

Naylor's career points to the fluidity between 'British' and 'colonial'
or 'settler' academia in this period. Yet fixing these categories has
been part of the project of national history since the 1960s. During
this period, historians writing about universities moved away from
portraying them as products of the progressive expansion of British
culture, and instead charted their independent course.[11] In the
former Dominions historical accounts assumed a national focus:

they both emphasised the distinctive qualities of colonial universities and presented their early achievements as key to the emergence of the independent nation, while at the same time casting them as dependent and imitative institutions that too often evidenced what A. A. Phillips in 1950 called the 'cultural cringe'.[12] Meanwhile, scholars interested in the dependent empire turned their attention to questions of educational 'development', power and cultural control in India and Africa.[13] Historians of British universities echoed this trend. In their landmark works, A. H. Halsey, Sheldon Rothblatt, Roy Lowe, and Robert Anderson all sought to explain the particular character of social and cultural hierarchies at home and focused their comparative studies on Europe and the United States.[14] In fact, other than Eric Ashby's 1963 'informal portrait' of the Association of Universities of the British Commonwealth, the last work to consider the universities of the settler empire of Canada, Australia, New Zealand and South Africa alongside those in Britain was the volume published by A. P. Newton in 1924.[15] As Daniel Gorman has written in another context, these historiographical shifts 'read imperial events within the frame of the birth of the nation', fragmenting the histories of British and settler universities, and locking scholars whose careers spanned continents within national frames of reference.[16]

But settler universities and the individuals who worked in them were both local and global actors. They were rooted in specific social and political communities and also wayfarers on international routes of scholarship. Like Kapil Raj's work, this study aims 'to reconsider simple models of metropolitan centre and remote periphery' by investigating the ways in which institutional structures, and experiences of travel and social connection shaped the lives and careers of men like Naylor.[17] It is therefore part of the vibrant body of scholarship that since the 1990s has focused on networks as a way of understanding the relationships between specific sites, imperial rule and the production of knowledge and culture.[18] Yet as Simon Potter points out, if networks are to be a useful concept in imperial history then their limitations, objects and ends, together with their constructed nature, need attending to.[19] Following Frederick Cooper, this book is concerned with the ways in which the networks of the past, like those of the present, were 'filled with lumps, places where power coalesces surrounded by those where it does not, places where social relations become dense amid others that are diffuse'.[20] Consequently it focuses on what David Livingstone and Charles Withers have called the 'complex social and technical mechanisms influencing science's movement across space'.[21] Specifically, it analyses the institutional and social practices employed by universities and academics across the British settler world. Despite growing bodies of work on imperial networks, postcolonial and transnational exchange, and the social construction of scientific knowledge, this is something that imperial historians, science studies scholars and university historians alike have long neglected.[22] Yet institutions and organisations were chief among the forces that worked to regulate and direct the reach and operation of imperial networks.[23] If we are to understand the intellectual history of the late nineteenth and early twentieth centuries, we need to know a lot more about those who made knowledge, and a lot more about the worlds that made them.

Thinking about the constructed character of academic networks, however, in turn necessitates a reimagining of the nature of intellectual and imperial space. Geographers such as Doreen Massey and David Harvey have argued that space should not be understood as a fixed entity through which we move, but rather as something that is made – socially, materially and imaginatively.[24] As contingent and created entities that reached in some but not all directions, connected some but not all people, and carried some but not all goods, long-distance networks conditioned the worlds in which people lived, how they experienced those worlds and the ways they understood them.[25] Networks fashioned relative and relational forms of space that did not accord with political borders or with physical topographies. Such perspectives recast the old geographies of empire and point to new alignments of proximity and distance measured by strength of feeling, closeness of friendship and access to power.

By paying attention to the nature and reach of academic connections, this study shows that the 'world' of British academia included the universities of the settler colonies. Thus, although it invokes Carl Bridge and Kent Fedorowich's concept of a 'trans-oceanic British world' that included the colonies 'set going' by mass migration from Britain, it points to a limited, exclusionary and irregular scholarly community that was made by very specific forms of long-distance social and institutional relations.[26] The frame of transnational history might initially appear a useful way of making sense of this more than local but not quite global world. However, as Ian Tyrrell points out, like national readings of the past, it too projects the boundaries of the post-imperial nation backwards onto a period in which no such nation existed.[27] The 1912 Congress delegates talked not just about empire but about what we might call the 'expansive British nation'. They saw themselves and their universities as belonging to what W. Peterson, the principal of McGill University, described as 'the national life of the whole British world'.[28] Only by paying attention to the connections that linked universities in Britain and the settler colonies can we start to understand what this meant.

The British academic world

The 1912 Congress was a conscious attempt to crystallise the ties that since the 1880s had linked the universities in the settler colonies of Canada, Australia, New Zealand and South Africa to those in Britain. These institutions often predated the English redbrick universities (see Appendix A). They were not set up by British officials, as in India and later Africa, but rather by self-confident settler elites who saw them as both symbols and disseminators of European civilisation in the colonies. Providing a classical and liberal (and often religious) education, they were designed to cultivate both the morals and the minds of the young men who would lead the economically successful colonial societies of the mid-nineteenth century. They presumed the universality and superiority of 'Western' knowledge and culture and established themselves as its local representatives, proudly proclaiming this position in the neo-gothic buildings they erected and the Latin mottos they adopted. Although they adapted old-world models, in their early years settler universities were very much local affairs. Fashioned by colonial politics and frequently funded by the state, they were small institutions that served the sons of the colonial elite.

However, in the 1870s imperial expansion and revolutions in transport and communication contributed to intensified forms of global interconnection that began to change this established relationship between culture and power. Under pressure to demonstrate their relevance to the socially diverse and rapidly expanding communities in which they were located, settler universities reasserted their position as institutions that straddled the local and the global. They did so in two ways: first, they expanded their educational franchise, opening their curricula to include science, law, medicine and engineering, and admitting women; and second, they established new links with 'universal' learning, investing in libraries and in mechanisms such as travelling scholarships and leave-of-absence programmes that were designed to carry their students and staff abroad. These innovations de-territorialised some of the structures that regulated knowledge in the colonies, and opened the way for settler universities to connect themselves to institutions abroad.

Settler universities undertook these changes in the context of a British university sector that was only reluctantly accommodating itself to the demands of the modern world. The expanding institutions in the settler colonies, with their relatively high salaries, professorial appointments, and openness to the professions and to pure and applied science, offered opportunities to aspiring scholars not widely available in Britain. Such men were sought after by universities in the colonies, but, faced with the difficulties of selecting candidates at a distance, in their appointment processes, settler universities relied heavily on the private recommendations of trusted individuals in Britain. Together with travelling scholarships and leave-of-absence programmes, this utilisation of personalised systems of trust helped extend abroad the informal networks at the heart of British academia. The expansive reach of these networks mapped the borders of a 'British academic world' that engaged with other academic communities in Europe and the United States, but that was nonetheless distinct from them.

Although the scholars who took up work in settler universities were acutely conscious of their distance from Britain, they also knew that they operated within a world of negotiable limitations. Time for research, funding, laboratory space, materials and access to the right kinds of people conditioned those working in metropolitan and settler universities alike. By nurturing their personal ties with colleagues in Britain, academics working in the colonies softened the tyranny of distance, creating social forms of proximity that reshaped and realigned it. As David Wade Chambers has argued in relation to science, 'some problems of isolation, supposedly related to distance, have more to do with social, cultural and economic factors than simply with accumulated mileage from some perceived centre'.[29] The personal relationships and connections of individuals were thus central to the workings of imperial academia. It was academic connections of this kind that underlay the 1912 Congress. Of the 158 official delegates from fifty-three universities who attended the meeting, at least sixty per cent had some direct experience of living or working in the empire, with many more connected through relations, colleagues or former students.[30] As the financier, philanthropist and Canadian High Commissioner, Lord Strathcona declared on the morning of its final day, the 'bonds which link us across the seas to each other are of the most intimate and personal character'.[31]

But when Congress delegates spoke of the imperial academic community, it was overwhelmingly to the settler universities that they referred. Reproducing hierarchical constructions of race that legitimised certain (white, western, gendered) kinds of knowledge at the same time as they erased others, this elision of the Indian and South Asian universities and colleges points to the exclusionary nature of British academic networks. Privileging raced and gendered forms of trust and sociability, the social and institutional practices that connected settler scholars to those in Britain simultaneously sidelined the empire's various 'others'. Women were systematically excluded from the spaces of academic connection and its attendant opportunities, even as their work enabled the attainments of their senior male colleagues.[32] Africans, Americans and Indians operated at the edges of British academic networks, and Europeans were only rarely admitted.[33]

Yet the British academic world was not impermeable. Small numbers of scholars from Europe found their way into settler universities, and Germany (and for Canadians, the United States) continued to be an important destination for study and research. The Afrikaans- and French- speaking universities in South Africa and Canada maintained separate ties with European institutions, and across the universities of the British academic world 'foreign' scholarship was widely read. In the early period especially, civil servants and lawyers who had worked in India returned to academic posts in the United Kingdom, while in the early twentieth century, missionaries, medics, archaeologists and others with experience in Africa, East Asia and the Middle East traded on their 'expertise' to acquire academic positions in the emerging social sciences.[34] Lateral traffic of all kinds flowed between Britain's settler, dependent and commercial empires, while alternative ties – including among anti-colonial nationalists from India, Ireland and the Boer Republics – were forged by those on the edges of British networks.[35] And neither was the British academic world uniform. Within the settler sphere distinct axes of travel emerged. These ran not just between the different Dominions and Britain but also between particular settler universities and particular regions or institutions in the United Kingdom: academics at the University of Cape Town, for example, had strong connections to the universities of Scotland.[36] Nearer to the United States, Canada came to function as something of a 'hinge' between the British and American academic worlds, and it was not uncommon for British scholars who ended up in the United States to have first spent time working north of the border. Moreover, local ties retained their importance. As some of the best recent work in the history of science shows, negotiation and active collaboration – with book dealers, instrument makers, local (including indigenous) collectors, agricultural agencies, professional bodies and a hinterland of (often female and often invisible) assistants – were crucial to the way that settler scholars, like their metropolitan contemporaries, made knowledge.[37] Porous borders, uneven topographies and unequal scholarly economies underpinned the workings of settler and British universities alike.

In this light the British academic world seems to resemble a sophisticated tool of social and imperial rule. Even as it exploited and appropriated work undertaken by the European, female, local and subaltern workers who constituted the shadow world of British universities, the academic establishment in Britain also cultivated the scholarly dependence of settler universities: drawing into the metropole the best colonial graduates and sending out young British guns to 'cut their teeth' abroad before recruiting them back again. Yet this was not how the settler universities saw it. They celebrated the departure of their graduates and welcomed the arrival of new recruits, aware that both helped connect them to the centres of British scholarship. They placed themselves alongside their provincial equivalents conscious that, as David Knight has pointed out, 'many Britons could feel just as excluded as any Australians or Americans'.[38] The British academic world certainly had centres and peripheries, but these did not always map neatly onto metropole and colony. Its intellectual geographies were relational and affective as much as they were regional.

The First World War both exploited and enhanced these forms of academic connection. By mobilising the talents of many academics from the settler world and drawing them into the imperial capital, the conflict simultaneously strengthened the informal ties that linked British and settler scholars, creating expanded avenues for exchange in the interwar years. But during this period also came various forces that worked to erode the networks on which the British academic world depended. Settler universities began to feel the growing influence of American philanthropy, with institutions such as the Carnegie and Rockefeller Foundations funding numerous educational projects in the Dominions. At the same time, anti-colonial activists from Africa, the Caribbean and India – many of them based in London – challenged the forms of scientific racism that supported imperial rule. But it was the waves of refugee scholars that came to Britain in the wake of the rise of Nazism that really disrupted the mechanisms at the heart of British academic networks. Their arrival upset previous hiring customs and brought new connections and new ways of thinking. Together these contrary tendencies began to unravel the ties that held the British academic world together. Loosened further by wartime collaborations that pulled British scientists out of their Senior Common Rooms and across the Atlantic, the British academic world was finally unwound in the 1960s by the rise of nationalism in the Dominions, which reterritorialised the institutions of knowledge and repurposed the old forms of connection, turning them to new, national ends.

Outline

This book is about the social and institutional practices of British and settler English-speaking universities in the nineteenth and early twentieth centuries. It is not a history of colonial education. It does not take up issues associated with the emergence of disciplines, with the development of the curriculum, or with teaching and student-life, and it pays limited attention to the production of knowledge. Its reach is broad. As Edwardian educationalists were quick to point out, there was no such thing as a typical university. Established in very different communities, each bore the unique marks of their specific physical, political and social environments. I have focused on the oldest and arguably the most prominent of the secular, English-speaking institutions founded in Britain's settler colonies: McGill, Queen's and Toronto, in Canada; Adelaide, Melbourne and Sydney in Australia; the University of New Zealand and its constituent colleges in Auckland, Christchurch and Otago; and the University of Cape Town and the South African College which preceded it. This means I have not attended to the colleges of the National University of Ireland, to the French university sector in Canada or to the Afrikaans-speaking cluster of institutions in South Africa, whose connections with France and the Netherlands, and whose resistance to Anglophilic orientations, are evident upon even cursory investigation. It also means I have paid less attention to the religious institutions in Canada, to the universities of India and South East Asia (notably the University of Hong Kong), and to what might be called the second wave of settler universities – those established after 1900 in the Canadian West and in the newer colonies of Queensland and Western Australia, which focused explicitly on the professions, science and applied technology.[39] Individual academics present a still more diverse picture. They moved in all sorts of directions, read material acquired from a variety of locations, including Europe and America, and taught, lectured, researched – and increasingly also consulted – in regions across the globe. They also stayed firmly planted, founding regional journals and associations and consolidating local connections. Thus there will be stories that do not fit easily into the broad patterns I detail, and careers that seem to swim against the dominant currents I identify.

The book begins in the early nineteenth century, when the first universities were founded in Britain's second empire, and concludes in the period of decolonisation. During this century-and-a-half, universities underwent a series of revolutions that would have made them unrecognisable to the dons of the early 1800s. Among the changes that buffeted them were the forces of late Victorian globalisation. Associated with these new kinds of global integration were anxieties about foreign economic competition that, after the First World War, would result in a curtailment of free trade policies. Yet for universities these were shifts that enhanced rather than diminished the academic relationships that connected Britain and its settler world. By contrast, the Second World War would bring much more radical changes. Therefore, although it reaches beyond these dates, the main focus of this study is the period between 1850 and the outbreak of war in 1939.

Part I examines the foundation of universities in the settler colonies and charts their efforts to establish themselves in local communities before considering the changes that in the 1870s began to draw them into closer connection with Britain. Part II turns to the period between 1880 and the outbreak of the First World War, when these universities began to forge links with British academia. Its three chapters consider the connective mechanisms – the libraries, scholarships, leave-of-absence programmes, appointment practices and forms of institutional association – that helped to create new kinds of access and new patterns of mobility in this period. Part III goes on to explore the networks made by these connections, and the ways academics and universities used them, from the start of the century to the outbreak of the Second World War. It underscores the central role social connection played in making academic careers, making knowledge, and making the British university sector in this period. Part IV considers some of the forces that, from the 1930s, worked to erode the networks on which the British academic world depended. Finally, the conclusion draws together the key arguments of the book.

In questioning the relationship between the forms of sociability, space and knowledge practice that helped constitute the British academic world, this study examines a set of issues that are central to the way we understand the history of Britain and its empire. First, by identifying the networks that, from the late nineteenth century, connected settler universities with the imperial metropole, it contributes to ongoing debates about the influence of empire on British society. Second, in expanding the boundaries of British academia and in pointing to the long-distance social and personal ties that helped constitute it, the book also provides a new context for the writing of intellectual history. Third, as an examination of the structures and practices of universities and those who worked in them, this book serves as a case study of the role institutions played in creating the limited worlds of global connection that enabled, conditioned and regulated the hopes and experiences of those who lived both in Britain and abroad in the period before the Second World War. In the process it evinces the need for historians to confront the historiographical and conceptual challenges posed by pasts that, although displaced onto territories now considered foreign, were once familiar.

When Rosebery spoke at the first Congress of the Universities of the British Empire in London in 1912, he invoked a community of universities – geographically expansive, masculine, familial, connected and co-operating.[40] In doing so he pointed to an expansive but also exclusionary British academic world that has since been fragmented. If we are to develop a critical understanding of the inequalities that characterise our own entangled scholarly communities and the practices that define them, this is a world to which we need to pay close attention.[41] For it helped established uneven lines of global connection and irregular geographies of access that continue to condition higher education today.

Notes

1 *Congress of the Universities of the Empire, 1912: Report of Proceedings*, ed. Alex Hill (London: Hodder and Stoughton, 1912), p. 2.
2 *Ibid.*, pp. 72, 192.
3 Anne McClintock, *Imperial Leather: Race, Gender, and Sexuality in the Colonial Contest* (New York: Routledge, 1995); Mrinalini Sinha, *Colonial Masculinity: The 'Manly Englishman' and the 'Effeminate Bengali' in the Late Nineteenth Century* (Manchester: Manchester University Press, 1995); Catherine Hall and Sonya O. Rose (eds), *At Home with the Empire: Metropolitan Culture and the Imperial World* (New York: Cambridge University Press, 2006).
4 Duncan Bell, *The Idea of Greater Britain: Empire and the Future of World Order, 1860–1900* (Princeton, NJ: Princeton University Press, 2007); Charles Dilke, *Greater Britain, a Record of Travel in the English-Speaking Countries During 1866 and 1867*, 2 vols (London: Macmillan, 1868); John Robert Seeley, *The Expansion of England: Two Courses of Lectures* (London: Macmillan, 1883); James Anthony Froude, *Oceana, or England and Her Colonies* (London: Longmans, Green and Co., 1886).
5 Nicholas B. Dirks, *Castes of Mind: Colonialism and the Making of Modern India* (Princeton, NJ: Princeton University Press, 2001); Bernard Cohn, *Colonialism and Its Forms of Knowledge: The British in India* (Princeton, NJ: Princeton University Press, 1996); J. A. Mangan (ed.), *Making Imperial Mentalities: Socialisation and British Imperialism* (Manchester: Manchester University Press, 1990); J. A. Mangan, *Athleticism in the Victorian and Edwardian Public School: The Emergence and Consolidation of an Educational Ideology* (London: Falmer Press, 1986).
6 Donald Fleming, 'Science in Australia, Canada and the United States: Some Comparative Remarks', *Proceedings of the Tenth International Congress of the History of Science* (1964), pp. 179–96; Richard Symonds, *Oxford and the Empire* (Oxford: Clarendon Press, 2000), p. 274; J. S. Mill quoted in J. A. Hobson, *Imperialism: A Study* (London: James Nisbet, 1902), p. 56.
7 W. R. Crocker, 'Naylor, Henry Darnley (1872–1945)', *Australian Dictionary of Biography*, 10 (1986).
8 *Ibid.*
9 'Passengers by the Scharnhorst', *Sydney Morning Herald*, 15 Sept. 1906, p. 14; 'A Professor Abroad', *The Register*, 6 Mar. 1913, p. 15.
10 Crocker, 'Naylor, Henry Darnley (1872–1945)'; 'Prof H. Darley Naylor', *The Times*, 11 Dec. 1945, p. 6.
11 Spurred by Robinson and Gallagher's concepts of 'informal empire', 'the official mind' and 'collaboration', this new historiography saw imperial expansion as something driven by events on the periphery. John Gallagher and Ronald Robinson, 'The Imperialism of Free Trade', *Economic History Review*, 6, no. 1 (1953): 1–15; Ronald Robinson, *Africa and the Victorians: The Official Mind of Imperialism* (London: Macmillan, 1961). For the earlier view, see Arthur Percival Newton, *The Universities and Educational Systems of the British Empire* (London: W. Collins Sons, 1924); J. C. Beaglehole, *The University of New Zealand: An Historical Study* (Auckland: Whitcomb and Tombs, 1937).
12 As early as 1971, Douglas Cole remarked that a conceptual confusion hampered the study of nationalism in the settlement colonies – what 'nation' meant was deeply problematic. Emphasising the national dimension of their histories also entailed distancing them from an earlier iteration of the national story: one that that had

been not only Canadian or Australian but also British. Douglas Cole, 'The Problem of "Nationalism" and "Imperialism" in British Settlement Colonies', *Journal of British Studies*, 10, no. 2 (1971): 160–82; Arthur Angel Phillips, *A. A. Phillips on the Cultural Cringe* (Melbourne: Melbourne University Press, 2006). See, for example, M. Boucher, *The University of the Cape of Good Hope and the University of South Africa, 1873–1946: A Study in National and Imperial Perspective* (Pretoria: The Government Printer, 1974), pp. 258–64; R. J. W. Selleck, *The Shop: The University of Melbourne, 1850–1939* (Melbourne: Melbourne University Press, 2003), p. 26; Keith Sinclair, *A History of the University of Auckland, 1883–1983* (Auckland: 1983).

13 Eric Ashby, *Universities: British, Indian, African: A Study in the Ecology of Higher Education* (London: Weidenfeld and Nicolson, 1966); For Africa and India, see Clive Whitehead, 'The Historiography of British Imperial Education Policy, Part I: India', *History of Education*, 34, no. 3 (2005): 315–29; Clive Whitehead, 'The Historiography of British Imperial Education Policy, Part II: Africa and the Rest of the Colonial Empire', *History of Education*, 34, no. 4 (2005): 441–54; J. M. Fletcher, 'The Universities in the Age of Western Expansion. The Colonial Factor in Research and Higher Education: Leiden, 27–29 September 1991', *History of Universities*, 11 (1992): 268–9.

14 A. H. Halsey, *Decline of Donnish Dominion: The British Academic Professions in the Twentieth Century* (Oxford: Clarendon Press, 1992); A. H. Halsey, Martin A. Trow and Oliver Fulton, *The British Academics* (London: Faber and Faber, 1971); A. H. Halsey, 'Oxford and the British Universities', in Brian Harrison (ed.), *The History of the University of Oxford: Vol. 8, the Twentieth Century* (Oxford: Oxford University Press, 1994), pp. 577–606; Sheldon Rothblatt, *The Revolution of the Dons: Cambridge and Society in Victorian England* (London: Faber and Faber, 1968); Roy Lowe, 'The Expansion of Higher Education in England', in Konrad H. Jarausch (ed.), *The Transformation of Higher Learning, 1860–1930* (Stuttgart: Klett-Cotta, 1982); Robert D. Anderson, *Universities and Elites in Britain since 1800* (London: Macmillan, 1992). See Harold Silver, '"Things Change but Names Remain the Same": Higher Education Historiography 1975–2000', *History of Education*, 35, no. 1 (2006): 121–40.

15 E. Ashby, *Community of Universities: An Informal Portrait of the Association of Universities of the British Commonwealth, 1913–1963* (Southampton: The Association of Commonwealth Universities, 1963); Newton, *The Universities and Educational Systems of the British Empire*.

16 Daniel Gorman, *Imperial Citizenship: Empire and the Question of Belonging* (Manchester: Manchester University Press, 2006), p. 12.

17 Kapil Raj, 'Introduction: Circulation and Locality in Early Modern Science', *British Journal for the History of Science*, 2010, no. 43 (2010): 513–17, p. 516.

18 For imperial historians, see A. L. Stoler and F. Cooper, 'Between Metropole and Colony. Rethinking a Research Agenda', in A. L. Stoler and F. Cooper (eds), *Tensions of Empire: Colonial Cultures in a Bourgeois World* (Berkeley, CA: University of California Press, 1997); C. Hall, 'Introduction: Thinking the Postcolonial, Thinking the Empire', in C. Hall (ed.), *Cultures of Empire: A Reader* (Manchester: Manchester University Press, 2000); A. Burton, 'Introduction: On the Inadequacy and the Indispensability of the Nation', in A. Burton (ed.), *After the Imperial Turn: Thinking With and Through the Nation* (Durham, NC: Duke University Press, 2003), pp. 1–26. For global and transnational historians, see Deborah Cohen and Maura O'Connor, 'Comparative History, Cross-National History, Transnational History: Definitions', in Deborah Cohen and Maura O'Connor (eds), *Comparison and History* (London: Routledge, 2004); Ian R. Tyrrell, *Transnational Nation: United States History in Global Perspective since 1789* (Basingstoke: Palgrave Macmillan, 2007).

19 Simon J. Potter, 'Empire, Cultures and Identities in Nineteenth- and Twentieth-Century Britain', *History Compass*, 5, no. 1 (2007): 51–71, p. 58.

20 Frederick Cooper, *Colonialism in Question: Theory, Knowledge, History* (Berkeley, CA, and London: University of California Press, 2005), p. 91.

21 Charles W. J. Withers and David Livingstone, 'Thinking Geographically About Nineteenth Century Science', in David Livingstone and Charles W. J. Withers (eds), *Geographies of Nineteenth Century Science* (Chicago, IL: University of Chicago Press, 2011), p. 12.

22 For work on imperial networks and science, see Joseph Morgan Hodge and Brett M. Bennett (eds), *Science and Empire: Knowledge and Networks of Science in the British Empire, 1800–1970* (New York: Palgrave Macmillan, 2011); Livingstone and Withers (eds), *Geographies of Nineteenth-Century Science*. Work on postcolonial and transnational exchange includes Arjun Appadurai (ed.), *Globalization* (Durham, NC: Duke University Press, 2001); Parama Roy, *Indian Traffic: Identities in Question in Colonial and Postcolonial India* (Berkeley, CA: University of California Press, 1998); Inderpal Grewal, *Home and Harem: Nation, Gender, Empire and the Cultures of Travel* (London: Leicester University Press, 1996); S. B. Cooke, *Imperial Affinities: Nineteenth-Century Analogies and Exchanges Between India and Ireland* (New Delhi: Sage Publications, 1993). For work on the social construction of knowledge, see Nicolaas Rupke, 'Putting the Geography of Science in Its Place', in Livingstone and Withers (eds), *Geographies of Nineteenth Century Science*, p. 439; see also Charles W. J. Withers, 'Place and the "Spatial Turn", in Geography and in History', *Journal of the History of Ideas*, 70, no. 4 (2009): 637–58; Diarmid A. Finnegan, 'The Spatial Turn: Geographical Approaches in the History of Science', *Journal of the History of Biology*, 41, no. 2 (2008): 369–88; David N. Livingstone, *Putting Science in Its Place: Geographies of Scientific Knowledge* (Chicago, IL: University of Chicago Press, 2003). For the networks and the history of education, see Gary McCulloch and Roy Lowe, 'Introduction: Centre and Periphery – Networks, Space and Geography in the History of Education', *History of Education*, 32, no. 5 (2003): 457–9; Joyce Goodman, Gary McCulloch and William Richardson, 'Introduction: "Empires Overseas" and "Empires at Home": Postcolonial and Transnational Perspectives on Social Change in the History of Education', *Paedagogica Historica*, 45, no. 6 (2009): 695–706.
23 Simon J. Potter, 'Webs, Networks and Systems: Globalization and the Mass Media in the Nineteenth- and Twentieth- Century British Empire', *Journal of British Studies*, 46 (2007), 621–46, p. 634.
24 Doreen B. Massey, *For Space* (London: Sage, 2005); David Harvey, *Cosmopolitanism and the Geographies of Freedom* (New York: Columbia University Press, 2009).
25 David Lambert and Alan Lester, 'Introduction: Imperial Spaces, Imperial Subjects', in David Lambert and Alan Lester (eds), *Colonial Lives across the British Empire: Imperial Careering in the Long Nineteenth Century* (Cambridge: Cambridge University Press, 2006); H. Michie and R. Thomas (eds), *Nineteenth Century Geographies: The Transformation of Space from the Victorian Age to the American Century* (New Brunswick, NJ: Rutgers University Press, 2002); Gary Bryan Magee and Andrew S. Thompson, *Empire and Globalisation: Networks of People, Goods and Capital in the British World, C.1850-1914* (Cambridge: Cambridge University Press, 2010).
26 Carl Bridge and Kent Fedorowich, 'Mapping the British World', *Journal of Imperial and Commonwealth History*, 31, no. 2 (2003): 1–15, p. 11; Carl Bridge and Kent Fedorowich (eds), *The British World: Diaspora, Culture, and Identity* (London: F. Cass, 2003). See also Tamson Pietsch, 'Rethinking the British World', *Journal of British Studies*, 52, no. 2 (2013).
27 I. Tyrrell, 'Reflections on the Transnational Turn in United States History: Theory and Practice', *Journal of Global History*, 4 (2009): 453–74, p. 461.
28 *Congress Proceedings, 1912*, p. 46.
29 David W. Chambers, 'Does Distance Tyrannize Science?' in Roderick Weir Home and Sally Gregory Kohlstedt (eds), *International Science and National Scientific Identity: Australia between Britain and America* (Dordrecht: Kluwer Academic, 1991), p. 20.
30 Seventy-five of the delegates were from universities in England, Scotland, Ireland and Wales (of whom at least twelve had worked or seriously travelled in the Empire); sixty-three were from universities in Australia, Canada, New Zealand or South Africa; and twenty were from institutions in India or Hong Kong. *Congress Proceedings, 1912*, pp. xxix–xxxv.
31 Strathcona in *Congress Proceedings, 1912*, p. 308.
32 Hannah Gay, 'Invisible Resource: Wiliam Crookes and His Circle of Support, 1871–81', *British Journal for the History of Science*, 29, no. 3 (1996): 311–36. See also Alison Prentice, 'Boosting Husbands and Building Community: The Work of

Twentieth-Century Faculty Wives', in Paul Stortz and E. Lisa Panayotidis (eds), *Historical Identities: The Professoriate in Canada* (Toronto: University of Toronto Press).

33 Steven Shapin has pointed out that the circulation of knowledge is inescapably bound to questions of trust. Adi Ophir and Steven Shapin, 'The Place of Knowledge: A Methodological Survey', *Science in Context*, 4 (1991): 3–21, p. 15; Steven Shapin, *A Social History of Truth: Civility and Science in Seventeenth-Century England* (Chicago, IL: University of Chicago Press, 1994), pp. 34–8, 410–14. There is an extensive literature on trust in various contexts. See, for example, Charles W. J. Withers, 'Reporting, Mapping, Trusting: Making Geographical Knowledge in the Late Seventeenth Century', *Isis*, 90 (1999): 497–521; Paul S. Adler, 'Market, Hierarchy, and Trust: The Knowledge Economy and the Future of Capitalism', *Organization Science*, 12, no. 2 (2001): 215–34; Marek Kohn, *Trust: Self-Interest and the Common Good* (Oxford: Oxford University Press, 2008).

34 The Archaeologist Flinders Petrie is just one example. When Amelia Edwards, his patron at the Egyptian Exploration Society, died in 1892, she endowed a chair in archaeology and philology for him at University College, London. See Margaret S. Drower, *Flinders Petrie: A Life in Archaeology* (Madison, WI: University of Wisconsin Press, 1995).

35 For example, see Elleke Boehmer, *Empire, the National, and the Postcolonial, 1890–1920* (Oxford: Oxford University Press, 2005), and Leela Gandhi, *Affective Communities: Anticolonial Thought and the Politics of Friendship* (New Delhi: Permanent Black, 2006).

36 Howard Phillips and Hector Menteith Robertson, *The University of Cape Town 1918–1948: The Formative Years* (Cape Town: UCT Press, 1993).

37 Simon Schaffer *et al.* (eds), *The Brokered World: Go-Betweens and Global Intelligence, 1770–1820* (Sagamore Beach, MA: Science History Publications, 2009); Steven Shapin, 'Placing the View from Nowhere: Historical and Sociological Problems in the Location of Science', *Transactions of the Institute of British Geographers*, 23, no. 1 (1998): 5–12.

38 David Knight, 'Review of N. Reingold & M. Rothernberg (Eds.), *Scientific Colonialism: A Cross-Cultural Comparison*', *Historical Records of Australian Science*, 7, no. 1 (1987): 134–6.

39 For the history of Hong Kong University, see Peter Cunich's *A History of the University of Hong Kong, Vol. 1, 1911–1945* (Hong Kong: HKU Press, 2012).

40 *Congress Proceedings, 1912*, p. 2.

41 Richard Drayton, 'Where Does the World Historian Write From? Objectivity, Moral Conscience and the Past and Present of Imperialism', *Journal of Contemporary History*, 46, no. 3 (2011): 671–85.

PART I

Foundations: 1802–80

CHAPTER ONE

Building institutions:
localising 'universal' learning

To a visitor from Britain the original buildings of many of the universities established in Australia, Canada, New Zealand and South Africa appear reassuringly familiar. With ivied cloisters and neo-gothic edifices they seem to stand as tangible signs of the exportation of old-world traditions to the new. But it would be a mistake to see these early universities as little more than transported institutions. As F. H. Chase, a professor of Divinity at the University of Cambridge, declared in 1903, in the settler colonies 'inherited tradition' was 'modified in the light of experience' to create 'many types of universities', each 'largely determined by its previous history and by its environment'.[1] Although the history of British settler universities is dominated by this tension between local conditions and imperial connections, in the period of their foundation it was the former that predominated.

Local foundations

The first universities founded in British North America were established by settlers from Britain and loyalists fleeing the American Revolution. They sought to perpetuate in colonial communities the privileges the Established Church enjoyed in England. As the 1802 statutes for King's College in Windsor, Nova Scotia, stipulated, '[n]o member of the University shall frequent the Romish mass, or the meeting Houses of Presbyterians, Baptists, or Methodists, or the Conventicles or places of Worship of any other dissenters from the Church of England ... or shall be present at any seditious or rebellious meetings.'[2] As colleges that provided a classical education to students who were required to affirm the 39 Articles, the 'King's Colleges' these settlers established in Windsor (1789), New Brunswick (1800, Royal Charter 1828), and Toronto (1827, opened 1843) borrowed heavily from the model of un-reformed Oxford – with its residential colleges, confessional criteria and classical curriculum.[3] This was also the model initially proposed in Australia. In the mid-1820s Thomas Scott – secretary to the Bigge Commission of Inquiry into the conditions of settlement in the colony – suggested the establishment of a comprehensive scheme of education under the control of the Church of England, ranging from elementary schools through to universities.[4]

However, these attempts to extend to the colonies the monopoly over education that the Established Church enjoyed in England provoked strong opposition from the numerous Presbyterian, Roman Catholic and nonconformist groups that also comprised colonial communities. In Sydney the Scott plan fell into abeyance, while in British North America two other kinds of institution arose to claim university status.[5] The founders of both Dalhousie in Nova Scotia (1818) and McGill in Montreal (1821) looked not to Oxford but to Edinburgh. Non-residential and non-sectarian, in Edinburgh teaching was delivered through lectures, and the curriculum included medicine and the sciences. Open 'to all occupations and sects of religions', both Dalhousie and McGill planned to offer courses in the natural and physical sciences as well as classics and theology.[6] 'If Dalhousie College [will] acquire usefulness and eminence,' declared its President, Thomas McCulloch, 'it will be not by an imitation of Oxford, but as an institution of science and practical intelligence.'[7] Third, alongside these Scottish-inspired foundations, an array of denominational colleges also emerged that modelled themselves after the nonconformist theological training colleges in Britain and the United States.[8] Founded in the 1830s and 1840s and funded by the donations of parishioners, these institutions aimed to train preachers and teachers by providing a classical and religious education in a residential setting. Yet in their early years all three kinds of university struggled to survive. Attracting tiny numbers of students, they lacked both money and materials. In the economic downturn of the early 1840s the denominational colleges only just managed to remain afloat, Dalhousie did not become fully functional until it was refounded in 1879, and McGill consisted only of the local medical school until it acquired a faculty of arts in 1843.

Things changed significantly in the improved economic conditions of the 1850s.[9] But better times produced conflicting impulses. On the one hand they brought a social and economic dynamism which in turn attracted money, confidence and migrants, resulting in the extension of responsible government and in turn the franchise. But on the other hand they also provoked uncertainty among established colonial elites who were anxious to ensure that social order did not crumble in the face of new forms of economic and political power. The history of the foundation and organisational design of settler universities records both these influences. In the context of intense debate in Britain about the form universities should take, colonial governments increasingly involved themselves in the foundation and reconstitution of a new wave of institutions.

In 1849 the Legislative Assembly of Ontario passed a bill that re-fashioned the Anglican King's College in Toronto into a secular, state-sponsored and faculty-based body called 'the University of Toronto'. However, with the other local denominational colleges resisting the government's plans for them to merge with the new institution, in 1853 the model of the University of London was proposed as a compro-mise.[10] Founded in 1836 as way of reconciling the 'Godless institution on Gower Street' later known as University College London (1826) with the rival King's College established by the Church of England (1828–29), the University of London was a secular body that awarded degrees solely on the basis of examination performance, to students taught in affiliated colleges. Following the example of London, in Toronto the provincial parliament turned the former King's College into 'University College' and proposed that, together with the denom-inational colleges, it should prepare students to sit the exams of a degree-confirming institution called the 'University of Toronto'. But the religious colleges were sceptical about this plan and only affiliated themselves slowly.[11] The complex politics of the colony meant that the original concept of a state-funded university that included professional schools was replaced by one that consisted of an examining institution and a government-run Arts college – albeit an Arts college in which history, geology, modern languages, natural history and engineering were also taught.[12]

Under the force of different local politics, in Sydney a separate com-promise emerged. In 1849 a local politician and landowner, William Wentworth, had introduced a bill to the New South Wales Legislative Council proposing the foundation of a university along the lines of that in London. But in the course of its passage, the bill was modified to allow the University Senate to establish its own secular, non-sectarian, state-endowed liberal arts college that would be staffed by the univer-sity professors and compete with colleges run by the various denomi-nations. However, when the first professor of classics, John Woolley, arrived in 1852, fresh from contemporary debates about reform taking place in Oxford, he discarded this notion and argued that the Univer-sity of Sydney should be reconstituted as a teaching *and* examining institution.[13] This was not a settlement that pleased the churches. Objecting to the diminution of their role, they campaigned hard until the university agreed on a compromise in the form of the University Colleges Act (1854). It gave land to each of the denominations to es-tablish residential colleges, but prevented them from conducting any teaching. As Woolley himself explained to a parliamentary committee of inquiry in 1859, the result was a new sort of institution:

> in this University we are trying an experiment which is a very difficult one ... that is, to unite the general secular teaching of the University with independent denominational Colleges, which are independent in their own sphere. It is a very difficult scheme, which has never been tried before anywhere.[14]

In contrast, in South Africa and New Zealand the London examining model had greater success as a solution not only to religious diversity but also to diffuse colonial populations animated by fierce provincial loyalties. As in Canada, in New Zealand the first efforts to establish higher education had been sponsored by the churches. A university was central to the plans of those who settled in Wakefield's Church of England Colony at Canterbury in the late 1840s, and equally important to the settlement scheme of the Scottish migrants who in the same decade founded communities in the South Island. However, when the Presbyterian Church in Otago endowed two chairs in the mid-1860s, the central colonial parliament responded by introducing its own *University Endowment Act*. This led the Province of Otago to pass an ordinance that formally founded a university, which in turn led the colonial parliament in 1870 to establish a rival 'University of New Zealand'. But the British Secretary of State was unwilling to grant two Royal Charters to the small colony. The foundation in 1873 of a third institution – an Anglican College in Christchurch called Canterbury College – hastened compromise between them. In 1874 both Canterbury and Otago became affiliated as founding members of the federal 'University of New Zealand'; a body that granted degrees in arts, law and medicine to students who had undergone a course of study at one of what would eventually be four constituent colleges.[15]

Similarly in South Africa, the model of London served as a boon to colonial nationalists wishing to centralise tertiary education. From 1858 students who had studied in a number of Cape Town's teaching establishments were able to sit 'higher' examinations set locally by the 'Board of Public Examiners in Literature and Science'. But in 1873, following the extension of responsible government, the newly elected Cape parliament converted this board into the 'University of the Cape of Good Hope'. An examining body fashioned after the University of London, it was designed to grant degrees to students taught in teaching colleges spread across the country. However, although in the 1870s a number of schools secured the government grants issued to centres that educated such students, in this period only the South African College and Stellenbosch School conducted serious collegiate-level work.

English-language degrees in arts (with broad-based courses modelled after London), law and medicine and certificates in land surveying were issued, but in the 1870s and 1880s student numbers remained small, and scholarships as well as the prestige of a European degree encouraged many students to travel to abroad for their studies.[16] Like the other universities established or re-established in the British settler colonies in the middle part of the nineteenth century, the University of the Cape of Good Hope was forged by the vicissitudes of local politics.

Taking a variety of forms, these settler universities all sought to localise the universal culture taught in British universities. This education was liberal in the sense that it sought to develop a student's moral and intellectual faculties through broad study, enabling him (and in the early period, colonial students were invariably male) to take up whichever occupation he might choose. But it was also liberal in that it presupposed another kind of liberty that was social and financial as well.[17] Universities in Britain differed in the kinds of learning they thought best constituted this education: Oxford placed the emphasis on classics, Cambridge on pure mathematics, the Scottish universities on moral philosophy, and London on a cross-section of arts, languages and sciences. But in practice all made some accommodation with the sciences and with the world outside their walls: for example, Cambridge introduced a Natural Sciences Tripos in 1851, and all three institutions prepared graduates for careers in the Church or the public schools, in law or medicine, the Civil Service or public life. Yet regardless of their various accents, the liberal and humane education they each provided emphasised the cultivation of character and culture as preparation for a life of political and social responsibility. The early settler universities assumed these same aims, seeking to shape those who would lead colonial society with an education worthy of the metropole. Most retained a focus upon the classical curriculum and continued to have Latin and Greek as entrance requirements. Although some, such as Melbourne, also offered science subjects, these were usually built into a broad-based arts degree. As the University of Adelaide's first chancellor said in 1877, the task of the settler universities was to direct 'the studies and [form] the character of the governing classes' and 'help elevate the middle class to higher civilization, the result of a more intellectual education'.[18]

This kind of liberal education was relatively easy to transport to colonial locations. As John Langton, the vice-chancellor of the University of Toronto, pointed out in 1860, the 'ordinary text-books used in education, the classical authors in various languages, the books of reference in common use, are not so numerous as to be beyond the reach of any College, or even of many private individuals'.[19] It could be carried out in modest rooms, by professors who had trained using almost the same books as their students. If, in the second part of the century, this static curriculum was increasingly being supplemented by branches of knowledge that were very much on the move, the early colonial universities remained focused on their role as local providers of the humane and liberal learning that worked to maintain the social and cultural hierarchies of their communities.

Settler universities were further drawn into local contexts by their need to build paying constituencies. In their early days they struggled to find students who could pass their entrance examinations and therefore sought ways to foster secondary education. Across Britain and the empire, university entrance tests served as the leaving certificate in secondary schools. In contexts in which secondary education was still largely dominated by private and denominational institutions, the university matriculation examination exerted a discernible influence upon the school curriculum. Settler professors were active in inspecting secondary schools with several tertiary bodies – including the South African College at Cape Town, Victoria College in Upper Canada and Acadia College in Nova Scotia – themselves growing out of such institutions.[20] But settler universities were also instrumental in the establishment of new feeder schools. Egerton Ryerson of Victoria College, Toronto, helped to design the state education system in Upper Canada in the 1840s, and Principal Woolley of the University of Sydney convinced the colonial government in New South Wales to establish the state-endowed and secular Sydney Grammar School in 1854.[21] In the 1860s a system of school and university bursaries was also extended by his successor, Charles Badham.[22] From their foundation settler universities established a relationship with the local secondary school system that, in most places, lasted into the second part of the twentieth century.

The same impulse pushed early settler universities to engage with public audiences. Funded by the subscriptions of parishioners, the denominational colleges in Canada were especially good at this. Throughout the nineteenth century their professors and principals gave public lectures and toured the parishes delivering sermons, sometimes canvassing for their own salaries.[23] Their libraries and museums were open to students and members of the community alike, and their graduates, who went on to fill the pulpits of the district, provided tangible evidence of their value. Similarly, the institutions established after 1850 by newly created colonial parliaments had to satisfy both the tax-paying public and the local government. In many universities professors offered public lectures. Evening classes in logic and composition were held at Dalhousie from 1841, and at McGill in 1855 the principal, J. W. Dawson, gave public lectures on zoology, natural philosophy, chemical engineering, paleontology and 'the Chemistry of Life'. In these ways, settler universities sought to demonstrate to their publics the value of the humane and liberal education they offered.

Scientific research was something that still largely took place outside the structure of the colonial university. Academic scientists were among a broad field of investigators attached to botanic gardens, natural history museums and government surveys, and working independently as collectors and explorers who looked abroad for recognition. As Daniel Wilson, the Professor of History and English at Toronto, wrote in 1856,

> such students of science as Canada has, stand, to a great extent, isolated in relation to each other, and look mainly for the appreciation of their labours to their scientific brethren in Europe. If Mr Logan meets with copper or coal in the course of this geological survey, he communicates it to Canada, and all her journals give welcome circulation to the fact; but if palaeontological researches among our Canadian strata disclose novel truths in relation to the structure of the *Graphalite*, he goes to Paris or to London with the discovery, and communicates it to his scientific brethren ... through the medium of English Societies' Transactions.[24]

Yet if Wilson's comments highlight the way Canadian scientists looked to Europe, they also point to the located nature of their work. The ability of early settler scientists to contribute to the global taxonomic project depended upon their relationship with their local environments.[25] For example, Ferdinand von Mueller, the abrasive director of Melbourne's Botanic Gardens, built an international reputation in the 1860s, which was premised on his ability to source – using a network of local collectors – species of plants unknown to his patrons in Europe.[26] International acclaim was thus contingent on local expertise, giving scientific investigators every reason to link themselves to particular regions even as they looked abroad for validation. Although removed from their fellow-workers, colonial researchers knew they had the ground – literally and therefore also intellectually – to themselves. As Loring Bailey, the professor of chemistry at the University of New Brunswick, wrote in 1861, 'I have the satisfaction of knowing that I work in a comparatively unexplored field and hope to lay a good foundation here, upon which in the future others may build.'[27]

What colonial scientists needed, thought Wilson in 1856, were publications that would 'furnish a means of intercourse among themselves, as well as an interchange of thought and discovery with the scientific world at large.' He hoped that the *Canadian Journal* – the publication of the Royal Canadian Institution, established in 1852 – might under his editorship serve the purpose. But the *Canadian Journal* was just one of several publications founded in Canada in the 1850s.[28] Reflecting the self-confidence engendered by the extension of responsible government, the middle of the century witnessed the birth of numerous such journals and societies in the settler colonies. In Australia, branches of the Royal Society were established in New South Wales (1850) and in Victoria (1854), with both beginning to publish their *Proceedings* in the 1860s; and from 1857 the *Cape Monthly Magazine* served the various literary and scientific institutions that had grown up in Cape Town in the 1830s. Important as forums for settler scientists, Saul Dubow has argued that these journals functioned as crucial sites for the construction of colonial identity among the growing middle classes.[29] Like universities, they too were part of the process by which settlers sought to localise institutions of knowledge and cultural production in this period.

Changes at home

However, in the 1870s settler universities came under growing pressure from rapidly developing colonial societies to demonstrate their relevance. Still struggling for student numbers, and often also reliant on government grants, these demands were not something they could afford to ignore. If universities were to survive they needed to establish their legitimacy, and this meant widening their educational remit. An 1878 resolution of the Senate of the University of Sydney expressed clearly this new awareness. Although its members 'did not abate anything of their estimate of high classical attainments', they expressed their conviction that 'the University of such an industrial community … should adapt itself more closely to the various views of its students concerning the occupations which shall constitute the future industry of their lives.' The Senate therefore resolved to

> gladly give opportunities for special preparation within the University, or in connection with it, for all the educated professions and for those technical occupations which are associated with science.[30]

The 1874 foundation Act of the University of New Zealand had actually made provision for degrees not just in arts, but also in law, medicine, music and science.[31] But when the Charter granted to them by the British Government only allowed for the first four, New Zealand banded together with Melbourne and Sydney in a joint petition. After 1882 students at all three universities (together with the University of Adelaide) were able to take degrees in the pure and applied science subjects that were coming to be seen as crucial to colonial development.

Change of this nature in Canada was more halting, and despite being on the books at Victoria from 1875 and Dalhousie from 1878, degrees in science were not generally offered in Canadian universities until after the First World War. However, provision for specialisation in science was frequently made within the Bachelor of Arts programme and, by the early 1890s, Dalhousie, New Brunswick and Queen's all had a number of science chairs, while McGill and Toronto could boast fully fledged departments. In South Africa too, science subjects were increasingly taught within the arts course, while specialised MSc and DSc degrees were instituted in 1906.

This new focus on science was part of a broader rapprochement between the universities and the professions. Although the ability to grant degrees in law, medicine and music had been enshrined in most of their original Charters, these were privileges that the early settler universities had not widely taken up. Instead, professional training had been controlled by independent professional institutions and conducted in proprietary schools. But from the 1870s and 1880s the settler universities began more actively to seek to incorporate these powerful knowledge communities. This was a move that in 1878 the Senate of the University of Sydney thought would prove universally advantageous. First, it would benefit prospective students, affording them new opportunities for training and advancement; second, it would assist the University, by increasing student numbers; and third, it would profit the professions, 'elevating' them through their association with the university.[32] Thus, by embracing professional education, the members of the Sydney Senate sought to position their institution as the ultimate credentialising body in a society that – like those across the industrial world – was increasingly coming to value certifiable expertise.[33]

What the Senate members did not recognise, however, was that the 'elevation' they envisaged would not necessarily be appreciated by the older training bodies they were seeking to displace. This was particularly the case with law. Although law degrees had been granted by numerous settler universities from their foundation, often very little teaching had actually been undertaken by professors, and the universities' involvement had been confined to that of examining institutions. In the 1870s and 1880s many of the larger universities did begin to offer teaching, but without the recognition of the various law societies this was of little practical benefit to students.[34] In some places formal recognition was granted more readily than others and, although by the 1890s schools of law had been established in Melbourne and Adelaide, and in most of Canada, South Africa and New Zealand, it was not until after the First World War that the universities succeeded in fully bringing legal education into their ambit.

Medicine was a different story. It was originally taught in separate, often privately run medical schools. Institutions such as McGill and Otago (notably, both based on the Scottish model) had been built upon such schools, but other universities seeking to enter the field of medical education found themselves in competition with them. In the 1860s and 1870s the Victoria faculty of medicine in Toronto and that at Queen's in Kingston had actually folded.[35] But the importance of clinical training and the increasing emphasis placed upon scientific research – attended by a need for expensive laboratories and equipment – pushed the colonial medical establishments towards rather than away from the settler universities. In the 1880s, a faculty of medicine was already flourishing at McGill, and by 1890 there were also schools of medicine at Dalhousie, Manitoba, Toronto and Western Ontario, many of which had or would incorporate the proprietary schools with which they had formerly competed. Similarly, in Adelaide, Melbourne, Sydney and to some extent also Otago, the universities' previously halting engagement with medical education was in the 1880s transformed into the establishment of fully fledged faculties and schools. Although in South Africa university medicine was not established until after the foundation of teaching universities in 1916, agitation for them began long before this date.[36] Across the settler world these medical schools grew quickly, attracting significant numbers of students and entrenching their place within the universities.

In rapidly developing communities, settler universities also observed the demand for highly skilled engineers and sought to position themselves as the institutions best placed to provide for their training. From 1873 a government-supported School of Practical Science began operating in Toronto in close association with the University, and diploma courses in engineering were revived at McGill in 1871 and established in New Brunswick in 1889. Engineering degrees were offered at Sydney from 1884, Melbourne from 1888 and Canterbury in New Zealand from 1885. In South Africa mining courses were established in association with the South African College and Victoria College in Stellenbosch from the mid-1890s with degrees in engineering granted from 1899.[37] But if establishing courses was one thing, attracting students was another. Universities initially had to compete not only with local schools of mines and technical colleges but also with the preconceptions of employers who thought the university course not sufficiently practical. Yet by the 1890s the incorporation of medicine – and in Australia also law – had helped to establish a university degree as the marker of economic and social standing. Together with government recognition, this proved attractive to both students and professional associations alike, and by 1900 engineering too had become firmly ensconced within settler universities.

As the century turned, universities across the settler empire widened their curricula even further. At the same time as the decline in student numbers and government funding brought about by the depression of the 1890s provided colonial institutions with a powerful incentive to develop their vocational and utilitarian offerings, the desire for social recognition propelled additional professional groups into the universities' arms. By 1914 settler universities variously offered diplomas or degrees in veterinary science, dentistry, agriculture, architecture, education and commerce as well as law, medicine and engineering.[38] Indeed, in this period a number of new universities were established which, from their inception, emphasised a vocational and applied as well as a traditional liberal education. Saskatchewan (1907), Alberta (1908), and British Columbia (1908); Tasmania (1890), Queensland (1909) and Western Australia (1911), all offered the practical and applied training that had come to be seen as essential to colonial development.

Having widened their curricula, settler universities also expanded their academic constituencies by extending the academic franchise, both to women and to the middle classes.[39] In New Zealand, the founding 1874 Act of the federal university was actually silent on the question of gender, and female students were admitted from its inception. The University of Adelaide perhaps wished this had been the course it too had pursued. In 1874 the local legislature had passed an Act that gave the university power to grant degrees to women. However, when application was made to the British Government, the Colonial Secretary warned that Letters Patent were not likely to be granted unless this clause was removed: 'Her Majesty's Government', wrote the Colonial Secretary, John Wodehouse, Earl of Kimberley, 'think it preferable that the constitution of the University of Adelaide should not, in the first instance at all events, contain so considerable a departure from the principles and procedures of the Universities of Oxford and Cambridge'.[40] Although the university decided to remove the clause, by the time the revised draft reached England in 1878 the University of London had itself begun to admit female students (first degrees conferred in 1882), and the Queen had changed her mind regarding Adelaide. This enabled a wave of reform across the settler colonies and the 1880s witnessed the extension of university education to women both in Britain and abroad.[41]

Moreover, by the 1890s the efforts of the founding generation of settler academics in building the school sector were beginning to pay off. In most colonies this period witnessed the passing of various pieces of legislation designed to extend free, compulsory and secular primary education and to institute state-funded secondary schools.

Universities and academics were often closely involved with this reform. In New South Wales, William Windeyer – the University of Sydney's first elected Member of Parliament – together with Professor Charles Badham, pushed for the expansion of state-supported grammar schools.[42] In the larger colonies in particular these measures significantly expanded the universities' student base, integrating them into co-ordinated educational systems that provided a path along which students could progress from primary school, through secondary education, to take a degree. Bringing a university education within the reach of students from the middle classes, the extension of public primary and secondary schooling helped entrench settler universities as fundamental parts of colonial communities.

The universities' accommodation of the changing needs of colonial societies ensured their importance to them. Not only did it help legitimate institutions that had previously served only the wealthy male elite, it also helped generate much needed income. In the 1880s increased government support – and sometimes donor bequests as well – bolstered their financial resources, while the incorporation of new subjects and the admission of women helped to attract larger numbers of paying students. The boom days, however, were not to last. When world-wide depression struck in the 1890s and government money dried up, settler universities were forced to cut back their expenditure and cope as best they could. But for the most part they did not go under, and this survival in the face of considerable financial difficulty attests the extent to which settler universities had successfully established themselves within their respective colonial societies. Standing at the head of comprehensive educational systems, conferring status upon the professions and attracting ever-larger numbers of students, they were now seen as an essential index of the maturity of settler communities. More secure in their place at home, by the end of the nineteenth century settler universities increasingly began to look for recognition abroad.

Changes abroad

James Belich has called the 1880s and 1890s a period of 're-colonization', in which the 'tightening of economic relations' between Britain and the settler colonies 'correlated with a tightening of other kinds of relations as well'.[43] The settler universities' turn to Britain in this period was both a product and a driver of these changes. Their attempts to reposition themselves as members of an expansive British academic community must be seen as part of the broader integrative processes reshaping both the empire and the world at the end of the nineteenth century.

In the 1870s and 1880s new technologies began to revolutionise global transport and communication. By the 1860s steam-powered ocean vessels had come to dominate passenger and freight transportation across the Atlantic, and by the 1880s, following the opening of the Suez Canal in 1869, they had largely taken over longer-range routes to Australasia and East Asia as well. Journey times were dramatically reduced: the transatlantic crossing, formerly thirty days, now could take as few as ten; the trip to Australia fell from three months to one. Moreover, cheaper steel enabled the building of larger ships, which in turn lowered passenger and transport prices.[44] By the turn of the century, travelling between Britain and the settler colonies was quicker and cheaper than it had ever been and this facilitated the more frequent movement of all sorts of people, including academics. The acceleration of transportation in turn improved communications. Letters travelled faster and more often, and undersea telegraph cables connected Britain to North America in the 1860s and to Australasia in the 1870s. Although the telegraph was too expensive for widespread individual use, governments as well as other organisations such as universities were eager adopters. Moreover, the formation of newspaper syndicates made events in Britain more accessible to colonial readers.[45] Moving people and information around the world, these developments meant that by the end of the century universities and academics in the settler colonies could expect to stay in much closer touch with Britain than ever before.

These technological changes helped drive a growing acquaintance with the idea of 'research'. Emerging in Germany in the early nineteenth century, the Humboldtian notion of scientific research had long been resisted in the ancient English universities. But by the 1880s this was beginning to change. The rise of the chemical and electrical industries in Britain had created a demand for scientific innovation and educated labour. Aware of Germany's growing industrial might, British politicians and men of business called upon universities to style themselves more closely after German institutions.[46] The increasing complexity of all the disciplines meant they were no longer as accessible to the amateur or dilettante as they previously had been: laboratories, publications, specialised knowledge, equipment and skills were all becoming more and more important. Not only did science now require investments that only large organisations such as universities could afford, but the changing politics of knowledge meant that these were investments that universities could not afford to neglect. If they were to sustain their claim to be credentialisers of knowledge, universities had to remain at its expanding edge. Institutions in the settler world were as subject to these pressures as were their cousins in Britain. From the end of the century on, the larger universities in Canada and Australia – and later South Africa and New Zealand – began to make cautious provision for research. It by no means displaced the primary role teaching played in the life of settler academics, but those who pursued research were pulled into ever closer contact with their fellow-workers abroad.

At the same time, a growing awareness of Germany's economic power was leading many British commentators to think in new ways about the settler colonies.[47] Since 1868 the Royal Colonial Institute had provided a platform for those who advocated closer political union with the self-governing colonies, but the publication of J. R. Seeley's *The Expansion of England* (1883) and J. A. Froude's *Oceana or England and her Colonies* (1886), and the foundation of the Imperial Federation League in 1884, all point to an intensified concern with the issue in the 1880s. However the movement was divided over which of the many models of imperial union should be pursued, and in 1893 the League dissolved.[48] In its wake there arose a proliferation of extra-parliamentary pressure groups, most of which claimed to be non-political, proposing various forms of 'practical unity': defence, trade, emigration, the judiciary – all these were issues around which closer imperial unionists began to agitate.[49] But even as these proposals for imperial union proliferated, some commentators expressed concern that they misjudged the political feeling of the self-governing communities of the settler colonies. In 1905 Richard Jebb argued for the need to take account of what he called 'colonial nationalism'.[50] Consequently, in the early years of the new century, numerous imperial groups turned to the idea of sentimental union and sought to institute schemes that would instead foster what was seen as the already existing cultural and ideological affinity between Britain and the settler colonies.[51] Education was the focus of many of these, and the Imperial Studies Group (c.1887), the Victoria League (1901) and the League of the Empire (1901) all emerged in this period.

In the context of these changes, across the British settler world a new type of teaching institution emerged. In Britain the 1870s and early 1880s witnessed the foundation of a number of centres located in industrial regions such as Birmingham and Sheffield that asserted the professional and vocational nature of their education.[52] Together with the regional colleges that prepared students to sit the University of London's examinations, they served a middling social stratum which – without the social background or necessary patrons – needed to rely on hard qualifications.[53] In South Africa too, the early years of the new century saw the University of the Cape of Good Hope shelter the development of a number of new teaching colleges: Victoria College in Stellenbosch (1881); the Transvaal Technical Institute in Johannesburg (1903), which became the Transvaal University College (1906); Rhodes University College, Grahamstown (1904); University College, Pretoria (1908); and Natal University College (1909).

However, even as these teaching colleges flowered, the disadvantages of the system of centralised examinations which they supported were swiftly becoming apparent: these imposed a uniformity that encouraged rote-learning and were not conducive to innovative teaching. In 1880 Owens College, Manchester (established in 1851), broke away from London and combined with Yorkshire College in Leeds and a projected college in Liverpool to form a new federal university, the Victoria University of Manchester. Unlike an examining institution in that it required students to be taught in constituent colleges by professors who were also responsible for their assessment, this new type of institution reflected the move away from the *laissez-faire* notion of a marketplace of talents towards one in which specialised knowledge was imparted by those already qualified. In 1887 it became the model for the University of Toronto, in 1893 for the University of Wales and in 1908 also for the National University of Ireland, formed from the former colleges of the disbanded Royal University.[54] In 1900, and again in 1910, the University of London itself was reformed, and centralised faculties were established with responsibility for monitoring academic standards within its affiliated institutions. After 1910 the University of London operated both an 'internal' programme, regulating the teaching of its students, and an 'external' programme, offering degrees by examination only. With the exception of this latter scheme, by the First World War the model of the examining university – which was so prominent in the middle part of the nineteenth-century – had disappeared in Britain. Although it survived in India, New Zealand, and South Africa, it did so in increasingly hostile conditions.

In its place arose a type of university that laid greater emphasis upon teaching and upon the scientific, professional and applied subjects that were beginning to be seen as central to national and imperial development. This new emphasis was reflected not just in the new federal universities but also in the emergence in the early twentieth century of independent, unitary, degree-granting institutions, with responsibility for both teaching and assessment. In England, the civic colleges began to assume full independent status, while in Canada a number of the religious colleges were reconstituted as non-denominational bodies, with their curricula expanded and Royal Charters granted to them.[55] At the same time, provincial legislatures – especially in the new communities in the Canadian prairies – began to endow public universities. Influenced by the English red-brick institutions as well as by the American state universities, these sought, in the words of Henry Marshall Tory (who had helped establish McGill College in Vancouver), to 'avoid the mistakes of the past, ... [by] start[ing] on a teaching basis'.[56] In South Africa too, a 1916 Act of Parliament created independent universities out of the preparatory bodies in Cape Town, Johannesburg and Stellenbosch that had previously served the Cape of Good Hope University.[57]

Funded by local government and industry and offering courses in an ever-increasing range of disciplines, whether in England or the settler colonies, in many ways all these institutions might be thought of as what A. H. Halsey has called 'provincial' universities. According to Halsey, for most of the twentieth-century only Oxford and Cambridge functioned as 'national' academic institutions, feeding and fed by 'the national elites of politics, administration, business and the liberal professions'.[58] All the rest, including the University of London, were in his view 'provincial' – aiming 'to meet the needs of the professional and industrial middle classes ... [and taking] most of their students from their own region'.[59] Although the London School of Economics, with its close connection to metropolitan elites, may be an exception, this description certainly fits Sydney and Toronto just as well as it does Manchester. Not only did such institutions provide a professional and practical as well as liberal education to students from their own region, but as Chapter 2 shows, they also began to feed the best of these into the 'national' universities of Oxford and Cambridge, and to a lesser extent London and Edinburgh. Although they continued to devote energy and resources to consolidating, extending, and often also placating their local colonial constituencies, it was as members of this expansive British academic community that, from the 1880s, many settler universities sought to define themselves.

⚬

The authority of settler universities rested principally upon their role as local agents of 'universal' culture and learning. Built by colonial elites as a way of maintaining the established social order, the gargoyles and turrets that decorate their original buildings were part of their early performance of this role. As proud assertions of the maturity of colonial societies and, at the same time, anxious agents in the quest to cultivate the culture and character of those who would lead them, in their early years settler universities were very much local institutions that sought to territorialise the structures of universal scholarship and turn them to parochial purposes.

When the content and social function of 'universal' culture began to change in the 1870s, however, the ways that universities performed their at once local and global role started to shift as well. Settler communities began to demand that their universities should be more than cultural incubators of a narrow elite. As revolutions in communication and transportation, together with changing economic and political circumstances, led settler societies to think in new ways about their place in the rapidly globalising late Victorian world, universities in the colonies were forced to reassess the way they performed this role. By embracing science and the professions and extending their academic franchise they reasserted their position as institutions that credentialised universal knowledge. This shored up their financial position and their local legitimacy. But, unlike the largely static classical curriculum, scientific research was a dynamic and rapidly expanding field of study. No longer content with gargoyles and gowns, from the 1880s settler universities began to look for new ways to demonstrate their connection and contribution to 'universal' scholarship.

Notes

1 Chase in 'Official Report of the Allied Colonial Universities Conference', *The Empire Review*, 6, no. 31 (1903): 71–128, p. 79.
2 Quoted in F. W. Vroom, *King's College: A Chronicle, 1789–1939* (Halifax, NS: Imperial Publishing Company, 1941), p. 41.
3 They were joined later by Bishop's College in Quebec (1843, Royal Charter 1852) and Trinity College in Ontario (1853), both also Church of England foundations.
4 John Thomas Bigge, 'Report of the Commissioner of Inquiry into the State of the Colony of New South Wales', *Parliamentary Papers*, 20 (1822).
5 C. Turney, Ursula M. L. Bygott, and Peter Richard Chippendale, *Australia's First: A History of the University of Sydney*, 2 vols (Sydney: University of Sydney in association with Hale and Iremonger, 1991), pp. 15–25.
6 Quoted in Newton, *The Universities and Educational Systems of the British Empire*, p. 14; Peter B. Waite, *The Lives of Dalhousie University* (Montreal: McGill-Queen's University Press, 1994), p. 15.
7 Quoted in Robin Sutton Harris, *A History of Higher Education in Canada, 1663-1960* (Toronto: University of Toronto Press, 1976), p. 33.
8 Upper Canada Academy (later Victoria College) was established in Ontario by the Wesleyan Methodist Church (1836); Acadia College in Nova Scotia by the Baptists (1838; degrees granted from 1840); Queen's University, Kingston, by the Presbyterians (1841); Mount Allison College, New Brunswick, by the Wesleyans (1843; Royal Charter 1858); and the College of Bytown (now the University of Ottawa) by the Missionary Oblates of Mary Immaculate (1848). In French Canada the Université Laval (1663) followed the pattern of universities in Latin America; it was founded first as a Catholic seminary and from 1852 fashioned after the example of the University of Paris.
9 James Belich, *Replenishing the Earth: The Settler Revolution and the Rise of the Anglo-World, 1783–1939* (Oxford: Oxford University Press, 2009), pp. 88–9, 306–55.
10 Martin L. Friedland, *The University of Toronto: A History* (Toronto: University of Toronto Press, 2002), pp. 30–42.
11 Knox College became affiliated informally in 1853 and formally in 1885, St Michael's in 1881 and Wycliffe in 1885. In 1877 the University Manitoba was also established as an examining institution with the sole power of conferring degrees to students

taught in affiliated colleges.

12 On denominational politics in Ontario, see A.B. McKillop, *Matters of Mind: The University in Ontario, 1791–1951* (Toronto: University of Toronto Press, 1994).

13 E. I. Carlyle, 'Woolley, John (1816–1866)', *Oxford Dictionary of National Biography* (Oxford University Press, 2004), accessed 27 Feb. 2007, www.oxforddnb.com/view/article/29958.

14 *Report from the Select Committee on the Sydney University 1860*, quoted in Turney, Bygott and Chippendale, *Australia's First*, p. 92.

15 Auckland College joined in 1882 and Victoria University College at Wellington in 1897. See J. C. Beaglehole, *The University of New Zealand: An Historical Study* (Auckland: Whitcomb and Tombs, 1937), pp. 101, 117.

16 Travelling scholarships are discussed in Chapter 2. Boucher, *The University of the Cape of Good Hope*, p. 58.

17 Michael Jan Sanderson, 'Introduction', in Michael Sanderson (ed.), *The Universities in the Nineteenth Century* (London: Routledge and Kegan Paul, 1975), pp. 1–5.

18 Chancellor Bishop Short in 1877, quoted in Walter George Keith Duncan and Roger Ashley Leonard, *The University of Adelaide, 1874–1974* (Adelaide: Rigby, 1973), p. 8.

19 Langton before the 1860 House of Assembly Committee of investigation into the University of Toronto, quoted in Robert Blackburn, *Evolution of the Heart: A History of the University of Toronto Library up to 1981* (Toronto: University of Toronto Library, 1989), p. 34.

20 Until the late nineteenth century the colleges that prepared students to sit the exams of the University of the Cape of Good Hope functioned as glorified secondary schools, teaching students at both pre- and post-matriculation level.

21 In 1853 McGill assumed control of the High School of Montreal (established 1843) and in 1857 established the McGill Normal School. Stanley Brice Frost, *McGill University for the Advancement of Learning: Vol. 1, 1801–1895* (Montreal: McGill-Queen's University Press, 1980), pp. 161; 192–3.

22 Geoffrey Sherington and Julia Horne, 'Modes of Engagement: Universities and Schools in Australia, 1850-1914' in Peter Cunningham, Susan Oosthuizen and Richard Taylor (eds), *Beyond the Lecture Hall: Universities and Community Engagement from the Middle Ages to the Present Day* (Cambridge: University of Cambridge, Faculty of Education, 2009), p. 137; Roderic Campbell, 'The Modest Hospitality of a Scholar: Badham and the First Bursaries', *University of Sydney Archives Record* (2005): 13–22.

23 R. S. Longley, *Acadia University* (Wolfville, NS: Kentville Publishing, 1938), pp. 45–65, 94–5.

24 Quoted in Harris, *A History of Higher Education in Canada*, pp. 83–4.

25 See Jim Endersby, *Imperial Nature: Joseph Hooker and the Practices of Victorian Science* (Chicago, IL: University of Chicago Press, 2008).

26 Deirdre Morris, 'Mueller, Sir Ferdinand Jakob Heinrich Von (1825–1896)', *Australian Dictionary of Biography*, accessed 3 Aug. 2011, http://adb.anu.edu.au/biography/mueller-sir-ferdinand-jakob-heinrich-von-4266/text6893.

27 Harris, *A History of Higher Education in Canada*, p. 79.

28 In the 1850s the Literary and Historical Society of Quebec (established 1824) increased the hitherto haphazard publications of its *Transactions*; the Natural History Society of Montreal (established 1827) began to publish the *Canadian Naturalist and Geologist* in 1857; the Canadian Institute (established 1849) established the *Canadian Journal* in 1852. Other professional journals included in Montreal: the *Montreal Medical Gazette* (Apr. 1844 to Mar. 1845), the *Canadian Medical Journal* (1852–53) and the *Medical Chronicle* (1852–59); in Toronto: the *Upper Canada Journal of Medical, Surgical and Physical Science* (Apr. 1851 to Sept. 1854). See *Ibid.*, p. 81.

29 Dubow, *A Commonwealth of Knowledge*, pp. 35–78.

30 University of Sydney Archives (USA), *Minutes of the Senate*, G1/1/3 July and 7 Aug. 1878.

31 Beaglehole, *The University of New Zealand*, 109–10.

32 USA, *Minutes of the Senate*, G1/1/3 July and 7 Aug. 1878

33 See Harold James Perkin, *The Rise of Professional Society: England since 1880* (London: Routledge, 1989).

34 This was particularly the case in Canada, where lectures were offered at McGill (c1850s), Laval (1878), Dalhousie (1883) and Toronto (1889). Similarly at Sydney, degrees were granted from 1864, but until the foundation of the Law School in 1890 the faculty functioned as little more than an examining board. Though a Law School wasn't formally established in Melbourne until 1873, from 1861 it had offered a LLB, which was recognized by the Law Society. See Selleck, *The Shop*, p. 64.

35 Harris, *A History of Higher Education in Canada*, pp. 161–2.

36 See Boucher, *The University of the Cape of Good Hope*, p. 76. J. A. Louw, 'A Brief History of the Medical Faculty, University of Cape Town', *South African Medical Journal*, November (1979): 864–70.

37 See Friedland, *The University of Toronto*, pp. 80–4; Boucher, *The University of the Cape of Good Hope*, pp. 74–5.

38 Veterinary Science (Laval, McGill, Melbourne, Sydney); Dentistry (Melbourne, New Zealand, Sydney, Toronto); Agriculture (Adelaide, Melbourne, New Zealand South Africa, Sydney, Toronto); Architecture (Melbourne, Sydney, Toronto); Education (Melbourne, Sydney, Toronto); and Commerce (Manitoba, McGill, New Zealand, Sydney, Toronto).

39 Julia Horne and Geoffrey Sherington, 'Extending the Educational Franchise: The Social Contract of Australia's Public Universities, 1850–1890', International Standing Conference for the History of Education, delivered in 2008.

40 Quoted in Duncan and Leonard, *The University of Adelaide, 1874–1974*, pp. 13–14. Letters Patent were granted along the original lines, in March 1881.

41 Degrees were granted to women at Melbourne and Victoria (1883), Acadia and Queen's (1884), Adelaide, Dalhousie, Sydney and Toronto (1885), Trinity (1886), McGill (1888), Manitoba and New Brunswick (1889). In many cases women had been admitted to attend university courses before they were entitled to earn degrees.

42 Three were established at the regional centres of Maitland, Goulburn and Bathurst. See E.W. Dunlop, 'The Public High Schools of New South Wales, 1883–1912', *Journal of the Royal Australian Historical Society*, 51 (1965): 60–64; Sherington and Horne, 'Modes of Engagement'.

43 Belich, *Replenishing the Earth*, pp. 9, 206–9, 462, 207.

44 *Ibid.*, pp. 108–12; Daniel R. Headrick, *The Invisible Weapon: Telecommunications and International Politics, 1851–1945* (New York: Oxford University Press, 1991).

45 Simon J. Potter, *News and the British World: The Emergence of an Imperial Press System 1876–1922* (Oxford: Clarendon Press, 2003).

46 See, for example, Mark Pattison, 'Review of the Situation', 1876, in Michael Sanderson (ed.), *The Universities in the Nineteenth Century* (London: Routledge and Kegan Paul, 1975).

47 See Andrew S. Thompson, *Imperial Britain: The Empire in British Politics, C.1880–1932* (Harlow: Longman, 2000).

48 See Ged Martin, 'The Idea of Imperial Federation', in Ronald Hyam and Ged Martin (eds), *Reappraisals in British Imperial History* (London: Macmillan, 1975), p. 130.

49 Thompson, *Imperial Britain*, p. 26; Bell, *The Idea of Greater Britain*.

50 Richard Jebb, *Studies in Colonial Nationalism* (London: Edward Arnold, 1905).

51 James Greenlee, 'The ABCs of Imperial Unity', *Canadian Journal of History*, 14, no. 1 (1979): 49–64, p. 49.

52 Michael Jan Sanderson, 'Introduction' in *Ibid.*, p. 5.

53 These included Owens' College, Manchester (1851), Yorkshire College, Leeds (1887), University College in Bristol (1876), Dundee (1881), Mason Science College, Birmingham (1875), Firth College, Sheffield (1879), and University Colleges in Aberystwyth (1872), Nottingham (1881), Cardiff (1883) and Bangor (1884). In 1907 the parallel stream of teaching institutions clustered in the last quarter of the century around the Royal College of Science and the Royal School of Mines in South Kensington, London, also affiliated with the University of London. On professionalisation more broadly, see Perkin, *The Rise of Professional Society*.

54 Initially the University of Wales comprised Aberystwyth, Bangor and Cardiff Colleges, and these were joined in 1920 by Swansea. Cork and Galway and Dublin joined

the National University of Ireland, while University College, Belfast, became the independent Queen's University. Also influenced by this model was the University of Durham, which became affiliated in 1880 with the Newcastle College of Physical Science and Newcastle Medical School. In 1892 University College, Reading, was established in connection with the University of Oxford.

55 Birmingham (1900), Liverpool (1903), Leeds (1904), Victoria University of Manchester (1904), Sheffield (1905) Bristol (1909) and Reading (1926). After the Second World War, Nottingham (1948), Southampton (1952), Hull (1954), Exeter (1955), Leicester (1957) and Newcastle (1963) all received Royal Charters. Toronto Baptist College became McMaster University in 1887 and the Anglican Western University of London Ontario became the University of Western Ontario in 1908.

56 Tory to Alexander Cameron Rutherford (Premier of Alberta), 6 Mar. 1906, quoted in Walter Hugh Johns, *A History of the University of Alberta, 1908–1969* (Edmonton: University of Alberta Press, 1981), p. 10.

57 The University of South Africa was also established as a federal university incorporating Grey University College at Bloemfontein, Huguenot at Wellington (Cape Province), Natal at Pietermaritzburg, Rhodes at Grahamstown, Potchefstroom, and Transvaal University College at Pretoria. Over the course of the first part of the twentieth century they too would become independent.

58 A. H. Halsey, 'Oxford and the British Universities', in Brian Harrison (ed.), *The History of the University of Oxford* (Oxford: Oxford University Press, 1994), pp. 575, 580.

59 *Ibid.*

PART II

Connections: 1880–1914

CHAPTER TWO

Forging links abroad:
books, travelling scholarships, leave of absence

Speaking in London in 1903, the vice-chancellor of the University of the Cape of Good Hope, Sir John Buchanan, alluded to the travelling scholarships his institution had recently established for South African graduates. 'We in the Colonies', he explained, 'are very desirous that our best young men should be able to pursue their postgraduate studies in [Britain], and to attain to the high excellence in the different branches of science, physics, chemistry, and other cognate branches of learning which they can only now get by going abroad.'[1] Buchanan's comments point to the emergence of changing patterns of academic territoriality at the end of the nineteenth century.[2] Conscious of the growing importance of new and dynamic forms of knowledge, from the 1880s many of the large settler universities began look beyond their local constituencies, investing in mechanisms that were designed to connect them more closely to scholarship abroad. By increasing the flows of academic people, information and resources to and from the colonies, settler universities sought to create relative and relational forms of proximity that might ameliorate some of the isolation imposed by their territorial location.

Books and libraries

Importing books was one way for settler universities to extend their temporal and spatial reach. Although the Australian and Indian universities had begun to send their *Calendars* to the Bodleian and British libraries in the 1850s, it was only in the 1880s that settler universities realised that wide-scale publication exchange offered a relatively inexpensive way for them to build their own collections. In 1889–90, McGill exchanged publications with thirty universities; in 1892–93 Strathclyde received thirty-eight publications; and in 1904–5 Sydney traded a total of seventy-eight *Calendars* with institutions overseas.[3] Even the University of New Zealand's Auckland College was in 1895 reporting exchanges with seventeen overseas universities. By listing these exchanges in their *Calendars* and *Annual Reports*, the universities in the settler colonies began to proclaim their imperial and international standing to the communities in which they were located.

But with only their *Calendars* to send, settler universities were limited in their acquisitional reach. The development in this period of university printing houses was in part a response to this need for additional publications to send abroad. As Robert Blackburn has pointed out, the University of Toronto Press began in just this way. On Valentine's Day 1890 a fire destroyed all but one hundred of the University of Toronto's estimated 70,000 volumes. As part of its reconstruction, the university issued a request for book donations, receiving approximately 20,000, 10,000 and 10,000 gifted volumes from Britain, Germany and the United States respectively. In order to continue a relationship with the many foreign societies and academic institutions that had made these contributions, Toronto wanted to send something back in return. However, all it had was its *Calendar*. This problem was solved in 1897 with the establishment of *University of Toronto Studies*. Aided by funds from a legislative grant, in return for copies to use for exchange, the university librarian sponsored and managed a scheme that brought to press research undertaken by the university's members.[4] Similar motives underpinned the foundation of university presses in South Africa (1914) and Melbourne (1921), while Sydney published in 1914 a *Bibliographical Record* that it sent to numerous institutions in Britain and the United States.[5] From the end of the century, several settler universities also began to print accounts of the research output of their staff in their *Calendars*.[6] By producing items for exchange in this way, settler universities not only increased their library holdings, they also promoted themselves as centres active in research that could keep company with institutions in Britain and abroad.

But fostering publication exchange only went part of the way to improving university library collections. Beginning in the 1880s, the larger settler universities also began to increase their purchase of books and journals published abroad. The critical reports of the Carnegie Commissioners into library conditions in the British Dominions, published in the early 1930s, have cast a long shadow over assessments about the state of colonial libraries. With few exceptions these reports described university libraries in Australia, New Zealand, South Africa, and to some extent Canada, as unprofessional, inaccessible and underfunded.[7] However, while that assessment is not necessarily inaccurate, it only presents part of the picture. An examination of the expenditure of settler universities shows that from the 1880s many were actually increasing the amount they devoted to the purchase of books.[8] At Sydney the library allocation doubled between 1880 and 1890, while at Toronto the book fund increased from 2,600 Canadian dollars per annum in 1880, to $6,000 in 1896, rising again to $14,400 in 1907 and $34,932 in 1921–22. This was a growth well above the rate of inflation. In South Africa too, there were hints at progress: although in 1929 the principal of the University of the Witwatersrand still thought the library at his institution could 'hardly be said to exist', the *Calendars* of the South African College reveal (slowly) growing holdings since the end of the nineteenth century.[9] By 1914 universities such as Sydney, McGill, Toronto and, to a lesser extent, Queen's and Adelaide, could boast radically expanded collections. In all these places, libraries were becoming much more professionalised, with many universities regularising their management and appointing full-time librarians. Only in New Zealand did the period not witness some effort to improve college libraries.[10]

In many cases these settler universities were helped along in their project of library expansion by the generosity of local benefactors. Thomas Fisher's bequest to Sydney's library in 1885 dramatically reversed its fortunes, while the benefactions of Molsen, Redpath, Macdonald and Osler to McGill (1876, 1881, c.1898 and 1919), the Barr Smith family to Adelaide (beginning in 1892), R. S. Stuttaford to the South African College (1909) and James Douglas to Queen's (c.1918), were equally crucial.[11] It is likely that in making their bequests Fisher and the Barr Smith family had been influenced by the visit of C. W. Holgate. Having toured the Australasian colonies in 1884, he had written a report for the Library Association of the United Kingdom in which he had noted that Adelaide's library 'had but few gifts of value, and in fact very few gifts at all', while Sydney's was 'sadly deficient in modern editions of the classics, and in scientific works it cannot be considered as being at all up to the mark'.[12] At Toronto it was the tragic fire of 1890 that stimulated library benefactions. In the days after the blaze an estimated 50,000 people arrived to inspect the damage. Moved by such spectacular loss, both the provincial government and the public rallied to support the library's reconstruction. According to both the library's historian, Robert Blackburn, and the university's president of the day, Daniel Wilson, the Toronto library emerged from the fire 'richer as well as larger'.[13] By 1909 it could boast nearly 130,000 volumes.

While the fire stimulated benefactions to Toronto's library, it also provided an opportunity for the university to reconsider the library's design. In June of 1890 Toronto's librarian set out on an American tour to learn about library management and in 1891 its architect visited

Cornell and the University of Pennsylvania, where large new libraries designed to accommodate research and seminar teaching were under construction.[14] The building unveiled in Toronto in 1893 reflected these influences: with room for 120,000 volumes and a fire-proof stack built entirely of cast-iron and lit by electricity, it also contained four 'seminary' rooms and a 'conversation room' for teaching and discussion, along the German model. At McGill too, the Medical School matched itself against developments in the United States, claiming by 1885 already to have 'the largest special library connected with any medical school on this continent'.[15] Influenced by the new role libraries were being accorded in America, where the seminar method of teaching was beginning to take hold, and spurred by the establishment of Johns Hopkins University in Baltimore as a primarily postgraduate institution, from the end of the century McGill and Toronto both prioritised their library collections.

If in Canada it was the example of American institutions that made clear to universities the fundamental importance of libraries, at the University of Sydney it was distance. Conscious of its physical isolation, Sydney sought to mitigate its circumstances by investing in the intellectual resources that would help bring European scholarship to Australia. As the librarian Robert Dallen wrote in his 1914 history of the University:

> in Australia the needs are more extensive and more pressing than those of similar institutions in Europe; we require a larger collection of books than any of the University libraries of the Old World; for in Europe, if a book is not immediately forthcoming, one may send for it to a library near at hand. Here we are remote from the great centres of culture. Our Universities and our libraries far apart, and all have special needs of money and of books.[16]

Comparison of the holdings of Sydney's Fisher Library with those of the library at the University of Birmingham suggests that, thanks to end-of-century investments, academics in Sydney had better access to British and European scholarship than their contemporaries in the Midlands. In 1901 the library at Birmingham University (the successor to Mason Science College) numbered 28,000 volumes and was financed by a total income of £593 14s.[17] In the same year at Sydney University, the library comprised some 52,000 volumes and spent £916 on books.[18] While in 1892 Sydney held subscriptions to at least 216 periodicals and transactions of scholarly societies, Birmingham in 1901 received approximately 120 of these. Both universities subscribed to the major British scientific periodicals (*Nature*, the *Proceedings of the Royal Society of London*, the *British Medical Journal*, *The Lancet* and the *Philosophical Magazine*), as well as a significant number of German and French scientific serials (including *Annalen der Chemie, Annalen der Physik, Archives de Zoologie* and *Annales de l'Institut Pasteur*). But Sydney's holdings also included a large number of American, British, French and German journals not available at Birmingham. These included *Archiv für Mikroskopische Anatomie, Bulletin de l'Académie de Médecine, Zeitschrift für Biologie, Science, American Geologist;* and major British publications like the *Journal of Anatomy and Physiology, Journal of the Royal Geographical Society* and the *Linnean Society Journal.* When it came to the humanities, readers in the Birmingham University Library were also far more restricted than those at Sydney's Fisher Library. Both libraries held subscriptions to *The Nineteenth Century,* the *Quarterly Review,* the *Revue des Deux Mondes,* the *Proceedings of the Royal Historical Society* and supplements of the *Dictionary of National Biography.* But while Birmingham subscribed to nine literary periodicals not available at the University of Sydney, Sydney subscribed to twenty-five not available at Birmingham.

Two decades later this disparity persisted. In 1921, Birmingham University Library numbered 75,000 volumes, and received fewer than 200 periodicals, whereas the Fisher Library at Sydney totalled 120,000 books and received 700 serial publications a year.[19] Such provisions were by no means universal, nor are they an accurate index of access to resources: staff at Birmingham could travel to Manchester, Oxford or London, and those at McGill or Toronto could in a day reach the better-provisioned American libraries on the East Coast. But what a comparison such as this does show is that settler universities' library holdings could be relatively good by comparison with those of their provincial contemporaries.

In this light, a closer examination of the Carnegie Report on the Australian university libraries reveals a more complex picture. What the Carnegie Commissioners saw as deficiencies – the absence of trained librarians, the lack of books on general subjects and the difficulties of access for undergraduates – in fact suggests that these university libraries were functioning very effectively as research collections. As Munn and Pitt wrote in 1935:

> The professor chooses all books for his own department and no one dares to interfere in any way with his selection. It is properly argued that the professor knows his field better than anyone else, but there are many instances in which he has selected books according to his personal interests alone. The library may thus comprise strong sections relating to the hobbies of successive professors without ever becoming a well-rounded general collection.

Indeed, at Sydney:

> The current issues of all periodicals are sent automatically to the professor to whose field they pertain, and are recalled by the library only if a student makes a demand for them. Entire files of many periodicals are retained by the professors ... It is estimated that at least 30,000 library books are at all times in their possession.[20]

Holgate had noted the same buying practice in 1884.[21] Though it did not necessarily meet the needs of undergraduates, this professorial control of the library budget meant senior academics working in Australian universities had what was effectively a personal budget that granted them access to the latest international scholarship. It meant that a professor such as W. H. Bragg, who was researching α-rays in early 1904 at Adelaide, could write to his fellow physicist, Ernest Rutherford, at McGill University in Montreal, confident that they both had read '[t]wo papers ... published in the December [1903] number of the *Phil Mag*'.[22] The settler universities' late nineteenth-century investment in library resources signalled their desire to participate in a new form of academic internationalism – one that was beginning to shift the geographies of intellectual consumption and production.

Leave of absence

Settler universities also sought to reconfigure their relationship with 'universal' scholarship by facilitating the mobility of their staff. At the end of the nineteenth century no practice of academic leave operated in Britain. 'I know of no English or Scottish University which has any regular system of sabbatic leave', declared Allen Mawer, the professor of English at Liverpool University, in 1921:

> All that we have is that occasionally, and in entirely sporadic fashion, three or six months' leave of absence is given to a professor who has grown old in the service of his University and is perhaps in danger of a serious breakdown.[23]

As Heike Jöns shows, before 1914 the number of such applications made for academic purposes was very low, and the period of leave granted only ever a short one.[24]

But settler academics felt keenly their distance from British and European centres of scholarship. As research grew in importance, their need to stay in touch with their overseas colleagues became more and more pressing. Canadian universities had endeavoured to address this issue by adjusting the length of the teaching year. At King's College in Toronto the council had in the 1840s scheduled the academic year so as, 'in these days of steam navigation [to] allow a visit to England'

during the long summer vacation.[25] Other Canadian universities followed suit. In fact, in 1931 Principal Currie still thought that because
McGill's 'summer vacations [were] so long, the need of a sabbatical
year does not arise to the same extent as in those institutions where
the terms [were] spread more generally over the whole year'.[26] These
four-month long vacations were put to good use by Canadian professors. During his tenure as professor of botany at Manitoba (1904–36),
Arthur Buller returned to England every summer to work at Birmingham University and the Botanic Gardens at Kew; in 1915 Toronto's
professor of physics Louis Vessot King took a house in Portland and
worked in the library at Harvard; and in the 1920s Spencer Melvin, the
professor of physiology at Queen's, 'spent several Summer vacations at
work in the Old Country'. From Cape Town, too, professors travelled
to Britain during the long vacation.[27]

Such measures, however, were not going to be sufficient to meet
the needs of the universities in Australia, where the return journey
to Europe alone took a number of months. Instead, almost from their
foundation, Australian universities recognised that granting their staff
leave to travel abroad would be mutually beneficial to both individuals and institutions. As early as 1860, the Senate of the University of
Sydney approved the application of John Smith, the professor of chemistry and experimental philosophy, to visit Europe for one year on the
grounds that it 'would be highly conducive to the interests of the University'.[28] Smith's estimated salary of £950 was to finance the whole
arrangement, with £350 going to pay his replacement, £300 to Smith as
an allowance and £300 to be used to purchase chemical apparatus for
the university. A year later the Senate similarly judged that 'the University would be much benefited by the information and experience
which the Professors would gain by occasional visits to Europe', and a
procedure of application was instituted.[29] Although not systematised,
this statement from the University of Sydney in 1861 enshrined a commitment to facilitating academic mobility that anticipated the formal
establishment of sabbatical leave at Harvard by nearly twenty years.[30]

These early precedents lay the ground for the formal institution-
alisation of leave-of-absence practices in Australian universities in the
1880s and 1890s. At Adelaide, Professor Horace Lamb's 1883 application led the university to pass new statutes that enabled the council,
'at its discretion [to] grant to any Professor, Lecturer, or any officer of
the University, leave of absence for any time not exceeding one year'.[31]
At Sydney in 1895 the Senate formally established a scheme whereby
periodic leave in the two terms immediately preceding or succeeding
the long vacation would be granted to a professor for 'the purposes
of making himself acquainted with the latest advances in his own

particular subject in Europe or in some other approved place at the discretion of the Senate'.[32] These moves enshrined the practice, hitherto informally in place, in which part of the professor's own salary was used to employ a substitute during his absence. Although the Australian universities did not grant leave automatically, minimised its cost to themselves and shied away from calling it 'sabbatical leave', they nonetheless recognised that enabling their professors to travel abroad for academic purposes was in their own best interests. Such schemes were seen, as the 1919 submission from the Sydney Professorial Board makes clear, as particularly necessary in Australia, where 'the geographical isolation of Australian from other education centres' meant that University teachers experienced special difficulties 'maintaining the necessary relationship[s] with corresponding teachers in Europe and elsewhere'.[33]

By the turn of the century a similar practice was beginning to emerge in the larger Canadian universities. As the president's secretary at Toronto reported to the ever-enquiring Carnegie Foundation for the Advancement of Teaching in 1909, although the University had 'no system by which professors [might] count upon a leave of absence for travel or study', there was nonetheless an established practice whereby leave of a year was granted to professors on an individual basis and 'the other members of their department arrange[d] to do their work, so that when their turn [came] a similar courtesy w[ould] be extended to them'.[34] And, with one important exception, this was the practice that was reaffirmed when in 1910 the enquiries of the Foundation led Toronto to re-examine 'applications for leave of absence and to the principle to be followed in General'. Consequently, the board of governors approved a policy whereby professors might attain leave 'on full salary in view of their long service', supplementing the previous arrangement whereby they received a two-thirds payment.[35] Although smaller institutions such as Queen's in Kingston were unable to match this financial generosity, from the late nineteenth century they too granted professors periods of extended academic leave, provided they arranged (and paid) for their own substitutes.[36] Like the Australian universities, these Canadian institutions did not call such practices 'sabbatical leave', yet these turn-of-the-century customs were in essence very similar to the sabbatical schemes formally established by settler universities in the 1930s.

The professorial mobility such provisions enabled was premised, however, upon the immobility of junior members of staff who were only rarely eligible for leave. The example of Harry Mandelbrote is revealing. As an undergraduate he had studied at the South African College before going to Oxford on a travelling scholarship and earning a first-class degree in history in 1914. When the war broke out and the professor at Cape Town, Eric Walker, was called up for service, Mandelbrote was appointed as lecturer. He remained in this role until Walker's departure for Cambridge in 1936 to take up the Vere Harmsworth Chair of Imperial History. Walker's election to this chair was facilitated by the three trips he made to Britain, in 1921–22, 1927 and 1930. During these absences, the teaching and administrative duties associated with the department fell to Mandelbrote, who already bore much of the lecturing and teaching load. He, however, had no opportunities for travel. Writing to Walker in 1931, Mandelbrote lamented the '18 years since [his] last visit to London', and the consequences for his career. 'I had forgotten it was as long as that,' replied Walker; 'it just shows how time slips away'.[37] With few positions available in South Africa, heavy teaching loads, and little prospect of travel, men such as Mandelbrote found themselves trapped in the local world of academic labour: a world upon which the mobility – and often also the knowledge claims – of their senior professors rested.

Notwithstanding these inequalities, those institutions that did not invest in leave programmes suffered, as the arguments of those who pressed for reform at the University of New Zealand in 1925 make clear. Noting that '[n]o provision ha[d] yet been made in New Zealand to enable University teachers to visit centres of learning', the reformers argued that, for scholars situated 'at the outpost of Empire – the very antipodes', there was an extra need for 'opportunities for re-inspiration'.[38] As the university's historian J. C. Beaglehole pointed out in 1937,

> The university teacher who comes to New Zealand should not feel that he is going into exile. Salary, narrowly considered, need be a subordinate matter ... The real importance attaches to the conditions under which the teacher works. Responsibility, access to adequate libraries, the technical and fructifying converse of his own kind, security and freedom; above all, and supremely important for both professors and lecturers, the regular and assured sabbatical year.[39]

Provisions for six months' leave after eight or ten years' service did nominally exist in the New Zealand colleges, on the condition that the professor concerned organised and paid for his own substitute. But in the years before the First World War this was only very rarely taken up.[40] New Zealand's long adherence to the examining model, and the low priority it placed upon research, did not help; it would not be until after the Second World War that a proper system of leave was developed. Yet New Zealand was alone in neglecting leave provisions. By 1916, even the newly constituted University of Cape Town provided funds 'to pay substitutes for members of staff going on leave, which was allowed after six years service', formalising a practice that had been operating at the South African college since the 1890s.[41]

It was finally the University of Cambridge Statutory Commissioners – acting in 1926 upon the rather vague recommendations of the 1922 Asquith Commission into the Universities of Oxford and Cambridge – who instituted the first system of year-long, periodic, paid academic leave in Britain.[42] In doing so they drew not just upon the example of America but also on that of the settler universities. For Asquith had staffed his Commission with a number of men who had been involved in the pre-war movement to bring together the universities of the British Empire. In fact, at the first Congress of the Universities of the British Empire in 1912 – a meeting attended by several of the men who would later work with Asquith – it was the University of Melbourne's J. W. Barrett who had explained to the audience the advantages of the Australian leave of absence system.[43] If the Cambridge commissioners initiated the first sabbatical programme in Britain, it was very much the settler universities who had led the way at the end of the previous century.[44] By enabling their staff to maintain connections with foreign scholars through periodic trips abroad, settler universities sought to resituate themselves as active participants in the world of international scholarship.

Travelling scholarships

Professors were not the only members of settler universities to travel abroad. For the best students, the route from colonial university to the ancient English institutions, or to London or Scotland, was seen as a natural path to follow. At Oxford, Cambridge and London colonial students undertook second BAs, at London and Edinburgh they enrolled in medical degrees, and after 1895 at Cambridge they gained 'Advanced Status' and took BAs by research. Although figures are problematic, in 1868 students from the empire already constituted sixteen per cent of those enrolled at the Edinburgh Medical School, and by 1913 their proportion had risen to thirty per cent.[45] According to Lawrence Stone, in 1885, eight per cent of matriculants at Oxford were from the British Empire and North America, while in 1898, just over five per cent of the undergraduates admitted to Trinity College Cambridge were empire-born.[46] Hilary Perraton has estimated that by 1921, between nine and ten per cent of full-time students studying in British universities came from overseas, with Canada, Egypt, India, South Africa and the United States constituting the top five sending countries.[47] Although most of these students were privately funded, like Harry Mandelbrote, a significant number were supported by 'travelling scholarships'.

Perhaps the most famous scheme of colonial scholarships was that established by the 1901 Will of the Cape Colony politician and mining magnate, Cecil John Rhodes. By bringing to Britain the most promising young men from America, Australia, Bermuda, Canada, Jamaica, New Zealand, Rhodesia, South Africa and – as an afterthought following the Kaiser's introduction of compulsory English lessons – Germany, Rhodes hoped to 'instil into their minds the advantage to the Colonies as well as to the United Kingdom of the retention of the Unity of the Empire' and effect 'the union of the English-speaking peoples throughout the world'. His Will did not make provision for students from India, East or West Africa, or Malaya, who were only included within the remit of the scheme after revisions in 1940 and 1953, respectively. At the heart of Rhodes' plan was his belief that the experience of living and studying together in a residential university would 'broaden [the] views' of his scholars, 'instruct them in life and manners' and in the process foster ties of mutual understanding that would serve to 'render war impossible'; for it was, wrote Rhodes, 'educational relations [that] make the strongest tie'.[48] Rhodes was less interested in the content of an Oxford education than in the affective ties built up by students during their time together. He saw his scholarships as a mechanism for fostering imperial loyalty among those who would become leaders.[49]

This was quite different from the logic that underpinned the other major colonial scholarship scheme of the period. The '1851 Exhibition' scholarships were set up in 1889 by the Commissioners charged by Royal Charter to direct the considerable profits of the 1851 Great Exhibition towards 'increasing the means of industrial education and extending the influence of science and art upon productive industry'.[50] Noting that 'the provinces' had played such a large part in supporting the Great Exhibition, the Commissioners felt that they 'had a just claim to receive [a] … direct benefit from the funds' and therefore stipulated that the scholarships were 'to enable the most promising students in provincial colleges of science to complete their studies either in those colleges or in the larger institutions of the metropolis'. But, as *Nature* reported in August 1890, when the scholarship committee considered the manner in which the grants were to be distributed, they determined that 'colonial institutions' should also be considered under the term 'provincial'.[51] Consequently, students from McGill and Toronto; Adelaide, Melbourne, Sydney and the University of New Zealand; the Queen's Colleges in Ireland; and the Royal College of Science in Belfast were placed alongside those from places such as Birmingham, Bristol and Glasgow. Indian universities were, notably, not included. Specifying that students should pursue subjects 'limited to those branches of science (such as physics, mechanics, and chemistry) the extension of which is specially important for our national industries', the 1851 Scholarship Committee envisaged a British nation that extended to the settler colonies. As Katrina Dean has pointed out, they 'equated the notion of fostering [English] provincial science with that of promoting colonial science'.[52]

Despite their different aims, in the early twentieth century both the 1851 Exhibitions and the Rhodes Scholarships were held up as examples of the kind of 'great system of scholarships' that should be established to attract colonial students to Britain.[53] In their wake numerous schemes were founded in Britain. In 1900 University College, Liverpool, established a 'Colonial Scholarship' in research bacteriology, as 'the first step towards a closer union with our Colonial Universities and ourselves'; and from 1912, Trinity College, Cambridge, instituted a 'Colonial Exhibition', permitting students who would 'profit by a further period of University study' to apply 'through the principal Authority of the University to which they belong[ed]'.[54] After the First World War, the University of Manchester sought to 'have classes for Colonial & American students to replace those formerly given in Berlin, Vienna &c' and wrote to colonial universities inquiring as to their needs, while a few years later the Royal Infirmary offered medical and surgical resident appointments 'to suitable medical graduates' from colonial universities. From 1922 Otto Beit established fellowships for scientific research tenable at the Imperial College of Science and Technology in London, and in 1924 ten scholarships were made available to graduates of colonial universities for study there.[55] Indian Government and Colonial Office scholarships, too, carried students from Africa and South Asia to Britain. But these scholarships aimed to create collaborators and administrators to serve in the various government services. Unlike those for settler students, they were not principally designed to foster the affective bonds of sentiment, nor to advance 'knowledge in the best interests of the Empire'.[56] None of these schemes, however, achieved the prominence or the prestige associated with the 1851 Exhibition and the Rhodes scholarships. It was not until the long-mooted plans for empire-wide student 'interchange' came to fruition in 1960 in the form of the Commonwealth Scholarships that another large-scale (and this time multi-racial) centralised programme emerged.[57]

But colonial students had been funded to study in Britain since long before the 1851 and Rhodes schemes came into existence.[58] Perhaps the most prominent of these nineteenth-century programmes was that managed by the Trust operating from 1865 under the terms of the Will of Dr John Borthwick Gilchrist, an officer in the East India Company and an Indologist. In the first instance, the Trust established grants for students from India, but in 1868 it widened the scheme to include other British colonies. Granted on the basis of performance in the University of London Matriculation examinations (held after 1858 in centres throughout the empire), Gilchrist Scholars received £100 per annum, which enabled them to study either at the University of Edinburgh or at University College, London. Alumni included Sir Robert Falconer (subsequently president at the University of Toronto), Walter C. Murray (president at Saskatchewan), and J. Gould Schurman (president at Cornell).[59] In supporting colonial matriculants finishing secondary school to attend university in Britain, the Gilchrist scholar-ships were similar to other travelling scholarships established in the years before the foundation of local universities – the Cape Colony's Porter (1865), Griffith (1871) and Jamison (1872); the Tasmanian Council of Education (1858); and the Natal (1884) scholarships, not to mention the Government and Colonial Office Scholarships in Africa and the West Indies.[60]

As settler universities grew up, however, they began to contest the right of the University of London to hold its matriculation examina-tions in their jurisdictions, seeing these metropolitan tests as a threat to their own local educational offerings.[61] The Trust had already made a concession to the Australian universities in 1868 when it agreed to offer scholarships, not on the basis of the London matriculation but to graduates of the universities of Sydney and Melbourne. Eventually the growing maturity of settler universities was perceived to diminish the need for the scheme altogether and at the end of the 1880s the Gilchrist Trust decided to disband its scholarships programme.[62]

But the foundation and growth of settler universities did not halt the flow of colonial students leaving to study abroad. Maurice Boucher has suggested that, in the case of South Africa, despite the existence of the University of the Cape of Good Hope, by the end of the century, 'more students attended universities overseas than ever before'. Far from arresting this movement of students, Boucher argues that the Cape University actually contributed to it by raising standards of education in the secondary schools through its matriculation exam.[63] Yet there was an additional way in which the University of the Cape of Good Hope contributed to the flow of young South Africans to universities in Britain. Like other settler universities in this period, the University of the Cape of Good Hope fostered the foundation of numerous scholar-ship schemes. The Porter, Griffith and Jamison funds mentioned above were converted into scholarships for Cape graduates and new schemes for travel were instituted alongside them. When in the 1890s Cecil Rhodes was thinking about the form his Will might take, there were already eight separate 'travelling scholarships' available for graduates from the Cape University. By 1914 the figure had risen to seventeen, with a further four available to students at the South African College. By 1940 the University of Cape Town had twenty-six travelling scholarships on its books.[64] The University of the Cape of Good Hope thus presented itself not as the apex of a self-contained local educational structure but instead as part of a wider system that included further education in Britain. As the Cape's vice-chancellor, John Buchanan, acknowledged in 1903, 'though we only examine we have endeavoured to stimulate the ambition of the best of our students and to induce them to pursue elsewhere their studies after obtaining our degree.'[65]

In Australia, too, this period witnessed the foundation of travelling scholarships designed to take the best university graduates on to further study in Britain. In fact, Thomas Hudson Beare, whose plan is said to have inspired Rhodes's scheme, was himself a recipient of one of them: the South Australian Scholarship, which was valued at £200 a year for four years and awarded on the recommendation of the University of Adelaide.[66] Also available to Adelaide students wishing to proceed to Britain were the Elder Overseas Scholarship, established in 1883 to 'support advanced musical training overseas', and the Angas Engineering Scholarship, established in 1888 'to encourage the training of scientific men and especially Engineers', as well as the 1851 Exhibitions. Before the institution of the Rhodes' scheme, the University of Sydney had at least five scholarships enabling its graduates to undertake further study abroad. By the end of the 1930s this number had increased to twelve. Additionally, after 1909 the Orient Line offered three free first-class passages to Europe to Australian and New Zealand university graduates.[67]

In New Zealand, the University of Otago began on the same path. The logic of the Sydney investment can be seen in the 1876 suggestion of the Otago professors. Establishing a postgraduate travelling scholarship would, they thought, 'open up the possibility of a distinguished career to successful students, and would tend to make the New Zealand University favourably known at other seats of learning'.[68] However, as so often in the history of the University of New Zealand, the professors' suggestion went unheeded in the midst of provincial wranglings with the federal university. After 1886, the John Tinline Scholarship took students in English abroad, but, as at Melbourne, in New Zealand the provision of travelling awards was not as generous as elsewhere.[69] Things improved after the turn of the century: Canterbury College established a Trinity College Cambridge scholarship in 1908; by 1911 there was an award taking women to Royal Holloway and a travelling scholarship in engineering; and after 1909 the Orient Company's gift provided further aid. After the First World War the pressures of research finally resulted in the foundation in New Zealand of additional travelling scholarships in arts, French, law and science, and in Melbourne of two travelling bursaries.[70]

Reflecting the benefactors' aims as well as those of the institutions whose students they benefited, travelling scholarships were a source of considerable pride, even to those settler universities where provision was light. Recipients of the awards were featured prominently in university *Calendars*, accounts of their work abroad were often cited in *Annual Reports*, and notices were printed in the local newspapers. For settler universities the progression of their graduates to British institutions stood as evidence of the quality of the education they provided. It showed they were recognised as members of the expansive British academic community of which they felt a part. But more than this, travelling scholarships helped connect settler universities to this community: as outlined in Chapter 5, those who held them served as vital conduits linking metropole and colony.

In Canada a different situation pertained. Some travelling scholarships were established at the University of Toronto around the turn of the century, with the George Paxton and the Flavelle as well as the 1851 Exhibition and Rhodes schemes carrying graduates to Britain, and some private efforts were made, as in the case of a fundraising campaign in 1911 to enable the brilliant classicist Charles Cochrane to study at Oxford. But these British-orientated programmes found it difficult to compete with the attractions of the universities in the United States.[71] Unlike British universities, which did not institute a PhD degree until after the First World War, universities in the United States offered doctorates, and this was something Canadian students were increasingly coming to value. From the late 1870s American universities attracted the majority of Canadian students wishing to undertake advanced graduate work. As Robert Falconer, the president of the University of Toronto, wrote in a letter to the vice-chancellors of the British universities in 1917:

> There has been an annual exodus [of Canadian graduates] for many years. Most of these students turned to the United States where they found conditions suitable to continue the work that has been completed for their first degree in the Universities of the Dominion. The Canadian degrees are well-known in the United States and little difficulty is experienced in securing recognition for them. As a rule also the expense was less than would be incurred in studying for the same length of time in Europe, and scholarships and fellowships were granted liberally by the American Universities.[72]

Confronted with this 'annual exodus' to the United States, and in the face of the lack of doctoral degrees in Britain, a number of Canadian universities took steps to institute their own research programmes.

From the 1880s they began to establish 'fellowships' designed to encourage original work at home.[73] The 1885 report of the Royal Society of Canada's 'Committee on the Encouragement of Original Literary and Scientific Work' lists two at Dalhousie, one at Trinity and nine at University College, Toronto. Moreover, by 1890 Acadia, Mount Allison, New Brunswick, Queen's and Toronto had all also approved PhDs, and though it was not until the turn of the century that they became in any sense operational, and then only really at Toronto and McGill, the establishment of the degree in Canada provided an incentive for students to stay at home that was absent in the institutions of the Southern Hemisphere.[74] Given the attractions of their American neighbour and without the alternative of a British PhD, the Canadian universities directed their resources, not towards travelling scholarships, but to the institution of their own research degrees.

As Falconer knew, however, the establishment of Canadian research degrees would only go part of the way towards providing an alternative to the American PhD. There would, he wrote to his fellow vice-chancellors and principals in 1917, 'continue to be many of the best graduates in each year who ... wish to complete their course in Universities outside Canada'.[75] Canadian universities much preferred their students to go to Britain. '[S]omething tangible' must be done, argued Professor Allen of the University of Manitoba in 1912, 'in order that the stream of students which constitutes a serious leakage from our Empire ... shall be diverted to our own British institutions'.[76] From the turn of the century Canadian academics could be heard in London arguing for the establishment of a British PhD to stop this 'leakage'.[77]

When the PhD was finally instituted in Britain, the Canadian universities set about creating the travelling scholarships that Falconer in 1917 had identified as so important: 'Only ... by the establishment of doctorates that may be obtained within a reasonable time and by subvention through scholarships', he wrote, 'can we hope that the stream of students which of late has set towards the United States will be diverted to the Universities of Britain.'[78] By 1922 five locally funded travelling scholarships were available for McGill students in addition to the 1851 Exhibitions and the Rhodes. By 1935 the total had risen to thirteen, while at Queen's in Kingston it was six.[79]

The scholarships fostered by settler universities differed from the more famous Rhodes programme in that they were premised, not upon the idea that study in Britain would further the cause of closer imperial union, but rather upon the conviction that their students were in fact already members of an expansive British academic community. In this they had more in common with the 1851 Exhibition scheme, which placed the settler universities alongside the English provincial institutions. Far from lamenting the departure of these students, settler universities both facilitated and celebrated it, taking considerable pride in the achievements of their graduate representatives abroad. Seeing themselves as feeder institutions in an emerging British professional system, they viewed travelling scholarships as means by which they could take up their membership of the wider British scholarly community.

—◆—

When in 1903 F. H. Chase, vice-chancellor of the University of Cambridge and president of its Queen's College, sought to describe the changes that characterised the academic world in which he lived, he reached for the example of medieval Europe. 'The foundations of the new learning in the sixteenth century were laid in the co-operation and mutual recognition of European universities', he contended, and it 'may be that future generations will regard the time now present as a second Renaissance': 'certainly it is a time remarkable for rapid educational progress ... [and] we are returning to the old principle of recognition and co-operation.' [80] But Chase thought the academic co-operation of his own period was significantly different from 'that which effected such great results in the sixteenth century'. It was both 'broader': there were 'many more subjects, many more types of universities, to deal with than were possible in those older days'; and it was also narrower: for Chase, the co-operation of the academic world at the turn of the twentieth century was 'not cosmopolitan', rather it was 'national and imperial'.

The policies of deterritorialisation pursued by the larger settler universities in the late nineteenth century connected what had previously been locally oriented institutions into a wider world of academic scholarship. But as Chase's comments suggest, this was principally neither an international nor a cosmopolitan world. Despite their purchase of European journals and notwithstanding professorial trips to Berlin and Leipzig, it was primarily to British universities that scholars from the colonies gravitated. The connective mechanisms established by settler universities in the period after 1880 functioned like bridges across the empire. They created opportunities for academics in the settler colonies and in Britain to make and maintain new sorts of relationships with each other – relationships that, as we shall see, would reshape the geographies of British academia.

Notes

1 'Official Report of the Allied Colonial Universities Conference', p. 91.
2 M. Middell and K. Naumann, 'Global History and the Spatial Turn: From the Impact

of Area Studies to the Study of Critical Junctures of Globalization', *Journal of Global History*, 5 (2010): 149–70; see also C. Maier, 'Consigning the Twentieth Century to History: Alternative Narratives for the Modern Era', *American Historical Review*, 105, no. 3 (2000): 807–31 and R.D. Sack, 'Human Territoriality: A Theory', *Annals of the Association of American Geographers*, 73 (1983): 55–74.

3 In 1889–90 McGill exchanged with twelve universities in the United States, eight in Canada, five in the UK, three in Scandinavia and two in Australia. Strathclyde exchanged with seven universities in the United States, fourteen in the UK, eleven in the Empire (of which five in Canada), five in Europe, and with the Imperial University in Tokyo. Sydney exchanged with twenty-three universities in the UK, twenty-one in the United States, fifteen in Europe, six in Australia, six in India, five in New Zealand, four in Canada, two in Japan, one in South Africa, and one in Venezuela. Auckland College exchanged with two universities in the UK, two in Australia, ten in the United States, one in Canada, and two in New Zealand. In 1890 Toronto was exchanging with fifty-three bodies and in 1901 Melbourne was exchanging Calendars with thirty-five universities. See *Annual Calendar of McGill College and University, 1890–91* (Montreal: 1890), pp. 197–205; *Calendar of the University of Strathclyde, 1892–93* (Glasgow: 1892), pp. 103–11; *Calendar of the University of Sydney, 1905* (Sydney: 1904), p. 384; Blackburn, *Evolution of the Heart*, p. 78; University of Melbourne Archives (UMA), *Library Accessions Books*, 103/123; *Auckland University College Calendar, 1896* (Auckland: 1896), pp. 57–8.

4 Blackburn, *Evolution of the Heart*, p. 98.

5 In 1914 the University Commissioners in South Africa argued for the establishment of a University Press on the grounds that the publication of research 'often enhances the reputation of the University from which it issues'. Though established in 1921, the origins of Melbourne University Press can also be found in exchange. Its stated 'main objective' was to produce 'high grade books, particularly those embodying the results of research in subjects peculiar to Australia; books that may have little sale but which it is essential should be available, for consultation purposes, in the libraries of the world.' This enabled 'a number of copies of each work so published' to be 'secured to the Central Library for exchange purposes with other institutions'. See Perceval M. Laurence (ed.), *Report of the University Commission* (Cape Town: Government Printers, 1914), p. 47; *Calendar of the University of Melbourne, 1925* (Melbourne 1924), pp. 861–2; *Bibliographic Record of the University of Sydney, 1851–1913*, (Sydney: University of Sydney, 1914).

6 See, for example, 'Annual Report, 1910–11', *Calendar of the University of Melbourne, 1912* (Melbourne: 1911), pp. 604, 619.

7 Ralph Munn, Ernest Roland Pitt, and Carnegie Corporation of New York, *Australian Libraries: A Survey of Conditions and Suggestions for Their Improvement* (Melbourne: Australian Council for Educational Research, 1935); Ralph Munn and John Barr, *New Zealand Libraries: A Survey of Conditions and Suggestions for Their Improvement* (Christchurch: New Zealand Library Association, 1934); Septimus Albert Pitt, *Memorandum: Libraries of South Africa, Rhodesia and Kenya Colony* (New York: Carnegie Corporation of New York: 1929); John Ridington, *Libraries in Canada: A Study of Library Conditions and Needs* (Toronto: Ryerson Press, 1933).

8 This is consonant with a wider growth in book sales in this period, especially to Australia. Magee and Thompson, *Empire and Globalisation*, p. 128.

9 Turney, Bygott, and Chippendale, *Australia's First*, Appendix 9 'Expediture Trends', p. 655; Blackburn, *Evolution of the Heart*, pp. 56–113; Laurence (ed.), *Report of the University Commission*, p. 46.

10 The serious neglect of libraries was noted by the University of New Zealand (UNZ) reformers in 1910, and the 1934 Carnegie report suggested little had changed: 'The college libraries of New Zealand do not even approach accepted overseas standards ... appear[ing] to be mere annexes to the colleges.' See Munn and Barr, *New Zealand Libraries*, p. 35; New Zealand University Reform Association, *University Reform in New Zealand* (Wellington, NZ: Whitcombe and Tombs, 1911), pp. 89–95.

11 Melbourne, meanwhile, limped along until a bequest from William Baillieu in 1936 radically changed its fortunes.

12 C. W. Holgate, *An Account of the Chief Libraries of Australia and Tasmania* (London: Chiswick Press, 1886), pp. 14, 43.

13 Blackburn, *Evolution of the Heart*, p. 66. 'We are on the whole gainers', Wilson wrote in his diary on 14 February 1892, two years after the fire. Quoted in Friedland, *The University of Toronto*, p. 153.

14 Blackburn, *Evolution of the Heart*, p. 89.

15 *Annual Calendar of McGill College and University, 1885–86* (Montreal: 1885), p. 104; Joseph Hanaway, Richard L. Cruess, and James Darragh, *McGill Medicine: 1885–1936* (Montreal: McGill University, 2006), pp. 12, 197; Peter F. McNally, ed., *Readings in Canadian Library History*, vol. 1 (Ottawa: Canadian Library Association, 1986).

16 Robert Ambrose Dallen, *The University of Sydney, Its History and Progress* (Sydney: 1914), p. 31.

17 University of Birmingham Archives (UBA), *Library Committee Minutes,* UA 15/3 October 1901; Eric W. Vincent and Percival Hinton, *The University of Birmingham: Its History and Significance* (Birmingham: Cornish brothers, 1947), p. 182.

18 Turney, Bygott and Chippendale, *Australia's First*, 'Appendix 9: Expenditure Trends', p. 655; H. E. Barff, *A Short Historical Account of the University of Sydney* (Sydney: Angus and Robertson, 1902), p. 129. The Accessions books for the Melbourne University Library for 1901 show that 57 per cent of the books purchased were published in the United Kingdom, 15 per cent in Europe and 11 per cent in the United States. UMA, *Library Accessions Books,* 1901–1911.

19 These included significant British journals such as *Mind* as well as German language publications like the *Neues Jahrbücher für Philologie* and American Journals like the *Political Science Quarterly*. W. H. Dawson (ed.), *The Yearbook of the Universities of the Empire, 1921* (London: 1921), pp. 18, 371; UBA, *Library Accessions Register,* 1920–21.

20 Munn, Pitt and Carnegie Corporation of New York, *Australian Libraries*, pp. 91, 94.

21 Holgate, *An Account of the Chief Libraries*, p. 24.

22 Science Museum Library Swindon Archives (SMLA), *Rutherford Correspondence,* vol. 1, Bragg to Rutherford, 19 Jan. 1904.

23 *Congress Proceedings 1912*, p. 388.

24 As Jöns also shows, although from 1884 Cambridge did have a leave of absence provision, its intention was only to make professors and readers more accessible for their students and colleagues. Heike Jöns, 'Academic Travel from Cambridge University and the Formation of Centres of Knowledge, 1885–1954', *Journal of Historical Geography*, 34, no. 2 (2008): 338–62, p. 344.

25 Friedland, *The University of Toronto*, p. 21.

26 Queen's University Archives (QUA), *Principal's Office,* 1251/box 19/Sabbatical Year 1931–64/Currie to Fyfe, 17 June 1931.

27 *Ibid.*, Sabbatical Year 1931–64/Spencer Melvin, Dept of Physiology, to Dean Etherington, 3 Jan. 1938; McGill University Archives (MUA), *Louis Vessot King,* MG 3026 C2/692, King to Rutherford, 27 July 1915; F. T. Brooks, 'Buller, Arthur Henry Reginald (1874–1944), Rev. V. M. Quirke', *Oxford Dictionary of National Biography* (2004), accessed 3 Aug. 2011, www.oxforddnb.com/view/article/32164; William Ritchie (ed.), *The History of the South African College, 1829–1918* (Cape Town: T. M. Miller, 1918), pp. 416–18.

28 Quoted in B. R. Williams and D. R. V. Wood, *Academic Status and Leadership in the University of Sydney, 1852–1987* (Sydney: University of Sydney, 2006), p. 79.

29 University of Sydney Archives (USA), *Minutes of the Senate,* G1/1, box 5/10 July 1861.

30 Walter Crosby Eells, 'The Origin and Early History of Sabbatical Leave', *Association of American University Professors Bulletin*, 48, no. 3 (1962): 253–6; Bai Kang and Michael Miller, 'An Overview of the Sabbatical Leave in Higher Education: A Synopsis of the Literature Base', *ERIC Document Reproductive Service*, No. ED 430 471 (1999).

31 *Calendar of the University of Adelaide, 1888* (Adelaide: 1888), 'Statutes Chapter VI – Of Leave of Absence'.

32 USA, *Minutes of the Senate*, box 5/10 Aug. 1895.
33 *Ibid.*, box 15/7 Apr. 1919. See also USA, *Minutes of the Senate*, box 6/6 Feb. 1922 and *Second Congress of the Universities of the Empire, 1921: Report of Proceedings*, ed. Alex Hill (London: G. Bell and Sons 1921), pp. 394–96.
34 University of Toronto Archives (UTA), *Carnegie Foundation*, A68-007, box 158/04/02, Falconer's Secretary to Bowman, 26 June 1909.
35 UTA, *Office of the President*, A1967-0007, box 21/Leave of Absence/23/Report of Meeting of a sub-committee of the Finance Committee, 10 Feb. 1910; box 51/Board of Governors/302/Falconer to the Board of Governors, 13 Feb. 1919.
36 Queen's University Archives (QUA), *Board of Trustees Minutes*, 1227 vol. 3: 1872–1912, 27 Apr.1898; QUA, *Personnel Files*, 2400, box 7/Robertson, Professor JK/ Robertson to AL Clark, 31 March 1931; QUA, *Principal's Office*, box 19/Sabbatical Year 1931–64. From the 1920s on Queen's professors received half pay. By the First World War most universities in Canada granted unpaid or partially paid leave, with paid schemes emerging in the 1930s. See Malcolm MacLeod, *A Bridge Built Halfway: A History of Memorial University College, 1925–1950* (Montreal: McGill-Queen's University Press, 1990), 98–9.
37 University of Cape Town Archives (UCTA), *Mandelbrote Papers*, BC576 /181/Walker to Mandelbrote, 24 Mar. 1931.
38 University Teachers Association of New Zealand, *Some Aspects of University Teaching in New Zealand* (Christchurch, 1925), p. 21.
39 Beaglehole, *The University of New Zealand*, p. 401.
40 In 1937 Beaglehole quoted a pamphlet by Arnold Wall (Professor of English at Canterbury College, 1898–1932) titled *The Future of the University* (unknown date), in which Wall remarked that 'one of the older Professors did not return Home till he had served 35 years; that another has served 40 years before returning at all; and that [he him]self served 29 years before [he] was able to return.' *Ibid.*, p. 402 fn.
41 UCTA, *Personal File of H.G. Galbraith*, AA1–156 Galbraith to the Registrar, 5 June 1920. For early leaves of absence, see Ritchie (ed.), *The History of the South African College*, pp. 431, 488, 517, 538.
42 Oxford still hesitated and although informal arrangements were in place in 1948, it was not until 1955 that a research leave scheme was institutionalised. See Jöns, 'Academic Travel from Cambridge University and the Formation of Centres of Knowledge'; Christopher N. L. Brooke *et al.*, *A History of the University of Cambridge: Vol. 4 1870–1990* (Cambridge: Cambridge University Press, 1988), pp. 352, 354; John Prest, 'The Asquith Commission', in Brian Howard Harrison (ed.), *The History of the University of Oxford: Vol. 8, the Twentieth Century* (Oxford: Clarendon, 1994), p. 27; Statute D.XII.1 *Statutes of Cambridge and Passages from Acts of Parliament Relating to the University* (Cambridge: Cambridge University Press, 1928), 40–1.
43 Commissioners W.H. Bragg, H.A. Miers, A. Balfour and A. Mansbridge were also involved in the organisation, acted as delegates, or delivered papers at the 1912 Congress, while E. Penrose, T. B. Strong, and Arthur Schuster were all listed as Congress members. See Barrett in *Congress Proceedings, 1912*, pp. 110–117.
44 As Professor Ernest Alton of Trinity College, Dublin observed in 1921, 'For a true Sabbatical Year, [British universities] have to look to the Universities of America and Australia.' *Congress Proceedings, 1921*, p. 401.
45 A. Logan Turner, *Sir William Turner, KCB, FRS: A Chapter in Medical History* (Edinburgh: Blackwood, 1919), pp. 152, 286. Sections of this chapter have been previously published as Tamson Pietsch, 'Many Rhodes: Travelling Scholarships and Imperial Citizenship in the British Academic World, 1880–1940', *History of Education*, 40, no. 6 (2011): 1–17.
46 Lawrence Stone, 'The Size and Composition of the Oxford Student Body, 1580–1910' in *The University in Society, Vol. 1*, ed. Lawrence Stone (Oxford, and Princeton, NJ: Oxford University Press, 1975), p. 101; *Admissions Books, 1882–1913* (Trinity College Cambridge Archives (TCCA). At Trinity College, of 199 undergraduate admissions for 1898, there were nineteen from outside the UK: four from Europe, two from the United States, three from India, two from New Zealand, three from Australia, two

from Cape Town and three from other places. This excludes advanced students. See also John Darwin, 'A World University', in Brian Harrison (ed.), *The History of the University of Oxford, Vol. III: The Twentieth Century* (Oxford: Oxford University Press, 1994).

47 Hilary Perraton, 'Overseas Students in British Universities 1900–2010: Practice Without Policy', paper delivered at the Institute of Historical Research, London (Mar. 2011) and personal correspondence with author.

48 Rhodes Will quoted in Philip Zeigler, *Legacy: Cecil Rhodes, the Rhodes Trust, and the Rhodes Scholarships* (New Haven, CT: Yale, 2008), Appendix 1.

49 See also E. T. Williams, 'The Rhodes Scholars', in M. G. Brock and M. C. Curthoys (eds), *The History of the University of Oxford: Vol. 7, Part 2, the Nineteenth Century* (Oxford: 2000), pp. 717–28; Anthony Kenny, *The History of the Rhodes Trust* (Oxford: Oxford University Press, 2001).

50 The majority of the funds were used to purchase eight-six acres of land in South Kensington. See *Calendar of the University of Sydney, 1892* (Sydney: 1891), p. 257; *Record of the Science Research Scholars of the Royal Commission for the Exhibition of 1851: 1891–1929* (London: The Commissioners, 1930), pp. 64–7.

51 'Establishment of Science Scholarships', *Nature*, 42 (28 Aug. 1890): 431–2.

52 Katrina Dean, 'Inscribing Settler Science: Ernest Rutherford, Thomas Laby and the Making of Careers in Physics', *History of Science*, 41 (2003): 217–40, p. 222.

53 Chase, p. 78; Warren, p. 100; Sir Arthur Rucker (Principal of the University of London), p. 95

54 UMA, *Council Minute Books*, UM174 vol. 11, 2 Apr. 1900; UMA, *Registrar's Correspondence*, UM312 1912/93/Trinity College Cambridge – Colonial Exhibitions, paper published by Trinity College Cambridge, 15 Nov. 1912.

55 UMA, *Registrar's Correspondence*, 1918/185/University of Manchester, letter from E. S. Reynolds, Prof[essor] Clinical Medicine, Manchester, to Sir Baldwin Spencer, 24 July 1918; UMA, *Registrar's Correspondence*, 1921/290/Manchester Royal Infirmary – Nominations for Internship, Frank G. Hazell (Manchester Royal Infirmary) to the Dean of the Sydney Medical Faculty, 6 May 1920. UMA, *Registrar's Correspondence*, 1922/53/Beit Fellowships. UMA, *Registrar's Correspondence*, 1924/279/Imperial College of Science and Technology Scholarship.

56 From 1886, six Government of India scholarships were awarded to students from the Indian Universities, and in 1904 provision was made for up to thirty Indian students at any one time to hold Government scholarships in technical subjects. Sumita Mukherjee, *Nationalism, Education and Migrant Identities: The England Returned* (London: Routledge, 2009), pp. 13–15, 114, 116, 119–121; *University of Calcutta Calendar for the Year 1907* (Calcutta: Baptist Mission Press, 1907), pp. 655–7; Thomas Babington Macaulay, 'Minute of 2 Febr. 1835 on Indian Education', in G. M. Young (ed.), *Macaulay, Prose and Poetry* (Cambridge, MA: Harvard University Press, 1957).

57 Hilary Perraton, *Learning Abroad: A History of the Commonwealth Scholarship and Fellowship Plan* (Cambridge: Cambridge Scholars Publishing, 2009), 5–18.

58 Pietsch, 'Many Rhodes'.

59 Scholarships were awarded to students from Australia, Canada, the Cape and the West Indies, and also to those from English colleges such as Owen's College in Manchester. 'Conditions of Scholarships Instituted by the Gilchrist Educational Trust for the Benefit of Youth Residing in the Dominion of Canada' (Gilchrist Educational Trust, 1880); *Calendar of the University of Sydney, 1886* (Sydney: University of Sydney, 1885), p. 199; U. J. Kay-Shuttleworth and David Herbert S. Cranage, *Gilchrist Educational Trust: Pioneering Work in Education* (Cambridge: Cambridge University Press, 1930); R. A. Falconer, 'The Gilchrist Scholarships: An Episode in the Higher Education of Canada', *Proceedings and Transactions of the Royal Society of Canada*, 27 (1933): 5–13, pp. 12–13; M. Boucher, 'The Gilchrist Scholarship and the University of London in the Early Development of Higher Education for the Cape Colony', *Historia*, 8 (Dec. 1968): 249–55; J. G. MacGregor, 'Letter Concerning the Gilchrist Educational Fund' (1895), Internet Archive, accessed 31 Mar. 2011, www.archive.org/details/cihm_29095.

60 Ashby, *Universities: British, Indian, African* (London: Weidenfeld and Nicolson, 1966).

61 UAA (University of Adelaide Archives), *Registrar's Correspondence*, S200/1905/ GH20, The Chancellor Sir Samuel Way to the Minister for Education, 8 Feb. 1904; see also Boucher, 'The Gilchrist Scholarship and the University of London', p. 252.

62 Falconer suggests they were withdrawn because of the growth of colonial universities, but also because the increasing importance 'of the postgraduate idea had put London out of date'. See *Calendar of the University of Sydney, 1886*, p. 199; Falconer, 'The Gilchrist Scholarships', p. 5; Kay-Shuttleworth and Cranage, *Gilchrist Educational Trust*, pp. 8–9.

63 Boucher, 'The Gilchrist Scholarship and the University of London', p. 58.

64 *Calendar of the South African College, 1907* (Cape Town: 1906), pp. 30–3; *Calendar of the University of the Cape of Good Hope, 1913–14* (Cape Town: 1913), pp. 296–304, 332–7; *Calendar of the University of Cape Town, 1940* (Cape Town: 1939).

65 'Official Report of the Allied Colonial Universities Conference', p. 89.

66 'Obituary: Sir T. Hudson Beare', *The Times*, 12 June (1940); 'The South Australian Scholarship', in *Calendar of the University of Adelaide, 1920* (Adelaide: University of Adelaide, 1919); Pietsch, 'Many Rhodes', pp. 7–8.

67 'The Elder Overseas Scholarship', University of Adelaide, accessed 30 Dec. 2010, www.hss.adelaide.edu.au/scholarships/elder_overseas_scholarship.html; 'University Statutes', in *Calendar of the University of Adelaide, 1940* (Adelaide: University of Adelaide, 1939); USA, *Accountant's Office*, G18/13; *Calendar of the University of Sydney, 1910* (Sydney: 1909), p. 287. After 1921 these three passages were shared between the P&O Company, the Blue Funnel Line, the Aberdeen Line and the Commonwealth Government Line.

68 Beaglehole, *The University of New Zealand*, p. 114.

69 *The New Zealand University Calendar, Vol. 29, 1901–02* (Wellington, Christchurch and Dunedin: Whitcome and Tombs, 1901), p. 50.

70 James Hight and Alice M. F. Candy, *A Short History of the Canterbury College* (Auckland: Whitcombe and Tombs, 1927), pp. 65, 95; Beaglehole, *The University of New Zealand*, pp. 278, 305; 'Annual Report, 1927–28', *Calendar of the University of Melbourne, 1929* (Melbourne: 1929), pp. 1016–17.

71 UTA, *Office of the President*, A1967-0007/21/09/'Charles Cochrane Scholarship'.

72 *Ibid.*, A1967-0007/45a/Falconer to the Vice-Chancellor of Liverpool, 6 Mar. 1917. In the years before 1900, thirty-nine Toronto graduates had gone to Chicago and nineteen to Johns Hopkins; Friedland, *The University of Toronto*, p. 178.

73 Research fellowships were also established in Australia in the years just before the First World War. See Roy MacLeod, *Archibald Liversidge, FRS: Imperial Science under the Southern Cross* (Sydney: Sydney University Press, 2010), p. 388.

74 'Report of the Committee on the Encouragement of Original Literary and Scientific Work', *Proceedings and Transactions of the Royal Society of Canada*, (1885): pp. xxix–xli. The PhD began to be offered at Toronto in 1897 and McGill in 1906. The Board of Graduate Studies was established at Toronto in 1915.

75 UTA, *Office of the President*, A1967-0007/45a/Falconer to the Vice-Chancellor of Liverpool, 6 Mar. 1917.

76 Principal Peterson (McGill) quoted in 'Official Report of the Allied Colonial Universities Conference', p. 83; Frank Allen in *Congress Proceedings, 1912*, p. 59.

77 For example, William Peterson (McGill) in 'Official Report of the Allied Colonial Universities Conference', p. 83; J. W. Barrett (Melbourne) in *Congress Proceedings, 1912*, pp. 67–8.

78 UTA, *Office of the President*, box 45a/letter from Falconer to the Vice-Chancellor of Liverpool, 6 Mar. 1917.

79 *McGill University Calendar, 1922–23*, (Montreal: 1922), pp. 89–92; *McGill University Calendar, 1935–36* (Montreal: 1935), pp. 373–8; *Queen's University Calendar, 1930–31* (Kingston: 1929), pp. 60–2.

80 'Official Report of the Allied Colonial Universities Conference', p. 79.

CHAPTER THREE

Making appointments:
access, exclusion and personalised trust

If importing books and facilitating scholarly mobility were some of the ways in which settler universities strove to reposition themselves in the period after 1880, then attracting professors was another. '[I]t all depends on the man,' declared Sir William Ramsay, professor of chemistry at University College, London, at the Allied Colonial Universities Conference in 1903; '[i]f we had … [great] men the students would come'.[1] But in their efforts to recruit 'great men', settler universities faced a number of difficulties. First, there was the problem of distance: how were colonial institutions to conduct the business of recruitment from afar? Second, there was the problem of selection itself: how should the merits of a potential candidate be assessed? For settler universities these two problems were intimately linked: the question of who could be trusted became especially important in the context of changing measures of expertise. Yet the academic appointment process has been neglected by imperial and educational historians alike.[2] Institutional histories, memoirs and biographies invariably speak of academic appointments in the passive voice, but behind such phrases lay a power-laden, historically contingent and largely unexamined world of access and exclusion that had a significant influence on the workings of British and imperial academia. Relying heavily on personal systems of trust, the appointments practices of settler universities worked to extend the networks of British scholarship beyond the British Isles, creating an expansive but uneven terrain that mapped the borders and shaped the contours of what we might think of as the 'British academic world'.

Selection practices

Steven Shapin has argued that the 'recognition of trustworthy persons is a necessary component in building and maintaining systems of knowledge, while [the] bases of that trustworthiness are historically and contextually variable'.[3] In the seventeenth and eighteenth centuries, gentlemanly codes of civility were fundamental to the constitution of scientific truth in Britain. But according to Niklas Luhmann and Anthony Giddens, in the nineteenth century this began to change. The complex conditions of modern life meant that trust formerly placed in individuals began instead to be placed in institutions.[4] As part of this shift, systems that valued merit and expertise increasingly came to replace personal patronage as the basis of appointment. The introduction of the written examination as a form of assessment in the middle of the century is often considered to have been particularly significant.[5] As Phillipa Levine writes, it meant that the 'criteria by which to judge quality and competence were gradually standardised'.[6] Bound up with the process of academic specialisation, by the second half of the nineteenth century it was the credentials of universities and professional societies, rather than the word of gentleman amateurs, that served as the guarantors of reliable knowledge.

In many ways this shift was reflected in the changing processes by which academic appointments were made in Britain. At the start of the nineteenth century, professorial chairs had been filled by various forms of political and religious patronage, while college fellowships were bestowed at the discretion of governing bodies and restricted to those who met certain regional, religious and educational qualifications. But in the middle of the nineteenth century this system of patronage came under attack. In the early 1850s the Oxford and Cambridge Royal Commissions abolished closed college fellowships, which instead began to be awarded on the basis of examination performance. Meanwhile, charges of nepotism in the 1830s instituted what might be seen as an analogous process of open competition for professorial appointments. University chairs began to be advertised, and candidates were required to present to the electors (who ranged from the Crown to all the members of a lay council or convocation) public testimonials from a wide range of figures both inside and outside academe. Ambitious to attract the very best candidates, settler universities also used this practice to select their original professors. The pages of *Nature* and the *Athenaeum* contain notifications of vacant chairs in the universities of Toronto and Sydney alongside those of University College, London, and the books of testimonials deposited in the Bodleian Library contain copies of applications to positions in Australia, Ireland and South Africa bound with those to Edinburgh and Oxford.[7]

However, the traditional story of a nineteenth-century transition from patronage to merit only partially explains the changes in academic appointments procedures that took place in this period. Older forms of privileged selection persisted. Not only was the process of presenting testimonials largely a codification of earlier patronage relationships, but it was also one that rested upon elaborate forms of covert canvassing in which candidates would race to solicit the support of the individuals they considered most influential. Under this system the election of a candidate was as dependent upon the various collegiate, religious, political and personal loyalties he could command as it was upon considerations of expertise or merit.[8] In the 1850s, for example, University College, Toronto, placed advertisements in the London papers, and candidates – many of whom had been approached by friends of the university in England – sent their written applications and testimonials to Canada. But the new constitution of 1853 stipulated that all appointments required government approval, and this had a discernible effect upon the selections made. The rejection of the biologist and future president of the Royal Society, Thomas Henry Huxley, in favour of the nearly 60-year-old Reverend William Hincks, professor of natural history in Cork and brother of the provincial premier, stands out only as the most egregious of these interventions.[9] Forms of patronage thus remained active in both settler and UK institutions into the twentieth century.

The Australian and New Zealand universities present a further complication. With the journey to Sydney or Melbourne taking three months, it was impractical for these universities' foundation councils to receive candidates' written applications and testimonials, as they did in Canada. The Australian universities solved this problem by vesting their trust in representatives and appointing selection committees that met in London.[10] To serve on such committees these universities wanted two kinds of people. First they wanted individuals living in Britain who were familiar with colonial conditions, and second they wanted the advice of what Canterbury College in New Zealand called 'commissions of eminent scholars'.[11] The membership of Sydney's and Melbourne's first London committees attests to this: both universities chose John Herschel (the prominent English scientist who in the 1830s had spent time at Cape Town), George Airy (the Astronomer Royal), and Henry Malden (the professor of Greek at London) to represent British science and scholarship, while the former secretary to Governor Fitzroy served as a local voice for Sydney, and Robert Lowe, a member of the New South Wales Legislative Council and Liberal MP in Britain, spoke for Melbourne. Although Australian university councils wanted the selectors on these London committees to be men distinguished by their scholarship, they were far less concerned about specific expertise: Herschel, Airy, Malden and Fitzroy/Lowe selected men to fill a range of disciplinary positions. London committees were, however, expected to be able to act as good judges of *character*; a quality that, as Stefan Collini has shown, underpinned so many Victorian educational ideals.[12] Melbourne's first chancellor, Sir Redmond Barry, made clear that he wanted the selection committee to find professors who had 'such habits and manners as to stamp on their future pupils the character of the loyal, well-bred, English gentleman', while Otago looked for a man 'of irreproachable moral character'. [13] And if Otago expressed a preference for candidates from the Scottish universities, both Australian universities sought first-class candidates from Oxford and Cambridge.[14] Therefore, although they employed the technology of 'open competition', early Australian and New Zealand universities both delegated their recruitment to men who had scholarly connections in Britain, and emphasised that gentlemanly character should be a criterion for selection.

However, in the context of increasing disciplinary specialisation and academic professionalisation, the principles for what constituted a good professor began to change. As settler universities expanded their curricula to include the professions and the applied (and later social) sciences, a gentlemanly character and a first-class examination performance in the universal liberal curriculum of Oxford or Cambridge was no longer seen as sufficient. Instead, disciplinary knowledge, together with competence in the methods by which it was acquired, became important. The old public modes of selection and the lay and generalist committees central to them did not lend themselves easily to the assessment of these qualities, and from the 1870s on they came under intense criticism. Although no exponent of twentieth-century research, in 1868 Mark Pattison, the Oxford scholar and rector of Lincoln College, condemned the fellowship examination as 'a wholly inadequate test of scientific merit' and called the presentation of testimonials, the 'least defensible' ... 'of all the modes of appointment'.[15] Specialised practical experience was taken to be a better index of ability in many of the new scientific disciplines.

But how were these skills to be assessed and evaluated? The fragmentation of the universal curriculum and the advance of disciplinary specialisation meant that generalists were no longer able to assess a candidate's merits. In the first decade of the twentieth century, the English civic universities began to employ an appointment system that relied on expert knowledge, convening disciplinary committees, which advised a university's governing body. However, this created another difficulty: if appointments were to be dependent on the recommendation of a few individuals, which individuals could be trusted? As J. J. Thomson, the director of the Cavendish Laboratory, wrote in 1912, '[t]here are some Professors whose geese are all swans, and others whose swans are all geese'.[16] Under these conditions, personal networks and private recommendations became crucial. As a group of New Zealand professors, seeking reform, wrote of the civic universities' new selection processes in 1911:

> when the list of available candidates is before them, the members of such a Committee will pay little attention to formal testimonials, but will form their judgment on special inquiries widely pursued; and their knowledge of the learned world will enable them to judge the value and character of the evidence they thus obtain; they will also interview likely candidates in an intimate and informal way.[17]

From the turn of the century, private knowledge and specialised expertise underpinned academic appointment in Britain's newer universities.

Yet personalised systems of trust were something settler universities had been using since the 1880s as a way of confronting the problem of distance. For junior posts, colonial 'God-professors' were frequently given unilateral powers of selection.[18] On the one hand this enabled individuals like Sydney's professor of medicine, T. H. Anderson Stuart, and Toronto's professor of history, G. McKinnon Wrong, to bring out from Britain men they knew personally. In the 1880s Anderson Stuart populated virtually his entire department with medical graduates from his old university, Edinburgh, while in the early 1900s Wrong did much the same with Oxford historians. But on the other hand such practices also facilitated the appointment of local or on-the-spot candidates. Such appointments were frequently expedient. In the 1880s and 1890s the best men that could be found by the colleges of the University of the Cape of Good Hope, which still provided pre-matriculation education, were usually graduates of British universities (most often from Scotland) who were already in South Africa. Local appointments could be opportunistic: for example, the future Nobel Prize-winning physicist Frederick Soddy was made senior demonstrator at McGill because he happened to visit the chemistry department when passing through Montreal.[19] Yet the process was also open to abuse. In Melbourne in 1884 the local newspaper levelled charges of nepotism at the university because one of the medical professors was assisted by his son, while another professor was in the process of trying to get his appointed.[20]

For more senior posts, however, the established settler universities contacted disciplinary specialists and asked for their private assessment or recommendation. Using this method, the Canadian universities had from the 1880s operated what effectively were search committees. Officially, the power of appointment remained with a university's governing body, to which recommendations would be made. But these were lay rather than academic bodies, and in practice (and sometimes also in statute) a great deal of power came to be vested in the principal or vice-chancellor who, in combination perhaps with the head of department and one or two other faculty members, conducted recruitment.[21] Each time an appointment came up, the committee or governing body either would 'invite [applications from] candidates or would proceed by method of calling someone already favourably known to them'.[22] The private recommendation of an applicant's colleague, supervisor, or head of department was taken to be more trustworthy than their public testimonials. By writing privately both to their friends in Britain and their colleagues in the United States, Canadian university principals looked both east and south, seeking out appropriately qualified men from England or Scotland, or Canadian graduates who since the 1870s had been undertaking graduate work in American universities.

University principals were central to this process and their archives overflow with voluminous 'private correspondence' regarding appointments. Letters to friends and colleagues – both in Britain and America – show them soliciting the names of likely candidates, inviting applications, checking endorsements and organising meetings. These archives point to the largely informal filtering process that preceded a recommendation to an appointment committee or governing body. In fact, on a number of occasions, McGill's Principal Peterson expedited this process by 'borrowing' the appointment lists of universities in Britain: 'There have been so many elections to Chairs on the other side of the water of late', he wrote to Professor E. B. Titchener of Cornell in 1904, 'that it is altogether unnecessary to make inquiries there, as I think we are well informed as to possible candidates.'[23] Often official advertisements were little more than fronts, as the letter in 1901 from Principal Peterson to the University of Manchester's Alfred Flux regarding the chair of political economy at McGill reveals. Flux and Peterson had been corresponding about the position for some time, and Flux had agreed to accept it. But 'it was felt', wrote Peterson, 'that it might be more satisfactory to those who have endowed the Chair, and who do not know how much has been accomplished already by private correspondence, if we followed the usual course of throwing the Chair open to all candidates'.[24] Those who responded to the advertisement in good faith must have been disappointed when Flux was eventually officially selected.

The consequence of this process was that a powerful principal could exercise significant sway in the making of appointments. But by the same token, an uninterested or poorly connected one could cause serious disruption, failing to act as a directing force on the powers of the governing body.[25] Indeed, it was perhaps the lack of interest in academic matters of Arthur Currie, McGill's principal between 1920 and 1933, that led the university to put in place statutory arrangements stipulating a Board of Selection for filling vacant chairs.[26] By contrast, Robert Falconer (principal from 1907 until 1932) was of great value to Toronto because of his extensive network of contacts both in Britain and America. George Parkin, the first secretary of the Rhodes Trust, was an old friend of his and served as something of an 'agent' in Oxford, as did William Osler until his death in 1919.[27] But Falconer's connections also extended to America. Sitting on the Board of the Carnegie Foundation, Falconer had reason to travel frequently to New York where he came into contact with many of the leading American university men. Yet it is clear from the tone of their correspondence that the presidents and principals of the Canadian universities were far less familiar with the university world in the United States than they were with that in Britain. In this period at least, their letters to Edinburgh or Oxford – to men with whom they had studied or worked – were full of a kind of intimacy absent from those exchanged with their southern neighbours.

Australian universities also made specialised personal knowledge much more central to their appointment processes after 1880. Although their governing bodies technically retained the power of final selection, they continued to rely on London selection committees whose recommendations carried enormous weight. But the ways in which these committees worked began to change. Instead of the old generalist panels, subject-specific selectors began to be appointed. Having some connection to these selectors gave candidates an enormous advantage, as the case of W. H. Bragg shows. When Horace Lamb, the foundation professor of pure mathematics at Adelaide, resigned to take up the chair at Owens College in 1885, the South Australian agent-general, Sir Arthur Blyth, asked Lamb to join the director of the Cavendish Laboratory, J. J. Thomson, and himself on a selection committee.[28] Bragg, who at the time held an assistant lectureship at Thomson's college in Cambridge, was on his way to attend one of Thomson's lectures when he was overtaken by the director himself, canvassing for the Adelaide post. Thomson asked Bragg if William Sheppard, the Senior Wrangler and an Australian, was applying for the position.[29] Bragg did not know, but asked Thomson if he might himself have a chance. Thomson, much to Bragg's surprise, replied that he would. This coincidence led Bragg to submit an application, and he was invited to attend an interview in London in December. From a field of twenty-three candidates, fifteen from Cambridge and fourteen of whom were Wranglers, Bragg was selected, and he left England to take up the chair of mathematics and experimental physics at Adelaide in 1886. In much the same way as the Canadian principals, the disciplinary experts appointed to the Australian selection committees engaged in an informal process of solicitation and encouragement, making judgments based on their personal knowledge of candidates. Such was the power of these London committees that a canny candidate working in an Australian university would not send his application across the hall to the registrar, but instead forward it all the way to London.[30]

Bragg's story highlights two further innovations introduced by the Australian universities in this period. First, although an Australian representative was retained on London committees, by the end of the century the return migration of some professors and the introduction of leave-of-absence schemes had helped create a growing pool in Britain of academic men who had themselves worked or studied in the colony.[31] This meant that the Australian universities now had a group of willing and – more importantly – trustworthy representatives in Britain on whom they could depend. Indeed, as the twentieth century progressed, a growing number of these men themselves became leading figures in British scholarship. The London committee for the University of Sydney's chair of physics in 1923 stands as an example. It included two Nobel Prize winners familiar with Australia (Professor Sir William Bragg and Professor Sir Ernest Rutherford), a former holder of the vacated Sydney chair (Sir Richard Threlfall), and a former professor of anatomy at Sydney and frequent member of its selection committees (Professor J. T. Wilson).[32] Increasingly, Australian universities were able to count on their own faculty and alumni to help make appointments from London.

Second, Bragg's selection for the Adelaide chair points to the emergence in the late nineteenth century of the interview as an authenticating tool that introduced a new and even more personal method of assessment. Employed since the mid-nineteenth century in the recruitment of men for the Indian Civil Service and developing as a feature of celebrity journalism in the 1880s, the history of the interview remains unwritten. In the academic world of the late nineteenth century it was as likely to take the form of a fireside chat as anything more formal, and it was seen by selectors as something that was only necessary in the absence of other forms of personal knowledge. In 1911, the agent-general for Victoria, who was responsible for organising the selection for a new chair of English for the University of Melbourne, made this clear. He reported that 'it was not thought necessary to ask [the short-listed candidates] to attend' an interview, because the members of the committee felt they knew all the gentlemen short-listed.[33] When the university sector remained small, such a coincidence was likely, but as the numbers of universities expanded in the early twentieth century, selectors could less frequently claim acquaintance with all the applicants. In this context the interview was adopted as a substitute for direct personal knowledge. For example, acting in 1919 on the advisory committee for the chair of physics at the University of Cape Town, Ernest Rutherford was led by the 'impossibility of forming a personal judgement on the large majority of the candidates' to suggest that the University in South Africa should employ the Australian system of an interview in London.[34]

However, Rutherford's suggestion was something that Cape Town resisted for two reasons. From the turn of the century the Cape university had set great store by the advice of professors at Edinburgh and Glasgow, and their judgment continued to be valued throughout the tenure of John Carruthers Beattie, the University's Scottish-born vice-chancellor (1918–37).[35] In 1919 Glasgow's Professor Andrew Gray had been asked to act alongside Rutherford and J. J. Thomson as an advisor, and allowing an interview in London would have sidelined him.[36] But the 1919 correspondence also indicates that the university in Cape Town did not wish to cede its jurisdiction over this powerful mode of assessment to its advisors in Britain. As the South African High Commissioner wrote to Rutherford, 'you will not forget that the appointment will be made by the University itself after it has the valued aid of the Committee's report and recommendations, and of course as far as candidates already in South Africa are concerned the University authorities may be assumed to have more personal knowledge than the Committee could possibly have.'[37] By limiting the committee – and the British applicants – to a judgment based only on the provision of written materials, the University of Cape Town reserved for itself the ability to override the London committee's recommendations. Yet the University's attempt to maintain local control of appointments was only partially successful, and in the interwar period the English-speaking South African universities used London selection committees with increasing frequency.[38]

It was the New Zealand colleges that were most sceptical of London committees. Although Otago and Canterbury had used committees in London and Scotland to select their foundation staff, the institution of the federal system in 1876 and the provincial rivalries it inflamed caused the college councils to assert their control over appointments. Although London advisory committees were still sometimes convened, the colleges maintained 'an attitude of hostility' towards them. Indeed, college councils reserved their 'absolute right to reconsider candidates who ha[d] been rejected' in England.[39] According to the group of reforming professors in 1911, the refusal to extend trust to London was at the heart of the colleges' recruitment problems, for the lay members who sat on local college selecting bodies had neither the special expertise nor the personal knowledge needed to properly evaluate applications:

> The Council will go through the testimonials, many of its members knowing nothing of the men who testify, and being quite unable to evaluate their testimony or to make allowance for, or go behind, the notoriously misleading phraseology of these unreal documents ... In such circumstances the decision is bound to be determined partly by paper qualifications, degrees and the like, which are always misleading, and partly by quite irrelevant considerations.[40]

This, the reformers thought, was 'the worst method which could be devised' in appointing candidates to university posts. Instead they pressed for the institution of the method that the newer civic universities in England were beginning to use. Although they recognised that such a system was not immediately replicable in New Zealand given its 'geographical circumstances', the reformers suggested that its virtues could be maintained by appointing 'a committee of selection in Great Britain'. The main drawback of such committees, they acknowledged, was that their 'members [we]re not deeply enough concerned in the matter to insure [sic] the exhaustive and thorough investigation of individual cases'; with sufficient care of selection, however, this was something they believed could be overcome.[41]

In their different ways, Canadian and Australian universities had in the last decades of the nineteenth century developed many of the features advocated by the New Zealand reformers in 1911. Moving away from a reliance on testimonials and generalist selectors, they had placed their faith in the private, personal recommendations of disciplinary specialists. While the Canadian universities did this through extensive search procedures that drew upon the connections of university principals and faculty members, the Australian institutions were able to depute their own former staff to act on their behalf. In doing so they overcame both of the difficulties identified by the New Zealand reformers. Thus, expansive systems of personalised trust underpinned academic appointment procedures in most of the settler colonies up until the Second World War.

By contrast, in India and South East Asia a wholly other system of selection was in operation. There it was civil servants rather than universities or academics that undertook the recruitment of professors. The colleges of the Indian universities had originally been staffed by British-born teachers. Under pressure from Indian nationalists, from the 1880s they were replaced by an increasing number of Indian graduates. But a British presence was retained in the form of a 'superior' graded Indian Educational Service (IES) comprising ninety-two members. This had been established by the government of India in 1897 and its members were recruited through a committee of the India Office in London. Positions were advertised and selection was based upon assessment of a candidate's written application, formal testimonials and – finally – an interview. Although the India Office endeavoured to stay in close touch with the English universities and the elite public schools, the civil servants who staffed its committees continued to place great weight on teaching capacity and manly character rather than research ability or specialised expertise.[42] As far as the India Office was concerned, the Indian universities – like the African institutions after them – remained closely tied to the civilising project, and a degree from Oxbridge together with good form on the river were ample qualifications for those who taught in them. Prizing administration over teaching (most of which was left to underpaid Indians), largely ignoring research and rewarding longevity of tenure rather than quality of performance, the conditions of tenure in the IES further worked to discourage the best scholars from applying to these posts. Attracting British recruits to the Indian Educational Service – which was less prestigious than the Indian Civil Service and less well remunerated – became even harder in the years after 1900, when the new civic universities in England provided opportunities at home for many who formerly would have applied.[43] As Calcutta's Professor C. V. Ramen commented in 1921, 'in the matter of the quality of the men sent out to us, we have been sadly disillusioned, and we have had painfully to learn the lesson of self-reliance'.[44] In the First World War, Indian teachers began to replace IES men, and from the 1920s the universities in South Asia were effectively Indianised. Although frequently required to have a British degree, these professors were selected locally rather than in Britain, and the private recommendations of British scholars were far less important in their recruitment.

Therefore, if the period after 1880 was one in which settler universities instituted appointment procedures that relied heavily on the personal recommendations of expert British academics, it was one in which the Indian universities moved in the opposite direction. The bureaucratic management of recruitment, the hierarchical imperial cultures that shaped selection criteria, and the rise of an Indian nationalist movement that contested the institutions of imperial rule meant that the systems of personalised trust, so crucial to appointment in the settler universities, played a minimal role in India. By extending British academic networks to the settler colonies, these appointment practices helped create an expansive academic community in which forms of proximity and distance were measured by personal relationships as well as by accumulated mileage.

Boundaries

At a primary level the selection practices of settler universities rein-scribed the 'global colour line' championed by late-Victorian writers such as J. R. Seeley, Charles Dilke and Charles Pearson.[45] Students from Africa, India and the West Indies often found it difficult to even gain admission to British universities. 'If I were a head of an Oxford College,' wrote one Colonial Office official in 1928, 'possessing my present knowledge of West African students, nothing on earth would persuade me to receive one of them'; '[w]ith Indian applications', explained one of the tutors at Corpus Christi College, Cambridge, 'we do not consider anybody who is not backed by the India Office'.[46] Although Indians were employed in the colleges of South East Asia and a small number of Africans found places on the staff at the South African Native College at Fort Hare in the Eastern Cape, it is difficult to find any trace of Indians or Africans applying for positions in settler universities and hard to imagine they would have been considered favourably if they had.[47] The exchange in 1900 between the India Office and Dadabhai Naoroji, the UK's first Indian MP and friend to many Indian scholars in Britain, highlighted just how difficult it was for 'Her Majesty's Indians subjects' to secure senior academic appointments even in India. While Naoroji was 'thankful to read' that, so long as they were 'distinguished graduates of Universities of United Kingdom', 'there [wa]s nothing to prevent the selection of the natives of India' for the Indian Educational Service, he nonetheless queried the lack of recognition accorded to Indian degrees, and perceptively noted that there remained a large question over 'how this eligibility of the Indian [wa]s to be practically given effect'.[48]

Yet the boundaries of the British academic world were not just racial. European- or American-born applicants were only infrequently ap-pointed to positions in settler universities. Although some Europeans did win chairs in the colleges of South and East Asia and to an extent also in South Africa and Canada where they were prominent in dis-ciplines such as languages and music, they were frequently confined to junior positions in the academic hierarchy. Americans were even fewer in number. Instead the professoriate at English-speaking settler universities was overwhelmingly 'British'. Between 1880 and 1930, ninety per cent of professorial appointments at Toronto, ninety-five percent of those at Cape Town and all of those at Sydney were born either in Britain or in the colonies.[49] This is not to say that scholarly collaboration and exchange with European and American scholars did not take place. In the late nineteenth century significant numbers of Europeans made research trips to the settler colonies, while settler academics frequently travelled to laboratories and libraries in Europe, and in Canada's case also the United States. The University of Sydney's investment in German-language journals alone attests the rich trade in international publications and the influence they carried. But for the most part these intellectual exchanges did not translate into employment.

Given language differences, it is perhaps not surprising that the numbers of European-born appointments to settler institutions were not high. However, this was an obstacle that did not apply to candidates from the United States. English-speaking and from a robust university sector, American candidates might have seemed good contenders for positions in settler universities. Australian chairs in disciplines that did not have a strong presence in British universities were frequently advertised in the United States and received significant numbers of American applicants; of the thirty-four candidates who put their names forward for the chair of dental science at the University of Melbourne in 1924, seventeen were from the United States.[50] But Americans were virtually never appointed to these positions, and American experience figured only marginally in the careers of Australian appointees.

In Canada American experience was looked upon more favourably. But, as in Australia, few Americans were appointed to positions in Canadian universities. In the shadow of the cultural and economic, not to mention military, might of the United States, Canadian universities asserted their British loyalty when it came to professorial appointments. In their search for new professors, for example, Toronto and McGill sought British-born candidates on the one hand, and American-trained Canadians on the other. It was thought that both would be more 'likely [than Americans] to understand the methods and needs of a Canadian University'.[51] But the preference for Canadian-born candidates also reflected a specifically local colonial politics. Led by James Loudon – the University's first 'home-grown' professor, and between 1892 and 1906 also its president – the self-styled 'nativist' movement that emerged in the 1870s had by the 1880s translated into a decisive shift in the balance between British- and Canadian-born professorial appointments at the University of Toronto. With Loudon as president, and the government still officially controlling appointments, seventy-five per cent of those selected for permanent positions at University College between 1889 and 1911 were not just Canadians but Toronto graduates.[52] Although the percentage of locally born appointments dropped following Loudon's departure, British-born professors would never again outstrip Canadians on the staff at Toronto. At Sydney the same shift occurred in the 1920s when the surge in national pride attendant with Australia's wartime contributions led to calls for 'native sons' of the University to come into their own and displace their British-born 'foster fathers' who were to recede appropriately into the background.[53] By contrast, up until the Second World War, the professoriate of the University of Cape Town remained dominated by British-born recruits (over sixty-five per cent), with South Africans only constituting ten to twenty per cent of all new appointments.[54]

This predominance of colonial-born professors at Toronto and Sydney might seem to signal a localisation of the trust systems fundamental to appointments procedures. But focusing only on birthplace hides the extent to which most of these 'native' professors had spent an extended period of time abroad, either as students or in employment. After studying or working in Britain or the United States, they were drafted back to their country of origin by the personal processes detailed above. On the one hand, the Toronto selection processes recruited a good number of Canadians with American experience (thirty per cent) and a significant number with European experience as well (until 1918 it also was thirty per cent, dropping to fifteen per cent in the 1920s).[55] But on the other hand, Toronto's informal search procedure recruited a professoriate that was characterised by significant British experience: thirty to forty-five per cent of the professors appointed in the period 1900–30 had spent time in Britain. Indeed, from the turn of the century there was a positive preference for British degrees, with the Canadian Universities Conference in 1911 'strongly express[ing]' its opinion that the Universities 'would greatly prefer to have professors who had pursued their post-graduate work in the United Kingdom rather than in the United States'.[56] At Sydney, meanwhile, reliance on London selection committees led to a professoriate that until 1940 was dominated by men with British experience: throughout the period over seventy per cent of all those appointed at Sydney had undertaken some work or study in the United Kingdom. And at Cape Town all of the professors had experience abroad, with eight-five per cent having worked or studied in Britain. Indeed, at Cape Town Scottish experience was particularly important, and it is striking that in the decade before the First World War, half of those appointed had spent time in Scotland.[57] Therefore, despite the predominance of the 'native-born' in places like Toronto and Sydney, throughout the period all these settler universities continued to appoint large numbers of academics with British experience.

While British race patriotism played a significant part in this, the selection processes that settler universities operated privileged those candidates who were connected to British scholarly networks. These were networks to which Americans did not belong. Speaking in 1921 of the period before the First World War, George McLean, the director of the American University Union in London, drew attention to this:

German Universities catered to us [Americans] at little cost, welcomed us with open hands and brought us into close contact with their greatest Professors. They acknowledged our credentials, initiated us into research and, with the exception of a few notorious Universities, made us work for our degrees, and sent us home with a measure of devotion to the Fatherland. Some of us caught a glimpse of the charms of the British Universities as we passed by, but no one beckoned us in.[58]

Although after 1901 Rhodes scholarships brought up to thirty-two American students annually to Oxford, reports from 1911 suggest that, unlike their settler contemporaries, these Americans remained on the edges of Oxford life. '[T]hey live a good deal apart', reported one college don, 'and have never identified themselves with the life of the college as the colonists have.'[59] They 'have not the same incentive to work as a colonist scholar,' pointed out another; the 'latter knows that honors gained at an English university will be of some help to him in after life', whereas '[the American] feels that his future career does not depend in any appreciable degree upon our examinations'.[60] Despite Rhodes' intentions, the universities of the United States operated as part of a separate academic world.

The case of Edinburgh-born Thorburn Brailsford Robertson makes this clear. In 1884 Robertson migrated to South Australia as a child with his parents. He attended the University of Adelaide where he studied physiology under Professor E. C. Stirling and mathematics under W. H. Bragg. Although Robertson initially considered becoming a mathematical physicist, he was unable to find a position in Australia and, without a travelling scholarship, he could not go to Britain. So in 1905 he accepted a position as assistant lecturer to the leading German-born American physiologist, Jacques Loeb, in the physiology department at the University of California at Berkeley.[61] Under Loeb, Robertson developed research skills and an interest in physio-chemistry that would influence him for the rest of his career. He obtained a PhD, married his old Adelaide professor's daughter Jane Stirling, and was appointed assistant professor of physiological chemistry and pharmacology on the departure of Loeb in 1910 and full professor in 1917.[62] At the end of that year Robertson accepted an invitation to lecture at Toronto and this in turn led to an offer of appointment there. Pulled by the lure of British connections as well as a generous salary, he accepted the chair of biochemistry and moved to Toronto in 1918.[63] But Robertson wanted to return to Australia. As he told T. H. Laby in 1919, despite receiving at Toronto 'much larger funds for research' ... 'after fourteen years of absence, I would rather accept a moderate opportunity to do good work in Australia than any sort of opportunity whatever in America or Canada'.[64] Before writing to Laby, Robertson had applied for a position at the newly founded Walter and Eliza Hall Institute for Pathology in Melbourne. Yet despite his qualifications, he was 'not very sanguine of obtaining the appointment'. This was because he had learnt that 'the choice [was] to be made in London, where experiences of the American School [were] not viewed with favour'. Robertson lamented the system that excluded scholars like him: 'I am', he wrote, 'handicapped by the comparative lack of development of my special subject in England', and by the 'system of application & selection by London committees which ... throws all Australian appointments into the hands of a few men' who, though they may be very good men, have an outlook 'necessarily ... limited in directions which chance to be foreign to them'.[65] 'In British circles', Robertson concluded, his 'long association with America' hampered his chances of employment. Cut off from British disciplinary networks, he had to rely on old family connections to obtain appointment in Australia: he finally took over his father-in-law's chair at Adelaide.

Built upon long-distance personal connections, the selection practices of British and settler universities drew the boundaries of a British academic world that included the settler colonies but that, for the most part, did not extend to Europe, India or the United States.

Contours

This British academic world had an uneven topography. The role played by personalised systems of trust in the making of appointments facilitated access for those with the right connections. It meant that particular schools and the recommendation of certain individuals could come to acquire especial weight, and well-connected candidates possessed significant advantages. The monopolisation of physics and mathematics appointments by Cambridge graduates provides only one example. As early as 1885 the Earl of Carnarvon and Lord Lieutenant of Ireland wrote complaining to the agent-general for South Australia: 'Irish Candidates for Educational posts have been frequently overlooked by the Colonial authorities, in mathematics especially, as these appointments are practically in the hands of Cambridge men'.[66] In physics a word from J. J. Thomson carried weight well into the twentieth century, and a recommendation from the New Zealand-born Ernest Rutherford could make or break a career. Indeed, between 1890 and 1930 these two men had a hand in virtually every physics appointment in the British settler world. Similarly, Scottish ties exercised a particular influence at Cape Town, Otago and Queen's University. When the Scottish-born philosopher, John Clark Murray, left Queen's for McGill in 1872, the recommendation of Glasgow's Edward Caird was enough to secure his student, John Watson, the post. In Canada, Watson maintained close connections not only with colleagues in Scotland but also with his Scottish contemporaries who had gone to work in the United States, and he employed these connections extensively when looking an assistant professor in 1912.[67] As these examples show, networks of personal connection became associated with particular institutions, investing each with an authority that conditioned recruitment and selection.

Settler universities were acutely conscious of the value of British scholarly ties and actively sought to recruit academics from within those circles. For example, weighing the merits of the British-born, Australian-educated and Chicago-employed Thomas Griffith Taylor as a possible head for Toronto's new department of geography in 1929, the professor of political economy, Harold Innes, felt that '[Griffith Taylor's] international reputation and strong connections in the United States, England (Cambridge) and Australia, Toronto and Canada [meant that he] would be placed at one stroke in a position to develop the subject under most favourable circumstances'.[68] Similarly at Melbourne, the selection committee for the 1924 chair of dental science recommended the appointment of F. C. Wilkinson, a graduate of and lecturer at the University of Liverpool, above the only 'suitable' Australian applicant – the Melbourne-trained James Monahan Lewis – on the grounds that '[Wilkinson's] medical education and associations [in Britain] would serve to influence dental education more along the lines of medical education'.[69] From this angle, the preference of settler universities for British candidates does not just signal their lack of faith in the merits of their own degrees: instead it was another mechanism by which they sought to connect themselves to scholarship in Britain.[70]

When the civic universities began to institute appointment practices that also relied on personalised systems of trust (in fact, their committees were often staffed by the same people who advised settler universities) the expansive nature of British academic networks also helped facilitate the movement of professors working in settler universities back to posts in Britain. The careers of the holders of the Sydney chair of chemistry provide a good example. Beginning with Archibald Liversidge (professor at Sydney from 1874 to 1907), four successive professors of organic chemistry proceeded from Sydney to British universities.[71] The story of their appointment is complicated, but shows just how entwined – and how important – expansive academic networks could be. Before his departure for the Davy-Faraday laboratory at the Royal Institution in London in 1907, Liversidge had been instrumental in organising the 1914 Australian meeting of the British Association for the Advancement of Science. It was at this conference that the British-born and trained Robert Robinson, who had been appointed to the newly created chair of organic chemistry in Sydney in 1912, met the leading British chemists of the day. The following year they supported him in his application for the newly created chair at Liverpool. Meanwhile, John Read – who was working under W. J. Pope at the Municipal School of Technology in Manchester, and then in Cambridge – was appointed Robinson's successor in Sydney.[72] In 1921 Robinson moved to St Andrews, but when his old student friend Arthur Lapworth took over as head of the Manchester department, Robinson moved to assume the position Lapworth had vacated – the Manchester chair of organic chemistry. On his departure from St Andrews, Robinson recommended as his replacement John Read – his successor at Sydney. The University of Sydney appointed to the empty chair John Kenner, from the University of Sheffield. His candidature had been supported by, among others, Professor J. F. Thorpe (who had been Robinson's old colleague at Owens College Manchester before his move to Imperial College).[73] When in 1927 the Manchester College of Technology was looking for a replacement for its chair of technological chemistry, Robinson's head of department, Lapworth – then occupying the chair of chemistry – invited Kenner in Sydney to take up the role.[74] To fill Kenner's empty chair, the University of Sydney appointed a London committee that consisted of Robinson and Read and W. J. Pope (now at Cambridge).[75] The man they recommended for the post was J. C. Earl, an Australian who had studied chemistry in Adelaide before serving in the First World War and then transferring to complete a PhD under Robinson at St Andrews. Since 1922 he had been lecturer at Sydney, under first Read and then Kenner. Robinson went on to hold the Waynflete Chair of Chemistry at Oxford and to receive in 1947 the Nobel Prize. As this extensive network of connection and appointment shows, although distance and institutional location always mattered, the settler universities could and often did operate as an integral part of the British academic sphere.

The possibilities opened up by these selection practices, in combination with the reduced time and cost of travel, created an academic population that – even outside the trips facilitated by temporary leave-of-absence schemes – was much more mobile than it had previously been. No longer was migration merely unidirectional: rather, return- and circulatory-migration increasingly also characterised the lives of academics working in settler universities. This was particularly the case for academics who went to Australia where, contrary to the assessment of Donald Fleming and others, a ticket to Sydney was not a one-way trip but rather a move that was one of the series of moves which constituted an academic life.[76] By the interwar period most professors at Sydney had, on average, relocated overseas two or more times (not including relocations within Britain or Australia). This figure is striking. It means that for every British-born and trained professor who moved permanently to Sydney (one relocation), there was another who had moved three times, and for every professor born and trained in Australia who remained there (no relocations), there was another who had moved four times. Movement along the Britain–Australia axis was much more common than movement between the universities of the new Australian nation.[77] Sydney professors, therefore, had significantly more experience of British universities than they had of other Australian institutions.

As the examples above suggest, academics moved along migratory axes that were particular to both their discipline and their country of origin. The age and position of the ancient English universities frequently made them important sites in multiple disciplinary networks, but in medicine and the sciences the Scottish institutions continued to exert a pull. At such places as Cape Town, Otago and Queen's, Scottish ties were particularly important. And if Australia, New Zealand and English-speaking South Africa looked predominantly to the United Kingdom, the Canadian universities came to function as something of a 'hinge' between the otherwise largely distinct British and American systems. Brailsford Robertson was not the only one to move along this route; R. M. MacIver, Griffith Taylor and Jacob Gould Shurmann were others who used Canada to move between Britain and America.[78]

However, although the priority that universities gave to personal knowledge facilitated the participation of some academics working in the universities of the settler empire, it also created a highly uneven and unequal terrain that excluded many others. The informal connections that underpinned academic appointments were forged by cultures of academic sociability that were not only raced, but gendered and classed as well.

By the turn of the century the opening up of the academic franchise had resulted in an increasing number of women graduates in the settler colonies, and some of these began to find academic employment as demonstrators or assistant lecturers in settler universities. Some travelling scholarships also took women abroad: to the women's colleges of Oxford and Cambridge, to Scotland, to the University of London, and in some cases to the United States.[79] Unforeseen vacancies and the Great War opened up still more opportunities, and as the 1920s progressed, women began to be appointed at the level of lecturer.

Despite these growing opportunities, for women the barriers to an academic career remained severe. In 1932, the percentage of professors who were women in Australian universities was zero. In Canada it was under one per cent. In Britain, New Zealand and South Africa the figures were only marginally higher, at 1.5, 3.8 and 1.4 per cent respectively.[80] For those who did find academic work, employment conditions were far from equal. At the University of the Witwatersrand, for example, women were paid fifteen per cent less than men at all levels of the university hierarchy, and faced compulsory retirement upon marriage or reaching the age of fifty-five.[81] In 1924 Margaret Hodgson – a lecturer in history – had contested these pay scales, but in the council debate that followed, Alexander Aiken's opinion that 'the work of women is not equal to that of men' won out and the provisions remained in force.[82] Hodgson was again defeated in her attempts to secure change in 1934 when she wished to marry. Despite waging a campaign that involved an appeal to the Minister of Education and resulted in the abolition of the unequal pay provisions, she was nonetheless forced to resign.[83] Across the British academic world perceptions about the gendered character of different branches of knowledge, in combination with theories of innate sexual difference and expectations about gender roles, restricted women's participation in academic life.[84]

Settler universities, like their cousins in Britain, were environments that fostered and rewarded masculine cultures of sociability.[85] Geoffrey Sherrington and Julia Horne have argued that in the 1880s Australian universities witnessed a 're-affirmation of the almost "aristocratic" ideal of character formation focused on the emergence of the male ideology of athleticism and celebration of the body and physical endeavour rather than the mind'.[86] The students imported this ethic from their schools and the early professors encouraged it by playing alongside them on the sports field. By the turn of the century it was being championed more broadly as a means of strengthening the bonds of empire.[87] In the settler university these forms of sociability were reinforced by the high incidence of British experience among the male academic staff. Looking back on his time as a young history lecturer at the University of Melbourne between the wars, Norman Harper attested to this when he talked about departmental parties at which he 'was often depressed by all those people who had been to Oxford or Cambridge, Athens or Thebes, London or Rome, who conducted in-conversations which left outsiders feeling like barbarians'.[88]

Women operated on the edges of these spaces. They were officially barred from membership of many professional and disciplinary societies: the British Physiological Society excluded them until 1915, and the Royal Society until 1945.[89] Thought to be financially sup-ported by their husbands and therefore less deserving of the positions, laboratory time and research money accorded to their brothers, they worked on the margins of both the formal and the informal structures that facilitated academic connection. Those who did manage to secure travelling scholarships found themselves either in the parallel realm of the women's colleges or in the homosocial cultures that dominated seminar, library and laboratory.[90] Women working in settler universities thus found it especially difficult to make the kinds of relationships that were so important for an academic career.

To navigate the highly gendered terrain of early twentieth-century academia, female scholars frequently required the backing of male colleagues. Baldwin Spencer at Melbourne and Edgeworth David at Sydney were particularly open to offering women opportunities, employing several in their departments. But as scholars such as Helena Pycior, Nancy Slack and Pnina Abir-Am have pointed out, it was a supportive marriage that most often enhanced a women's chance of doing academic work.[91] It was not uncommon for women students or assistants to marry their professors, and some formed 'collaborative' relationships that gave them space to work. Marriage to the Canadian astronomer Frank Scott Hogg, for example, enabled Helen Hogg to pursue her own research, while Edith Osborn not only helped her husband establish a department at Adelaide, but served as lecturer and demonstrator in the department of botany at Sydney following his appointment there as professor.[92]

Yet the example of Hogg – who worked in a junior capacity until her husband's death – also shows that even in such relationships women were rarely accorded full credit for the work they undertook.[93] More usually women were vital components of what Hannah Gay has called the 'underground economy' of academia.[94] '[T]he function of a wife, my lad,' wrote Donald Hunter, director of the (British) Medical Research Council's Department for Research into Industrial Medicine, to the South African medic, J. F. Brock, 'is to help you to get that [manuscript] into print'.[95] Women transcribed articles, ordered research and conducted experiments for their husbands, brothers and fathers in ways that went largely unacknowledged. They maintained and facilitated male sociability, conducting personal and professional correspondences and organising the afternoon teas, dinner parties and excursions to the country that fostered connections between academic men. As with Noel Annan's 'intellectual aristocracy', marriage played a central role in knitting together the affective relations of the British academic world.[96] Two of J. T. Wilson's daughters married Australians studying under him in Cambridge, while Rutherford's only daughter also married one of his students, Ralph Fowler, who would himself later hold the chair of theoretical physics at the Cavendish Laboratory. In these ways women joined Europeans in what we might think of as 'the shadow networks' of the British academic world. Although they were frequently enmeshed in long-distance ties, these were not of a kind that earned them a significant place inside settler institutions. Even as they participated in the scholarly project, women provided the poorly paid, under-recognised, and often locally based labour that both supported and enabled the mobility of the white, male and largely middle-class Britons appointed to senior posts.[97]

The expansive networks of the British academic world played an important role in shaping, policing and extending these racial, gendered and gentlemanly geographies. Unofficial information travelling along these networks determined who was and who was not admitted to them. One of the candidates who applied for the chair of physics in Adelaide in 1885 was passed over because it had been heard that he was considered 'not safe with the bottle'.[98] In 1905 Mr Price (of Harvard) appeared to Toronto's James Mavor to be 'too jeuvenile looking [sic] to take affective control of Toronto's large classes', and in Melbourne Esmonde Higgin's affiliation with the Communist Party meant he was, according to one of his supporters, 'regarded with deep suspicion'.[99] Similarly, 'while not knowing him personally', the members of the 1919 advisory committee for the Cape Town chair of physics 'felt [they] ought to mention' that they had 'heard somewhat conflicting reports of [Lewis Simons'] personality and his ability to get on with students'.[100]

This continuing emphasis upon character and the informal means by which it was assessed also created space for more insidious forms of discrimination, as the case of the Polish-born Lewis Berstein Naymier (later Namier) at the University of Toronto shows. While some anglicised Jews were able to find academic appointments in Australia, Canada and South Africa, those who did not obviously conform to British cultural expectations met a very different experience.[101] Naymier – whom the master of Balliol College, A. L. Smith, described as 'the ablest man we have had in economics and history for some years' – had been recommended by Smith in 1911 for a junior appointment in Toronto's department of political economy. But Godfrey Lloyd, a member of the department who was in England meeting candidates and who interviewed Naymier, seemed to take against him, preferring Gilbert Jackson who had a second-class degree from Cambridge as the 'safer choice'. 'Of course,' wrote Lloyd of Naymier, 'he is not in the least British', and the 'one definite drawback, about which opinions vary, is the extent to which his foreign accent affects his intelligibility'.[102] The head of department, James Mavor, was similarly minded.[103] In the end Jackson was awarded the position. But the same year the Toronto history department wanted to appoint a lecturer and Naymier's name was again put forward. Although he was strongly favoured by the outgoing post-holder Kenneth Bell, and in the face of Falconer's assertions that 'the fact of his being a Jew has not influence one way or another with us', once again Naymier's Jewishness – often discussed in terms of his 'difficult' accent – proved an obstacle. In particular, Joseph Flavelle, a member of the board of governors, 'did not like the choice of a Polish Jew as an interpreter of history ... who by his broken accent constantly proclaims it', and Naymier was again passed over.[104] Despite his evident ability and good Oxford connections, the combination of anti-Semitism, British race patriotism, and the weight given to personal assessments led Toronto to reject Naymier's application.[105]

The racial, gendered and – although not discussed in detail here – classed cultures of British academia were thus intimately bound up in the same processes that extended British networks to settler universities. In concert with, but also often in the face of, stated university policies, expansive personal networks shaped the composition and character of academic bodies.

*

Speaking in 1912, the one-time inspector-general of schools in Western Australia, Cyril Jackson, described the process of selecting new academic personnel:

> [S]upposing a Professor of Geology, or some other branch of science, is wanted, it is very difficult to know where such a man is likely to be found. One cannot possibly know all the staffs of the various Universities in England, and one has to do the best one can by writing to friends.[106]

This practice of 'writing to friends' was a crucial aspect of the making of appointments in settler universities. Personal relationships developed in such sites as common rooms and laboratories were carried with academics when they migrated. These trusted long-distance ties then become the channels that settler universities relied on when weighing the merits of potential candidates. As this chapter has shown, the official institutional practice of universities was premised upon the private knowledge and the personal relationships of their staff and students.

Yet the place universities accorded to private knowledge meant that their measures of expertise were contingent upon the cultures of academic sociability in which the friendships of their staff were formed. Not only were these cultures that were racially exclusive, they were also heavily gendered. Even as women were marginalised from the formal structures of academia, as correspondents, assistants and marriage partners, they provided much of the 'affective labour' on which the maintenance of academic relationships depended.[107] The technologies of selection used by settler universities therefore reveal a British academic world that was both expansive and exclusionary. They point to boundaries and contours and to routes of access and impasse that – from the end of the nineteenth century – began to be mapped not just by mileage but also by the density and reach of personal connections and by the cultures that supported them.

Notes

1 'Official Report of the Allied Colonial Universities Conference', p. 112.
2 Focus has generally centred on the type of candidates appointed. While some have seen those who took up colonial positions as scholars 'of the second rank' others have contested this assumption. For the first view, see Rothblatt, *The Revolution of the Dons*, pp. 264–6; Fleming, 'Science in Australia, Canada and the United States', p. x. For the second, see James Johnston Auchmuty, *The Idea of the University in Its Australian Setting: A Historical Survey* (Melbourne: 1963), p. 155; Richard Symonds, '"The Foundations of All Good and Noble Principles": Oxonians and the Australian Universities in the Nineteenth Century', in H. Morphy and E. Edwards (eds), *Australia in Oxford* (Oxford: Oxford University Press, 1998), p. 78.
3 Shapin, *A Social History of Truth*, p. xxv.
4 Niklas Luhmann, 'Familiarity, Confidence, Trust: Problems and Alternatives', in Diego Gambetta (ed.), *Trust: Making and Breaking Cooperative Relations* (New York: Basil Blackwell, 1988), pp. 97–8; Anthony Giddens, *The Consequences of Modernity* (Cambridge: Polity, 1991), pp. 29–34. See also Niklas Luhmann, *Trust and Power: Two Works*, trans. Howard Davis, John Raffan and Kathryn Rooney (Chichester: Wiley, 1979), esp. chs 3, 6 and 7. Stefan Collini has pointed to the broad historical shift from birth, to office, to achievement, to celebrity as the criteria that determined prominence in Britain from the eighteenth century to the present. Stefan Collini, *Absent Minds: Intellectuals in Britain* (Oxford: Oxford University Press, 2006), p. 475.
5 Christopher Stray, 'From Oral to Written Examinations: Cambridge, Oxford and Dublin, 1700–1914', *History of Universities*, 20, no. 2 (2005): 76–130; Keith Hoskin, 'Examinations and the Schooling of Science', in Roy MacLeod (ed.), *Days of Judgement: Science, Examinations, and the Organization of Knowledge in Victorian England* (Driffeld: Studies in Education, 1982); Rothblatt, *The Revolution of the Dons*, pp. 182–3; Sheldon Rothblatt, *The Modern University and Its Discontents the Fate of Newman's Legacies in Britain and America* (Cambridge: Cambridge University Press, 1997), pp. 148–76.
6 Philippa Levine, *The Amateur and the Professional: Antiquarians, Historians and Archaeolgists in Victorian England, 1838–1886* (Cambridge: Cambridge University Press, 1986), p. 158.
7 See, for example, 'Testimonials in Favour of Mr Daniel Wilson (Candidate for the Chair of History and English Literature in the University of Toronto)' (1851); 'Testimonials in Favour of T. P. Anderson Stuart (Candidate for the Chair of Anatomy and Physiology in Sydney University)' (1882).
8 See Christopher Stray, 'Flying at Dusk: The 1906 Praelections', in C. Stray (ed.), *The Owl of Minerva: The Cambridge Praelections of 1906* (Cambridge: Proceedings of the Cambridge Philological Society, 2005), pp. 1–12.
9 Friedland, *The University of Toronto*, pp. 48–9.
10 In the case of the University of Otago in New Zealand, a Scottish committee was appointed for the chair of mental and moral philosophy. It comprised three theologians from the Free Church and United Presbyterian College, and two philosophy professors.

11 James Hight and Alice M.F. Candy, *A Short History of the Canterbury College* (Auckland: Whitcombe and Tombs, 1927), p. 24.

12 Stefan Collini, 'The Idea of "Character" in Victorian Political Thought', *Transactions of the Royal Historical Society*, 35 (1985): 29–50.

13 Barry quoted in Selleck, *The Shop*, p. 31.

14 Who they got was another matter. Melbourne: Frederick McCoy (Irish – Trinity College Dublin and Cambridge; Queen's Belfast), William Hearn (Irish – Trinity College Dublin; Queen's Galway), William Wilson (English – Cambridge; Queen's Belfast), Henry Rowe (English – Cambridge). Sydney: Morris Birbeck Pell (American-born – Cambridge), John Smith (Scottish – Aberdeen), John Woolley (English – London and Oxford).

15 Pattison, *Suggestions on Academical Organisation*, p. 213.

16 *Congress Proceedings, 1912*, pp. 59–60.

17 *University Reform in New Zealand* (Wellington, NZ: Whitcombe and Tombs, 1911), p. 49.

18 For the phrase, see W. J. Gardner, *Colonial Cap and Gown: Studies in the Mid-Victorian Universities of Australasia* (Christchurch: University of Canterbury, 1979), pp. 56–67.

19 Leo Yaffe, *History of the Department of Chemistry McGill University* (Montreal: McGill University, 1978), p. 15.

20 Selleck, *The Shop*, p. 206.

21 MUA, *Office of the Principal, William Peterson*, RG2 c15-35/2/641/97/59/7 Feb. 1910. In the case of the University of Toronto it lay with the Minister of Education until the 1906 University Act substituted a (lay) board of governors for direct government control, giving responsibility to the principal to make recommendations for appointments, which would be made by the board. See Friedland, *The University of Toronto*, pp. 204–5.

22 MUA, *Office of the Principal, William Peterson*, c32/2/June 1900 – May 1901/2 Oct. 1900, Peterson to Prof. John Davidson (University of New Brunswick).

23 *Ibid.*, c33/5/Apr. 1903 – Jan. 1904/1 May 1903, Peterson to Prof. E. B. Titchener (Dept Psychology, Cornell).

24 *Ibid.*, c32/2/June 1900 – May 1901/18 Mar. 1901, Peterson to Flux.

See Friedland, *The University of Toronto*, pp. 234–5; Ian M. Drummond, *Political Economy at the University of Toronto: A History of the Department, 1888–1982* (Toronto: University of Toronto, 1983), pp. 18–19.

26 MUA, *Office of Principals, Arthur Currie, Arthur Eustace Morgan, and Lewis Williams Douglas*, RG2/c53/16 Sept. 1936, 'Memorandum: The Powers of the Senate with Respect to the Establishment of Chairs'.

27 For a discussion of 'agents', see Chapter 5.

28 Quoted in John Jenkin, *William and Lawrence Bragg, Father and Son* (Oxford: Oxford University Press, 2008), p. 64.

29 W. F. Sheppard went on to become a British civil servant. He continued his mathematical work and was interested in statistics by the eugenicist Francis Galton, publishing a series of papers on correlation between 1897 and 1907.

30 J. T. Wilson (demonstrator at the University of Sydney) did this in his application for Sydney's 1890 chair of anatomy. See USA, *J.T. Wilson Papers*, P162/series 1/3/'Letter of Application and Testimonials of James T. Wilson', 9 Sept. 1889. Later, Alfred Radcliffe-Brown (teaching at the time in Johannesburg) did the same thing in his application for the 1921 chair of anthropology at the University of Cape Town. UCTA, *Social Anthropology (1921)*, AA 157–330/22 Oct. 1920.

31 For example, after his move from the University of Sydney to take up the chair of anatomy at Cambridge in 1921, J. T. Wilson became a regular on the University's London selection committees

32 *Calendar of the University of Sydney, 1924* (Sydney: University of Sydney, 1923), p. 818.

33 UMA, *Registrar's Correspondence*, UM312/1911/34: English Chair, Agent-General reporting on London Committee to the Melbourne Chancellor, 19 June 1911.

34 UCTA, *Chair of Physics*, AA 1–156/South African High Commissioner to Rutherford, 7 Mar. 1919; Rutherford to High Commissioner, 13 Apr. 1919.
35 See UCTA, *Personal File of J. K. Wylie*, AA 1–156/J. Mackintosh (Edinburgh) to Currathurs Beatie, 7 Nov. 1923.
36 UCTA, *Chair of Physics*, Rutherford to South African High Commissioner, 13 Apr. 1919.
37 *Ibid.*, High Commissioner to Rutherford, 7 Mar. 1919.
38 Ritchie (ed.), *The History of the South African College*, pp. 416, 428.
39 *University Reform in New Zealand*, 46–54.
40 Article published in the Educational Supplement of the *London Times*, 4 Apr. 1911, quoted in *Ibid.*, p. 48.
41 *Ibid.*, p. 50.
42 C. Whitehead, *Colonial Educators: The British Indian and Colonial Education Service 1858–1983* (London: I. B. Tauris, 2003), p.17.
43 *Ibid.*, pp. 11–18.
44 *Second Congress of the Universities of the Empire, 1921: Report of Proceedings*, ed. Alex Hill (London: G. Bell and Sons, 1921), p. 367.
45 Marilyn Lake and Henry Reynolds, *Drawing the Global Colour Line: White Men's Countries and the International Challenge of Racial Equality* (Cambridge: Cambridge University Press, 2008).
46 National Archives UK (NAUK), *Colonies, General: Original Correspondence*, CO 323/1001/13/Colonial Gov[ernmen]t Schol[arship]s Admission to Brit[ish] Uni[versitie]s 1928/A. Fiddian, 28 Feb. 1928; Kenneth Pickthorn to the Educational Officer for West Africa, Colonial Office, 8 May 1928.
47 For a list of staff at Fort Hare, see Alexander Kerr, *Fort Hare 1915–48: The Evolution of an African College* (London: Hurst and Co, 1968), pp. 275–7.
48 British Library (BL), *India Office Records – Public and Judicial Department Papers: Annual Files*, IOR/L/PJ/6/555/file 2168, 1900/Naoroji to the Under Secretary of State, 29 June 1900.
49 Tamson Pietsch, 'Wandering Scholars? Academic Mobility and the British World, 1850-1940', *Journal of Historical Geography*, 36, no. 4 (2010): 377–87. Of the seventy-eight professors appointed at the South African College and the University of Cape Town between 1876 and 1930, only three (3.8 per cent) were born outside the Empire, with the birthplace of a further seven (8 per cent) unknown.
50 UMA, *Council Minute Books*, UM174/vol. 15, 20 Dec. 1909; UMA, *Registrar's Correspondence*, UM312/1909/23: Engineering – Chair; UM312/1924/162: Chair of Dental Science – Applications.
51 MUA, *Office of the Principal, William Peterson*, c26/Mathematics Chair 1903/James Harkness to Peterson, 14 March 1903; UTA, *Office of the President*, A1967-0007/box 56/490/Bonner to Falconer, 10 Dec. 1918.
52 Friedland, *The University of Toronto*, pp. 113–15.
53 Patricia Morison, *J. T. Wilson and the Fraternity of Duckmaloi* (Amsterdam: Rodopi, 1997), p. 325.
54 The rest were born elsewhere in the Empire (four of a total of 101 across the whole period) or in Europe (seven of 101).
55 In the period 1881–1900, sixty per cent of Toronto professorial appointments had spent time in Britain; in 1901–18, thirty per cent; and in 1919–30, forty-five per cent. Pietsch, 'Wandering Scholars?' supplementary tables.
56 UTA, *Office of the President*, A1967-0007/16/57/254/'A [printed] report of the preliminary Conference of representatives of the Canadian Universities held at Montreal, 6 June 1911'
57 The remaining Cape Town group looked to Europe, with three of the twenty professors appointed in the period 1876–1900 and five of the thirty-nine appointed in 1901–1918 undertaking their overseas experience there – about half in the Netherlands. The United States was unimportant until the 1930s when eight of twenty-three (34.7 per cent) professorial appointees had spent time there, though almost always going to Britain as well.
58 *Second Congress Proceedings, 1921*, p, 415.

59 '"Attractive but Restless and Volatile": American Rhodes Scholars', *New York Times*, 12 Mar. 1911.

60 *Ibid.*

61 Robertson later described his move to America as 'entirely forced upon [him] by [his] lack of opportunities in Australia'. UMA, *T.H. Laby Papers*, UM85/2/1/2/1919/ Brailesford Robertson to Laby, 23 Sept. 1919.

62 G. E. Rogers, 'Robertson, Thorburn Brailsford (1884-1930)', *Australian Dictionary of Biography* (2006), accessed 18 November 2007, www.adb.online.anu.edu.au/biogs/ A110429b.html.

63 UTA, *Office of the President*, A1967-0007/box 49, 'Robertson, Brailsford T.'.

64 UMA, *T.H. Laby Papers*, UM85/2/1/2/1919, Brailsford Robertson to Laby, 23 Sept. 1919.

65 *Ibid.*, UM85/2/1/2/1919, Brailsford Robertson to Laby, 23 Sept. 1919.

66 Quoted in John Jenkin, 'The Appointment of W. H. Bragg, F.R.S., to the University of Adelaide', *Notes and Records of the Royal Society of London*, 40, no. 1 (1985): 75–99, p. 85.

67 MUA, *John Watson Fonds*, 1064/1/Correspondence 1898–1925.

68 UTA, *Office of the President*, A1967-0007/287/'Memorandum re. Prof Griffith Taylor', 23 Mar. 1929.

69 UMA, *Registrar's Correspondence*, UM312/1924/162/Chair of Dental Science – Applications/'Report of J. W. Barrett on behalf of the London Committee', 19 Aug. 1924.

70 Selleck makes this argument in his history of the University of Melbourne. Selleck, *The Shop*, p. 504.

71 MacLeod, *Archibald Liversidge, FRS*, p. 388.

72 E. L. Hirst, 'John Read, 1884–1963', *Biographical Memoirs of Fellows of the Royal Society*, 9 (1963): 236–60.

73 *Calendar of the University of Melbourne, 1925* (Melbourne 1924), p. 826.

74 A. Todd, 'James Kenner, 1885–1974', *Biographical Memoirs of Fellows of the Royal Society*, 25 (1979): 389–405.

75 USA, *Minutes of the Senate*, G1/1/18/Committees of Advice/'Organic Chemistry: 1928', 8 Aug. 1927.

76 Fleming, 'Science in Australia, Canada and the United States', pp. 183–4; Auchmuty, *The Idea of the University in Its Australian Setting*, p. 34.

77 Pietsch, 'Wandering Scholars?' p. 386.

78 See Blackburn, *Evolution of the Heart*, p. 73. Principal Wilson tried to appoint Jacob Schurmann to take over the teaching of history at Toronto, but the scheme was thwarted by the Minister of Education, and Schurmann went instead to Cornell.

79 For example Gwynneth Buchanan, appointed junior demonstrator in biology at Melbourne in 1909, studied embryology under J. P. Hill at University College, London, and then went onto further research in the United States before returning to Melbourne as lecturer in zoology in 1925. Selleck, *The Shop*, p. 319. On women's academic mobility see Joyce Goodman *et al.*, 'Travelling Careers: Overseas Migration Patterns in the Professional Lives of Women Attending Girton and Newnham before 1939', *History of Education*, 40, no. 2 (2011): 179–96.

80 F. Perrone, 'Women academics in England, 1870–1930', *History of Universities* 12 (1993): 339–67. In Toronto Annie Laird and Clara Cynthia Benson were in 1920 granted the title of Professor in Household Science and Food Chemistry. But, with the exception of J. B. Brodie, who succeeded Laird in the 1930s, their ranks did not swell until after the Second World War. See also Marianne Gosztonyi Ainley, 'Gendered Careers: Women Science Educators at Anglo-Canadian Universities, 1920–1980' in Paul Stortz and E. Lisa Panayotidis (eds), *Historical Identities: The Professoriate in Canada* (Toronto: University of Toronto Press), pp. 251–8.

81 Bruce K Murray, *Wits: The Early Years: A History of the University of the Witwatersrand Johannesburg and Its Precursors, 1896–1939* (Johannesburg: Witwatersrand University Press, 1982), p. 328.

82 Quoted in *Ibid.*, p. 329.

83 Aiken quoted in *Ibid.*, pp. 330–4.
84 Ruth Watts, *Women in Science: A Social and Cultural History* (Abingdon: Routledge, 2007), pp. 142–3, 154–8; Carol Dyhouse, 'Social Darwinistic Ideas and the Development of Women's Education in England, 1880–1920', *History of Education*, 5, no. 1 (1976): 41–50; Katie Pickles, 'Colonial Counterparts: The First Academic Women in Anglo-Canada, New Zealand and Australia', *Women's History*, 10, no. 2 (2001): 273–98.
85 Margaret Gillet, *We Walked Very Warily: A History of Women at McGill* (Montreal: Eden Press Women's Publications, 1981), esp. p. 371; Pickles, 'Colonial Counterparts: The First Academic Women in Anglo-Canada, New Zealand and Australia', pp. 273, 275; Ruth Watts, 'Gendering the Story: Change in the History of Education', *History of Education*, 34, no. 3 (2005): 224–41; Kay Whitehead, 'From Youth to "Greatest Pedagogue": William Cawthorne and the Construction of a Teaching Profession in Mid-Nineteenth Century South Australia', *History of Education*, 28, no. 4 (1999): 395–412. For related work on the gendered nature of the professions in the nineteenth century, see M. C. Carnes and C. Griffen (eds), *Meanings for Manhood: Constructions of Masculinity in Victorian America* (Chicago, IL: University of Chicago Press, 1990); D. Deacon, *Managing Gender: The State, the New Middle Class and Women Workers, 1830–1930* (Oxford: Oxford University Press, 1989).
86 Sherington and Horne, 'Modes of Engagement', p, 134; Geoffrey Sherington, 'Athleticism in the Antipodes: The A.A.G.P.S. of New South Wales', *History of Education Review*, 12, no. 2 (1983): 16–28.
87 The 1921 chair of anthropology at the University of Cape Town imposed an age restriction of thirty-five and referees and selectors alike weighed candidates according to their 'colonial vigour' and ability 'to get on well with [their] fellowmen'. UCTA, *Social Anthropology (1921)*, AA 157–330/'Report by R. R. Marrett' [Dept of Social Anthropology, University of Oxford] 9 Mar. 1921.
88 D. Goodman, '"There Is No-One to Whom I Can Talk": Norman Harper and American History in Australia', *Australasian Journal of American Studies*, 23, no. 1 (2004): 5–20, p. 7.
89 Pickles, 'Colonial Counterparts', p. 275.
90 Watts, *Women in Science*, pp. 142, 144; Susan Squier, 'Conflicting Scientific Feminisms: Charlotte Haldane and Naomi Mitchinson' in Barbara T. Gates and Ann B. Shteir (eds), *Natural Eloquence: Women Re-inscribe Science* (Wisconsin, WI: University of Wisconsin Press, 1997); Harriet Zuckerman, Jonathan R. Cole, and John T. Bruer (eds), *The Outer Circle: Women in the Scientific Community* (New York: W.W. Norton and Co., 1991), p. 17.
91 Helena M. Pycior, Nancy G. Slack and Pnina G. Abir-Am (eds), *Creative Couples in the Sciences* (New Brunswick: Rutgers University Press, 1996); Roy MacLeod, 'Fathers and Daughters: Reflections on Women, Science and Victorian Cambridge', *History of Education*, 8, no. 4 (1979): 321–33; Regina M. Morantz-Sanchez, 'The Many Faces of Intimacy: Professional Choices among Nineteenth and Early Twentieth Century Women Physicians', in Pnina G. Abir-Am and Dorinda Outram (eds), *Uneasy Careers and Intimate Lives: Women in Science, 1787–1979* (New Brunswick: Rutgers University Press, 1987).
92 Marianne Gosztonyi Ainley, 'Marriage and Scientific Work in Twentieth Century Canada: The Berkeleys in Marine Biology and the Hoggs in Astronomy' in Pycior, Slack and Abir-Am (eds), *Creative Couples in the Science*, pp. 143–55. For Edith Osborn, see UAA, *Theodore George Bentley Osborn Records*, MSS 0020.
93 A. D. Thomson points to the dominance of husband and wife teams among early New Zealand women botanists. A. D. Thomson, 'Some Pioneer Women Graduates in Botany from Canterbury University College' (Centre for Studies in New Zealand Science History, date unknown), accessed 30 Sept. 2011, http://goo.gl/3wqZP. In regard to junior positions, see Carol Dyhouse, 'The British Federation of University Women and the Status of Women in Universities, 1907–1939', *Women's History Review*, 4 (1995): 465–85, p. 471.
94 Hannah Gay, 'Invisible Resource'. See also Prentice, 'Boosting Husbands and Building Community.

95 UCTA, *J. Brock Papers*, BC1041/A1/1/Hunter to Brock, 27 Feb. 1933.
96 Noel Annan, *The Dons: Mentors, Eccentrics and Geniuses* (Chicago, IL: University of Chicago Press, 2001). See Annexe: 'The Intellectual Aristocracy'.
97 See Marjorie R. Theobald, *Knowing Women: Origins of Women's Education in Nineteenth-Century Australia* (Cambridge: Cambridge University Press, 1996); Joyce Goodman and Jane Martin (eds), *Gender, Colonialism and Education: The Politics of Experience* (London: Woburn Press, 2002); Jenny Collins, 'Creating Women's Work in the Academy and Beyond: Carnegie Connections, 1923–1942', *History of Education*, 38, no. 6 (2009): 791–808; Perrone, 'Women Academics in England, 1870–1930.'; Catherine Hall, *White, Male and Middle Class: Explorations in Feminism and History* (London: Polity Press, 1992).
98 From Bragg's autobiography, quoted in Jenkin, 'The Appointment of W. H. Bragg, F.R.S., to the University of Adelaide', p. 84.
99 G. V. Portus quoted in Fay Anderson, *An Historian's Life: Max Crawford and the Politics of Academic Freedom* (Melbourne: Melbourne University Press, 2005), p. 75.
100 UCTA, *Chair of Physics*, AA 1-156/Chair of Physics/'Report on the Candidates for the Chair of Physics in the University of Cape Town'.
101 See also Frederick Gibson, *Queen's University, Vol. 2, 1917–1961* (Kingston and Montreal: McGill-Queen's University Press, 1983), pp. 199–202; Friedland, *The University of Toronto*, pp. 342–8; Michiel Horn, *Academic Freedom in Canada* (Toronto: University of Toronto Press, 1999), pp. 34–5, 136–8, 165–6; David Zimmerman, '"Narrow-Minded People": Canadian Universities and the Academic Refugee Crises, 1933–1941', *Canadian Historical Review*, 88, no. 2 (2007): 291–315.
102 UTA, *Office of the President*, A1967-0007/21/20/Lloyd to Mavor, 12 July 1911.
103 *Ibid.*, A1967-0007/21/20/Mavor to Falconer, 20 July 1911.
104 Friedland, *The University of Toronto*, p. 235.
105 In the end Toronto's loss was Manchester's gain, for Bernstein Naymier was to become Lewis Namier, professor at Manchester from 1931 and brilliant English historian of the eighteenth century. UTA, *Office of the President*, A1967-0007/21/02/307/Falconer to Prof. C. H. Hull (Cornell), 14 Sept. 1911; John Cannon, 'Namier, Sir Lewis Bernstein (1888–1960)', *Oxford Dictionary of National Biography* (Oxford University Press, 2004), accessed 4 Oct. 2011, www.oxforddnb.com/view/article/35183.
106 *Congress Proceedings, 1912*, p. 318. Cyril Jackson was educated at Oxford and worked in the 'New Education' movement in London before accepting a post as Inspector-General for Schools in Western Australia in 1896, where he reformed the elementary school system. He left Western Australia in 1903 for London and served as Chief Inspector to the Board of Education and in local government. He continued to consult for the Western Australian government and acted as agent-general in 1911–12. He died in 1924.
107 For a definition of 'affective labour', see Michael Hardt and Antonio Negri, *Multitude: War and Democracy in the Age of Empire* (New York: Penguin, 2004), p. 108.

CHAPTER FOUR

Institutional association: mutual recognition and imperial organisation

Appointed in 1902, George Parkin spent his first decade as secretary of the Rhodes Trust attempting to make the practical arrangements necessary for the establishment of the Rhodes scholarship scheme. This was a task that brought him into close contact with universities across Britain, the empire and the United States, and one that made him acutely aware of the absence of any systematic institutional co-operation between them. 'The old Universities go on their way', he told the delegates of the 1912 Congress,

> without any complete information about what is being done in the new; the new have to feel their own individual way along the untried paths of development, with little consultation between each other, and little ready opportunity to learn from the old. Engaged in a common task, the Universities lack the means for common and concentrated effort, for the comparison of experience, and for the ready exchange of ideas.[1]

In 1912 Parkin sought to improve this situation by proposing the foundation of a permanent organisation that would represent the universities of the British Empire in London. Like the scholarship scheme he was establishing, however, Parkin's effort to co-ordinate the universities of the empire grew out of connections that had been developing since the 1880s.

Reciprocal recognition

In 1861, Oxford, Cambridge and Trinity College Dublin established a system of mutual recognition in which they granted full rights of reciprocation to each other, enabling students to 'have the Terms kept ... at [Dublin or Cambridge] reckoned as if they had been kept at Oxford', and vice versa.[2] This system was called 'incorporation' and applied only to these three collegiate universities. But in 1887, Oxford instituted an additional policy that enabled select universities to apply for 'affiliated status'. Under this provision, students who had passed two years' worth of exams at 'affiliated' universities were exempted from the requirement to sit Oxford's *Responsions* examination (usually taken prior to or immediately after matriculation) and accorded the 'privilege' of reckoning 'the Term in which [they] matriculate[d] as the fifth Term from [their] matriculation'.[3] This shortened the period of necessary residence by one year and enabled such students to take a three-year Oxford undergraduate degree in only two years.

The 1887 Oxford statute, however, specified that 'affiliated status' was open only to universities 'situated in any part of the British Dominions other than the United Kingdom'.[4] Therefore, although the universities of Australia, the Cape of Good Hope and New Zealand, and several in Canada and India, had by 1900 all successfully made application for this privilege, English, Scottish, Irish, American and European universities were not eligible for it (see Appendix B).[5] Well might the principal of the University of Birmingham have called in 1903 for the mutual acceptance of examinations; whereas the study completed by a Birmingham student was not accepted by Oxford, that undertaken by a student in Sydney was.[6] Oxford's 1887 recognition of colonial degrees points clearly to an academic world that was not orientated along simple geographic lines.

In 1904 the University of Oxford passed statutes that reformed this system. In order to accommodate the arrival of a significant number of Rhodes Scholars from America, it broadened its criteria to enable 'foreign universities' as well as 'universities within the United Kingdom' to apply for 'affiliated status'. The older British universities were the first to take advantage of this new provision. By June of 1904, Durham, St Andrews, Glasgow, Aberdeen and Edinburgh had all acquired the privileges that settler and Indian students had been enjoying since 1887. Harvard was next, followed by several of the American and Canadian universities covered by the Rhodes scholarship scheme. But, despite Birmingham's protestations in 1903, it took nearly a decade for the newer British universities to apply for 'affiliated status', with the University of London gaining it only in 1912 and the Irish universities in 1914.

Although the 1904 Oxford statute opened up new avenues of access for British and foreign students, it instituted a new kind of obstacle for Indian scholars. By dividing students from affiliated institutions into two classes – junior and senior – the statute inscribed in regulation the racial divide that helped define the British academic world. 'Senior Students' were those from any affiliated institution – colonial, foreign or Indian – who had obtained an Honours degree, and were excused the need to sit the First Public Examination. Students from 'colonial' and 'foreign' universities who had completed two years of study, on the other hand, were deemed 'Junior Students', and were required to sit the First Public Examination. Yet in order for Indian students to be granted 'Junior' status they had to have obtained a complete Bachelor's degree.[7] All students were required to show proficiency in Latin and Greek, but a special provision was accorded to candidates who were not what the university termed 'European British subjects'. This awkward categorisation was, as *The Student's Handbook* helpfully pointed out, used to describe '[a]ny subject [or legitimate child or grandchild of such person] of His Majesty born, naturalized, or domiciled in the United Kingdom of Great Britain and Ireland, or in any of the European, American, or Australian Colonies or Possessions of His Majesty, or in the Colony of New Zealand, or in the Colony of the Cape of Good Hope or Natal'.[8] Instead of Greek, 'non-European British subjects' – essentially South and East Asians and students from the Middle East – were able to offer Sanskrit, Arabic, Pali or Classical Chinese.[9] Although this provision represented a concession to such students, it also racialised the category of 'British subject', officially dividing those of 'European' from those of 'non-European' parentage.

This redefinition of the colonial student was accompanied by a new institutional taxonomy. Whereas previously there had been one classification – 'affiliated status' – for which universities in all parts of the British Empire were eligible, the 1904 Oxford statute defined Indian and colonial universities separately. But, despite being located outside the British Isles, neither type of institution was considered 'foreign', which was a designation reserved for the universities of Europe and America. Adopted by most universities in the United Kingdom in the years before the First World War, this lexical division between Indian, 'colonial' and 'foreign' institutions enshrined wider contemporary racial and political discourses in university regulations.[10]

In contrast to Oxford's system of unequal recognition, the settler universities took more literally the words of their Letters Patent.[11] These declared that colonial degrees 'should be recognized as academic distinctions, and be entitled to rank, precedence, and consideration throughout the British Empire as if granted by any Univ. in the U.K.'[12] In reciprocation, the universities of Sydney, Melbourne, Adelaide and New Zealand, along with McGill and Bombay, admitted graduates from 'all the universities of the British Empire to which Royal Charters or Letters Patent have been granted' *ad eundem gradum* ('to the same degree'), while students still in the course of their studies were admitted *ad eundem statum* ('at the same level').[13] This practice had operated informally at Oxford in the first part of the nineteenth century, but Oxford had abandoned it in 1861 when the university instituted 'incorporation'.[14] Settler universities, however, saw it as valuable because it offered them a means of creating a critical mass of local graduates to serve as members on their early senates and convocation bodies.

Nonetheless, by the early years of the twentieth century many settler universities were beginning to feel that British institutions undervalued their degrees. Together with some of the English civic universities and colleges they began to push for an empire-wide policy of mutual recognition. This met with resistance from Oxford and Cambridge, which guarded closely the integrity of their own degrees and their unique residential requirements.[15] E. C. Pearce, the master of Corpus Christi College, Cambridge, went so far as to declare: 'Cambridge is not primarily a place of learning or a place of examination ... It is a place where you live for three years'.[16] In the end it was only the advent of graduate study in Britain that resolved the impasse between the old and new universities. '[L]eave the undergraduate ... to the University which has the student for two years out of three,' suggested Gregory Foster, the provost of University College London, in 1919, and instead place all the 'stress on the interchangeability of post-graduate students'.[17] With the new British PhD from 1918 granting *de facto* recognition of all undergraduate degrees, this was an approach that proved universally attractive, and Foster's recommendations formed the basis of the system of recognition still in place in British universities today.

Before the establishment of the British PhD, however, postgraduate study in Britain was something that, as James Bryce averred in 1903, was 'still imperfectly developed'.[18] Students wishing to pursue further study at Oxford were required to enter a College and gain admittance to the university by passing in Latin and Greek.[19] Writing to J. T. Wilson from London in 1890, the young Sydney travelling scholar, Grafton Elliot Smith, described these conditions as 'practically prohibitive'. There were, Elliot Smith wrote, 'far more rational' rules at Cambridge where, 'provided a man is accepted by the faculty as a 'Research Student' he is admitted ipso facto as a College member after producing moral certificates &c'.[20] Cambridge made this policy official in 1895, and research or 'advanced students' were able to enter without having to sit a language examination.[21] At the University of London a similar provision was instituted in 1902, while at Edinburgh any persons 'of good general education' wishing to undertake research could gain entry, whether graduates of other universities or not.[22] Such students were required to keep two, not necessarily consecutive, winter sessions. In the late nineteenth and early twentieth centuries, these provisions brought small but growing numbers of colonial graduates to these universities.[23] In fact, by 1903 the professor of mathematics at Cambridge, J. A. Ewing, considered the introduction of 'advanced student' status the most important change his university had recently made: it had brought to Cambridge 'not only from the home university colleges and universities, but more especially from the colonies, a band of most admirable young men, young men full of enthusiasm for their work, of much more than average ability, and it ha[d] left these men free to devote themselves to ... the most highly educative exercise that they c[ould] possibly choose'.[24]

This partial system of academic recognition stood in stark contrast to the status that many of London's professional societies accorded to the degrees of a wide range of settler and Indian institutions.[25] As preparation for admission, the Royal College of Surgeons accepted degrees not only from the universities of England, Scotland and Ireland, but also from the universities of Adelaide, Bombay, Calcutta, Laval, McGill, Madras, Melbourne, New Zealand, the Punjab and Sydney, and from the Imperial University of Japan and the Italian Royal Universities. Meanwhile the accredited non-metropolitan headquarters of the Royal Institute of British Architects reads like a list of the major cities of 'Greater Britain'.[26] Election to membership of organisations such as the British Medical Association and the Royal Society was open to individuals resident outside the United Kingdom, and although at the latter a distinction was drawn between 'Foreign' and 'British' fellows, the second category included 'any inhabitant of any part of the imperial territories, and any native Britisher living even beyond its borders'.[27] As with the 1851 Exhibition scholarships and the 1887 Oxford statutes, these professional societies drew the boundaries of 'British' scholarship in such a way as to include the settler world (and sometimes also India), while excluding Europe and America. Although loose and uncoordinated, the formal recognition that universities accorded each other at the start of the twentieth-century mapped a world in which special institutional relationships existed between universities in Britain and those in the settler colonies. These statutory geographies aligned with and reflected the social and institutional practices that helped mark out the borders of the British academic world.

The 1903 Allied Colonial Universities Conference

Despite the emergence of these forms of recognition, at the turn of the century there was, as Parkin suggested, very little sign of collective organisation among either the universities in the United Kingdom or those across the empire.[28] When British universities acted together, they did so mainly from immediate financial necessity. In Scotland, the Commission of 1858 recommended that the university courts liaise in

regard to changing their ordinances, and in England in 1887 the struggling colleges that prepared students for the London examinations met
to apply for financial aid from the government.[29] But this was as far as
nineteenth-century university association in Britain went. In settler
contexts too, universities had little contact with each other. Neither
in Canada nor in Australasia had there been any serious effort to bring
those institutions located in various colonies and provinces together.
The Allied Colonial Universities Conference, held in London in early
July 1903, thus represented the first form of multilateral association
of universities either in Britain or in the empire. Like the 1887 Oxford
statute, it drew the boundaries of the British academic community
not around the British Isles, but around what it saw as the racial and
cultural community of Britain and its settler empire.

Given the absence of official university co-ordination, it is perhaps
not surprising that the event began as a much more informal gathering.
It was the brainchild of the Canadian novelist and Conservative MP
for Gravesend, Sir Gilbert Parker. In November 1902 he had attended
a dinner in London for graduates of Trinity University in Toronto
and, moved by the sense of fellow-feeling at the event, had decided
it would be a good idea to host a similar dinner for all graduates of
settler universities living in Britain.[30] Such an event would, Parker
hoped, 'contribute, though perhaps indirectly, to the educational advancement of the Empire'.[31] To help organise the proposed dinner, he
recruited his old friend Clement Kinloch-Cooke, editor of the recently
established journal, the *Empire Review*. In April 1903 they placed a
notice in *The Times* advertising their intention of hosting 'an Allied
Colonial Universities Dinner' in London in July that same year.[32] This
same notice suggested that the proposed dinner would be preceded by
a conference 'when subjects of interest and important to University
life in all parts of the King's dominions w[ould] be discussed' and asked
graduates wishing to attend to get in touch.[33]

But these tentative plans of April 1903 were still a long way from
resembling what a few months later became the first multilateral conference of British universities. Whereas Parker had initially proposed
a dinner for colonial graduates preceded by a conference, the events
that eventually transpired amounted to a representative gathering
of universities and series of social occasions that were attended by
public luminaries including the Canadian High Commissioner (Lord
Strathcona), the Colonial Secretary (Joseph Chamberlain), and the
British Prime Minister (A. J. Balfour).[34] In fact, the account of the conference dinner published in the *Official Proceedings* almost seems to
suggest that colonial graduates were included as an afterthought. In
the audience of four hundred, wrote Kinloch-Cooke, were:

university delegates, many heads of colleges, and men prominent in educational and scientific work. The more important of the learned societies sent their presidents, and the different departments of State their chief permanent officials. Every profession was represented, and among the company were bishops, judges, men in the front rank of literature and journalism, as well as several members of both Houses of Parliament, and many graduates and undergraduates of Colonial universities.[35]

Between April and July, Parker's dinner for colonial graduates had grown into an Edwardian imperial convention, complete with the round of parties and 'inevitable dinner[s]' such an event usually entailed.[36]

The political events of 15 May 1903 go a long way to explaining this mutation. On that date in Birmingham Town Hall, the Colonial Secretary, Joseph Chamberlain, proposed 'a treaty of preference and reciprocity' with the colonies that stunned the nation.[37] The Liberal opposition were outraged at this attack on the doctrine of free trade, and the government divided into pro- and anti-Chamberlain factions. As the Liberal Imperialist R. B. Haldane pointed out to his constituents a few weeks later, the issue 'had submerged almost every other' and it was 'increasingly difficult to get the attention of the public to any other topic'.[38] Parker too launched into the fray. On 29 June he made the trip to Gravesend to outline his views to the Conservative members of his constituency and he willingly lent his significant speaking talent to Chamberlain's cause.[39] 'I am in the midst of the battle here,' he wrote during June to his old friend W. N. Ponton in Belleville, Ontario, and '[t]here are far more temptations to speak than I can yield to.'[40]

Parker's enthusiasm for tariff reform was not surprising given that the empire was a cause with which he had long profitably associated himself. Born in 1860 in what his biographer described as 'the backwoods of Canada', he began his career as a school teacher in Ottawa. But after ordination as an Anglican deacon, in 1881 he began a divinity course at Trinity College, Toronto, where he also served as professor of elocution. Giving up thoughts of entering the ministry, in 1886 Parker travelled to Australia, where he eventually became associate editor for the *Sydney Morning Herald.* In 1889 he finally settled in Britain where he became a writer. The success of his 1896 novel, *Seats of the Mighty* thrust Parker into London's social limelight and his popularity was still high when he was recruited by the Conservative and Unionist Party to contest the seat of Gravesend in the 'khaki election' of 1900. During the campaign he made a point of emphasising his imperial credentials and, in the charged context of the South African War, he was successful.[41] By the time the Coronation Honours were being announced and distributed generously throughout the British Empire, the novelist MP was one of the 'half-dozen best-known living Canadians': he became Sir Gilbert Parker.[42]

In the process of this ascent, however, Parker also acquired a reputation for ambition. He openly admitted his preparedness to cultivate friends who might be of use to him and was widely believed to be aspiring to the position of Canadian High Commissioner.[43] Indeed, in a 1905 letter to his friend the Canadian Prime Minister Wilfred Laurier, Parker was transparent about his desires. He asked Laurier if he might be considered as Acting High Commissioner, arguing that even a temporary appointment would 'help to strengthen [his] hold on public life' in London.[44] Such ambition was not always viewed favourably. Beatrice Webb's recollection of her husband's advice regarding the nature of their own social engagements is telling:

> I don't think it is desirable that we should be seen in the houses of great people. Know them privately if you like, but don't go to their miscellaneous gatherings. If you do, it will be said of us as it is of Sir Gilbert Parker – in the dead silence of the night you hear a distant but monotonous sound – Sir Gilbert Parker, climbing, climbing, climbing.[45]

In the atmosphere created by Chamberlain's tariff reform speech, Parker's proposed dinner for colonial graduates offered him the chance to capitalise on the two most controversial issues of his day. For before Chamberlain's speech had engulfed the political sphere, British politicians had been intensely divided over the Education Bill, passed into law in 1902.[46] As the Prime Minister A. J. Balfour later pointed out, Parker's conference brought together 'two subjects, each which, separately, ha[d] been exercising the minds, at all events, of people on this side of the Atlantic – the ideas of education and the ideas of Empire'.[47] A representative conference of university delegates from all parts of the British Empire would, in the environment of tariff reform, embody exactly the kind of imperial union that both Chamberlain and Parker wished to promote. Parker seized this opportunity and, in only the week before the dinner was scheduled to take place, telegraphed the Australian universities with a last-minute invitation to send a representative to what he now billed as a gathering of delegates from the universities of the empire.[48]

Parker's 'imperial' vision, however, was one that was very much dominated by exclusionary racial discourses. Not only were the Indian universities not invited to his conference, but at the event itself speakers repeatedly affirmed what they saw as the racial and cultural bonds linking the settler colonies and Britain.[49] A. J. Balfour boasted of a 'community of blood, of language, of laws, of literature', but James Bryce was even clearer:

We have two aims, and those two aims are closely bound together. One aim is to develop the intellectual and moral forces of all the branches of our race wherever they dwell, and therewith also to promote learning, science and the arts by and through which science is applied to the purposes of life. The other aim is to strengthen the unity of the British people dispersed throughout the world.[50]

With statements like these, the representatives at the conference gave voice to their expansive conception of what R. B. Haldane called 'the great British nation in its different parts'. Pointing to the migration of scholars between Britain and the settler colonies, they highlighted the already existing connections between British universities at home and abroad. As F. H. Chase, the vice-chancellor of the University of Cambridge, argued, '[t]hese universities are already closely connected. We have not to create an affinity between them'. Referring to the need for the 'specialisation of studies', for student interchange, for the mutual recognition of degrees and even for a British research degree, Chase and others saw it as 'the business of [the] Conference to recognize [the] affinity [of the British and colonial universities] and to make it effective for practical purposes'.[51] They saw themselves as formalising and facilitating the extant informal relationships between individual academics, and the loose bilateral relationships between institutions.

This urge to give official form to existing connections resulted in the conference's resolution to establish a 'representative Council' in order to promote relations 'between the principal teaching universities of the empire'.[52] Borrowing the contemporary language of efficiency, speakers argued that the interests of the 'whole nation' would be served by better incorporating the resources of its various parts. 'The key-note of all the speeches', wrote the University of London's R. D. Roberts a few years later, 'was the need for co-operation and even for federation'.[53] Yet in the heat of the 1906 tariff reform election this plan for a representative council fell into abeyance. Although a year and a half after the event Parker was still hoping that 'another Conference may be held', little came of his plans.[54]

The notion of educational federation was, however, revived by the League of Empire at the Imperial Conference on Education in 1907. Since 1904 the League had been acting as the London agent for a number of colonial boards of education, and its 'History Section' had been working on a 'graded series of text-books on the Empire'.[55] According to *The Times* correspondent in 1907, the success of these books had led the League to wonder if 'a still greater result [for the cause of Imperial Federation might] be attained by the holding of a Federal Conference, expressly for the purpose of establishing a system of [educational] co-operation throughout the Empire'.[56] With this aim in view the League drafted an agenda, the first item on which was a proposal for the federation of the British Empire through education, and the second a plan for a permanent central bureau. But when it sent copies to the various colonial boards of education, few were enthusiastic. Many dismissed the idea of federation entirely, while others were unimpressed by the plans for a central bureau.[57] At the conference itself, every attempt to discuss schemes designed to centralise the curriculum were met with the delegates' 'grave misgivings' or outright rejection.[58] Although they freely acknowledged their shared connections and desire for more practical forms of co-operation, in 1907 it was clear that neither the universities nor the British and Dominion boards of education were, as James Greenlee has written, 'willing to submerge their autonomy in a centralized imperial system'.[59]

The 1912 Congress of the Universities of the British Empire

The University of London's extension registrar, R. D. Roberts, was careful not to make these mistakes when in 1910 he was appointed as organising secretary of the inaugural Congress of the Universities of the British Empire. In late 1909 the English civic universities and colleges had approached the University of London in the hope that it would host a 'Modern Universities Congress' with the aim of 'convey[ing] to the public mind, particularly at the seat of Government ... their claims to public support'.[60] The academic council of the University of London was sympathetic, but saw these aims as part of an imperial rather than a national discussion. It suggested they instead be raised within the context of an empire-wide universities' congress. The London senate duly adopted this suggestion, and elected a 'preliminary' committee that appointed Roberts as its organising secretary.[61]

In his approach to his task, Roberts placed imperial university co-operation on a new footing. Not only did he invite the Indian universities to what would become the 1912 Congress of the Universities of the British Empire, but from the beginning he included both them and the settler institutions in the planning process. He asked each university for 'a brief memorandum setting out [their] mature judgment on the more important subjects to come before the Congress'. The board of education in London followed this up with a detailed survey 'regarding the facilities for study offered by each University' to be collated and published in time for the meeting.[62] Unlike the 1903 and 1907 events, consultation characterised the 1912 Congress from its inception.

At Roberts' suggestion regional planning conferences were held. These meetings brought together the universities of the various colonies of the empire, often for the first time.[63] The British 'Home Universities Committee' was formed in November 1910. On it sat 'representatives of the British Universities', and over the course of the following eighteen months they met with the 'purpose of drawing up a preliminary list of topics for discussion at the Congress'.[64] Writing to the registrar of the University of Melbourne, Roberts (who was also secretary of the 'Home Committee') suggested that the universities in Australia might also have particular concerns that united them.[65] The Canadian universities, he went on to explain, were organising a 'preliminary conference to be held at Montreal in June [1911] for the purpose of considering the subjects for discussion at the Congress and ascertaining how far Canadian University opinion [wa]s agreed as to the more important subjects to be considered.' 'It would certainly seem', wrote Roberts, 'that some such plan in Australia might prove of great value'.[66] Acting on this suggestion, the Australian and New Zealand universities also arranged a 'preliminary Conference' that took place in Sydney in September 1911.[67] So useful were these meetings that, both in Britain and in the various settler colonies, regular national conferences grew out of them. As the report of the Canadian meeting predicted, 'one general result of the Congress – whatever effect its deliberations may have – will be that local conferences of representatives of Universities in different parts of the Empire will become a permanent institution'.[68] Although they would later form the foundation for national groupings, in 1911 these regional conferences effectively served as sub-committees that met as constituent parts of a wider imperial enterprise, helping feed information about colonial universities' wishes and concerns back to Roberts in London.[69]

This broad consultation process resulted in a congress agenda that was much more extensive and practical than those tabled in 1903 and 1907. The congress itself ran for three full days, with its proceedings, published later by the University of London, running to over 460 pages.[70] Issues that had been raised in 1903, such as the specialisation of studies, reciprocal recognition of degrees, and teacher and student interchange, this time made it officially onto the programme. Residential facilities, entrance requirements, remuneration, university extension, and the position of technical and professional education were also subjects discussed by delegates. These official sessions were accompanied by an extravagant social programme: in London the delegates – Darnley Naylor among them – went to the theatre, lunched with the Prime Minister and Prince Arthur of Connaught at the Savoy Hotel, and attended the formal reception at the University of London along with 2,500 other guests.[71] Tours to various universities across the United Kingdom ran both before and after the meeting: at Aberdeen delegates were entertained at luncheon in the Palace Hotel by the principal, G. Adam Smith; at Edinburgh they attended a concert arranged by the Union Musical Society; at Durham they toured the Castle; and at Oxford and Cambridge they were guests at the various colleges. These visits were accompanied by dinners, toasts and honorary degree ceremonies, and were frequently attended by delegates' wives and daughters, for whom separate programmes were also devised.

Designed to foster feelings of friendship and affinity between delegates, congress sociability thus reinforced and reflected the substance of congress discussion. For the organisers, as for the delegates, personal and private ties of friendship were inseparable from official organisational forms of connection. This association reflected the congress's commitment to the same expansive and racially exclusive conception of the British nation evident in 1903. In 1912, Lord Strathcona spoke of the great 'Anglo-Saxon Community', George Parkin alluded to 'our British people', and James Barrett talked about welcoming to Australia's shores 'people of our own race'.[72] Emphasising the existing personal and professional ties between universities located across the British settler world, the delegates in 1912 expressed their wish that these connections should be given what Oxford's P. E. Matheson called 'practical recognition'.[73]

The organisational form this 'practical recognition' took, however, was shaped by the delegates' deep commitment to university autonomy. As Matheson continued,

> if unity is a vital principle of our commonwealth of learning, that does not mean uniformity. Variety is one of the 'notes' of our political arrangements, and it is no less vital in our educational structure.[74]

Conscious, perhaps, of the failure of previous attempts at educational federation, when George Parkin proposed the foundation of a 'bureau' that would act as 'a connecting link between all our world-wide experiences', instead of speaking of federation, he assured delegates that '[i]ndividuality and independence rather than uniformity constitute the characteristic note of British Universities, and [that] anything that tends to unnecessary uniformity would be open to strong objection'.[75] The organisation he outlined would not hold a centralising agenda but would focus on building informal connections. Parkin suggested it might produce a 'University Year Book' that provided in one volume information about the specialisms, entrance requirements and staff of all the universities of the British Empire and serve as 'the missing link' between them.[76] It might collate information about approaching appointments and distribute it throughout the university world. It might arrange the temporary exchange of professors and distribute information about courses that would enable the 'interchange' of students, and it might organise another congress. More hesitantly, Parkin proposed some practical measures he thought might be also helpful – a common matriculation standard and a degree of specialisation between institutions – but his emphasis remained on they ways in which 'intimate co-operation' might be 'obtained by frequent and friendly consultation'.[77] This turned out to be a successful strategy. On its final day the congress unanimously endorsed Parkin's proposal and appointed a committee charged with the task of establishing a 'Central Bureau' that would act as a 'clearing house': 'an organ for the purpose of continuing [the] communication of knowledge and comparison of varied experience' begun at the congress.[78]

The Bureau's committee met for the first time on 28 January 1913 in the Bloomsbury buildings of the University of London. Comprising seven members nominated by the overseas universities (two from Canada, one each from Australia, New Zealand, the Cape and India, and one from the 'rest of the Empire') and seven representatives of the universities in the United Kingdom, it was the first ever organisation of British universities.[79] Renting a room in the Imperial Institute in South Kensington, the new 'Universities' Bureau of the British Empire' appointed a part-time assistant secretary, advertised itself as an appointments agency and began planning a second congress. In 1914 it also published the first edition of the *Universities' Yearbook*, which provided in one volume information about the courses, entrance requirements and staff of all the universities of the British Empire. For its first six years the Bureau was funded entirely by the voluntary subscriptions of its members, with suggested contributions of £50 a year from the bigger institutions, £25 from the smaller. Some universities were more enthusiastic than others: for four years Adelaide paid £20 per annum, the University of New Zealand £25, and Melbourne made an annual contribution of £60, while, as Ashby noted in his memoir, Cambridge initially declined to subscribe and Sheffield never made a payment.[80] Yet despite this varied commitment, the Bureau's early life was promising. Working within the bounds established at the 1912 Congress, it squared the circle of imperial co-operation and university independence by focusing on ways of fostering the already existing ties between academics working in British and settler universities.

According to George Parkin, the establishment of a central universities' bureau in 1912 was part of a much wider process in which the 'British people [were] being compelled to think in terms of the Empire':

frequent consultation between representatives of different parts of the Empire has become a necessity – vigorous attempts at co-ordination are being made – reorganization to meet new national conditions is admitted to be an imperative need. Our Universities cannot expect to escape this great movement of evolutionary development. Enormous national interests of an extremely varied kind are entrusted to them.[81]

But universities, and those concerned with them, had been thinking in terms of empire since at least the 1880s. Before the 1912 Congress, both the 1887 Oxford statute and the 1903 Allied Colonial Universities Conference had drawn the boundaries of the British academic community expansively, so as to include the universities of the settler colonies. These late Victorian and Edwardian forms of academic association gave official recognition to the web of informal ties being built by the empire's wandering scholars. They placed colonial universities alongside the institutions developing in provincial England, creating particular forms of acknowledgement and providing preferential routes of access that, alongside travelling scholarships and leave-of-absence programmes, in turn shaped the directions in which settler scholars travelled.

Yet, as decentralised forms of organisation, these early types of institutional association balanced imperial recognition against universities' desire to maintain their independence. In many ways the worlds mapped by their regulatory and fraternal reach were like the circumscribed landscapes of Victorian globalisation that Gary Magee and Andrew S. Thompson have argued were shaped by '[p]ersonal connections and social networks'.[82] Not only did cultural ties mould economic relations in the age of Victorian free trade, they also conditioned the associational geographies of British and settler universities in the era of high imperialism. The Oxford statutes and the proceedings of the Edwardian conferences show that – long before Parkin suggested his Bureau – the de-territorialised practices of settler universities, together with the long-distance personal connections enabled by them, had fashioned the official as well as unofficial boundaries of an expansive 'British' academic community.

Notes

1 *Congress Proceedings, 1912*, p. 310–11.
2 *Oxford University Calendar, 1901* (Oxford: Oxford University, 1900), p. 80; 'Incorporation at Oxford' (Oxford University Archives), accessed 10 Oct. 2011, www.oua.ox.ac.uk/enquiries/incorporation.html.
3 *Oxford University Calendar, 1901*, p. 83.
4 *University of Oxford First Supplement to the Historical Register: 1900–1920* (Oxford: Oxford University, 1921), p. 328. See note 5, below.

5 An 1880 statute did make provision for colleges within the UK or the British Dominions to apply to be 'affiliated colleges', but only on the condition that the University was represented on that college's governing body, and by 1900 only four colleges (St David's Lampeter; Nottingham; Firth College Sheffield; and Reading) had made application. *Historical Register of the University of Oxford, 1900*, (Oxford: Clarendon Press, 1900), p. 576.

6 Oliver Lodge in 'Official Report of the Allied Colonial Universities Conference', p. 191.

7 *Statuta Universitatis Oxoniensis* (Oxford: Oxford University, 1914), pp. 28–9.

8 *Ibid.*

9 *The Student's Handbook to the University and Colleges of Oxford* (Oxford: Oxford University, 1909), p. 238.

10 For example, in a paper delivered at the 1921 Congress, J. C. Maxwell Garnett invoked this distinction when, speaking of the new PhD, he said, 'It is to be hoped that these courses will receive graduates from other Universities at home, as well as from British and foreign Universities overseas.' J. C. M. Garnett, 'The Universities and Technological Education: Universities or Separate Colleges' in *Second Congress Proceedings, 1921*.

11 *The Yearbook of the Universities of the Empire, 1915* (London: Herbert Jenkins Ltd., 1915), p. 155. For Cambridge see *The Student's Handbook to the University and Colleges of Cambridge* (Cambridge: Cambridge University Press, 1902), pp. 232, 237–43. Edinburgh further reduced this requirement for students who had studied in other Scottish universities to one year, and accorded some teachers in settler universities status as 'extramural teachers', meaning that students who had taken their courses could count them towards an Edinburgh degree. See UCTA, *SAC Reports*, Report of the South African College Council, 1904

12 *Yearbook of the Universities of the Empire, 1915*, p. 15.

13 *Ibid.*, pp. 16–17.

14 'Incorporation at Oxford'.

15 See, for example, discussion at the 1919 Imperial Education Conference regarding the 'Interchangeability of Credit for Work done by Students Transferring from one University to another within Empire'. *Imperial Education Conference: Convened by the Chief of the Imperial General Staff, June 11–12, 1919* (London: His Majesty's Stationary Office, 1919), pp. 13–24.

16 *Ibid.*, p. 17.

17 *Ibid.*, p. 24.

18 'Official Report of the Allied Colonial Universities Conference', p. 73.

19 Oxford dropped Greek under pressure from the Asquith Commission (1919–1922). Prest, 'The Asquith Commission', p, 37.

20 USA, *J. T. Wilson Papers*, P162/3/4/Grafton Elliot Smith to Wilson, 7 Sept. 1890.

21 'Official Report of the Allied Colonial Universities Conference', pp. 87–8.

22 USA, *Minutes of the Senate*, G1/1/11/2 Feb. 1903.

23 In July 1914 there were approximately 92 students (68 men and 24 women) registered as preparing for higher degrees under Section 113 of the Statutes. Just under three-quarters were from the UK, just under a fifth from Colonial or Indian universities, with the remainder from 'foreign' institutions. *Yearbook, 1915*, p. 266.

24 *Ibid.*, p. 157.

25 Those listed in the 1915 *Yearbook* as being prepared to do so were: the Royal Institute of Architects, the Institute of Chemistry of Great Britain and Ireland, the Institution of Civil Engineers, the Institution of Electrical Engineers, the Institution of Mechanical Engineers, the Royal College of Surgeons, the Royal College of Physicians of London and the Royal College of Surgeons of England, the Royal College of Surgeons of Edinburgh, the Royal Faculty of Physicians and Surgeons of Glasgow, and the Royal College of Physicians of Ireland.

26 *Yearbook of the Universities of the Empire, 1915*, pp. 589, 576. These were located in Aberdeen, Adelaide, Birmingham, Brisbane, Bristol, Cape Town, Cardiff, Dublin, Dundee, Durban, Edinburgh, Exeter, Glasgow, Johannesburg, Leeds, Leicester,

Liverpool, Manchester, Melbourne, Montreal, Newcastle, Northampton, Notting-ham, Perth, Sheffield, Southampton, Sydney, Wellington, York.

27 R. W. Home, 'A World-Wide Scientific Network and Patronage System: Australian and Other Colonial Fellows of the Royal Society of London', in R. W. Home and S. G. Kohlstedt (eds), *International Science and National Scientific Identity* (Dordrecht: Kluwer Academic Publishers, 1991), p. 153.

28 Ashby, *Community of Universities*, p. 1.

29 The role of university finance – from increasing government involvement in Britain to scholarships such as the Rhodes – in bringing about association is a subject not explored in this book, though it could be an avenue for further investigation.

30 UAA, *Registrar's Correspondence*, S200/1903/156/letter from E. N. Fere and L. C. R. Arnott [Honorary Secretaries] 15 Jan. 1903.

31 *Ibid.*

32 Kinloch-Cooke remained editor of the *Review* until his death in 1944. He was the Conservative and Unionist Member of Parliament for Davenport from 1910 until 1923 and East Cardiff from 1924 to 1929. 'Allied Colonial Universities Dinner', *The Times*, 30 Apr. 1903, p. 4.

33 *Ibid.*

34 'Official Report of the Allied Colonial Universities Conference', p. 120.

35 *Ibid.*, p. 121.

36 'The Allied Colonial Universities Conference', *The Times*, 13 July 1903, p. 9.

37 Joseph Chamberlain, *Imperial Union and Tariff Reform: Speeches Delivered from May 15 to Nov. 4, 1903: With an Introduction* (London: G. Richards, 1903).

38 Haldane opposed Tariff reform. 'Mr Haldane on Preferential Tariffs', *The Times*, 3 June 1903, p. 4.

39 'Preferential Tariffs', *The Times*, 30 June 1903, p. 12. On one of these occasions, Parker attacked his former Conservative colleague Winston Churchill on the subject in his own constituency of Oldham. J. C. Adams, *Seated with the Mighty: A Biography of Sir Gilbert Parker* (Ottawa: John Coldwell Adams, 1979), p. 122.

40 Quoted in Adams, *Seated with the Mighty*.

41 Parker cited his imperial credentials in a letter published before the election in the *Gravesend Reporter*; he had, he wrote 'by wide experience, acquaintance with the resources and trade of that Empire which represents nearly one-fourth of the Earth's surface.' *Gravesend Reporter*, 22 Sept. 1900, quoted in *Ibid.*, p. 98.

42 *Ibid.*, p. 116.

43 According to his biographer, Gilbert Parker once admitted that 'when he was making a start and had very little he would go almost hungry for nearly a week in order to dine with someone he felt would be of use to him'. Letter to J. C. Adams from Gladys Parker Myers, quoted in *Ibid.*, p. 92.

44 Parker to Laurier, 5 Nov. 1905, quoted in *Ibid.*, p. 131.

45 Beatrice Webb, *Our Partnership* (London: Longmans Green, 1948), p. 294. Quoted in Adams, *Seated with the Mighty*, p. 126.

46 The Act abolished the school boards and handed over their duties to local educa-tion authorities (LEA) appointed by local county councils. The LEA would oversee secular education in all schools, including denominational schools that would be supported by aid from ratepayers. These measures were vehemently opposed by Nonconformists, backed by the Liberal party, who were forced to contribute through their rates to the teaching of religious doctrines in which they did not believe.

47 'Official Report of the Allied Colonial Universities Conference', p. 122.

48 USA, *Minutes of the Senate*, G1/1/11/6 July 1903. In a letter dated 17 August, and noted in the Senate Minutes, the agent-general reported that Gurney and Threlfall attended, but Scott was unable to due to illness.

49 'Official Report of the Allied Colonial Universities Conference', pp. 73, 76–77, 109, 118, 120.

50 *Ibid.*, Balfour, p. 122; Bryce, p. 177.

51 *Ibid.*, R. B. Haldane, p. 118; F.H. Chase, p. 178.

52 *Congress Proceedings, 1912*, pp. 310–11; 'Official Report of the Allied Colonial Universities Conference', p. 69.

53 'Official Report of the Allied Colonial Universities Conference', p. 115.
54 UAA, *Registrar's Correspondence*, S200/1905/22/7 Dec. 1904.
55 *Ibid.*, S200/1905/22/7 Dec. 1904. For more on the History Section, see J. Greenlee, *Education and Imperial Unity* (New York: Garland, 1987), p. 22.
56 'The Federal Conference on Education', *The Times*, 29 Mar. 1907, p, 6.
57 Greenlee, 'The ABCs of Imperial Unity', *Canadian Journal of History*, 14 (1979): 49–64, p. 58.
58 Quoted in *Ibid.*, p. 59.
59 *Ibid.*, p. 60.
60 University of London Archives (ULA), *University of London Minutes of Senate and Appendices, 1909–10*, ST 2/1/11/Minute 477 and 482.
61 *Ibid.*, ST 2/1/11/15 Dec. 1909, Minute 816; 23 Feb. 1910, Minute 1883; 15 June 1910, Minute 3206. R. D. Roberts was for a time also a member of another organisation associated with education and empire, the Colonial Office Visual Instruction Committee.
62 *Ibid.*, ST 2/1/11/3 Aug. 1911; 10 Nov. 1911.
63 The Australian universities appear to have had a one-off 'informal conference' in 1906 and to have considered then the establishment of a 'Joint Board'. UMA, *Registrar's Correspondence*, UM312/1906/12/Conference of Australian Universities.
64 *Ibid.*, 1912/25/'Congress of the Universities of Empire'/Henry Miers (Principal of the University of London) to the Vice-Chancellor of the University of Melbourne, 2 Aug. 1910.
65 *Ibid.*, Roberts to Melbourne Registrar, 1 May 1911.
66 *Ibid.*, 2 May 1911; 1 May 1911.
67 *Ibid.*, Tasmania Registrar to Melbourne Registrar, 21 July 1911. The Indian universities came together to for the Inter-University Board following a resolution passed at the 1921 Congress. See *Handbook of Indian Universities* (Bangalore: Inter-University Board, India, 1928).
68 UMA, *Registrar's Correspondence*, UM312/1912/25/'Report of the Montreal Conference between Canadian Universities', enclosed in letter from Roberts to Melbourne Registrar, 21 July 1911.
69 UMA, *Registrar's Correspondence*, UM312/1912/25/'Notes on the forthcoming Congress of the Universities of the Empire', 1 May 1911.
70 See *Congress Proceedings, 1912*.
71 *Ibid.*, pp. xiv–xxvi.
72 *Ibid.*, pp. 217, xxii, 307, 310; Ashby, *Community of Universities*, p. 6.
73 *Congress Proceedings, 1912*, p. 198.
74 *Ibid.*
75 *Ibid.*, pp. 312, 323.
76 *Ibid.*, p. 312.
77 *Ibid.*, p. 315.
78 UMA, *Registrar's Correspondence*, UM312/1913/61a/Alex Hill reporting on the first meeting of the Organising Committee of the Bureau, 18 Feb. 1913.
79 *Ibid.*, UM312/1913/61a/Alex Hill reporting on the first meeting of the Organising Committee of the Bureau, 18 Feb. 1913.
80 UAA, *Registrar's Correspondence*, Series 200/1914/208; Archives New Zealand (ANZ), *University of New Zealand Archives*, AAMJ Acc W3119/volume 7/Minutes of Proceedings of the Senate of the University of New Zealand at the Annual Session, Jan. 1917; UMA, *Registrar's Correspondence*, UMA312/1920/444/Alex Hill to Vice-Chancellor Melbourne, 28 Oct. 1920.
81 *Congress Proceedings, 1912*, p. 309.
82 G. B. Magee and A. S. Thompson, *Empire and Globalisation: Networks of People, Goods and Capital in the British World, c1850–1914* (Cambridge: Cambridge University Press, 2010), pp. 14–15.

PART III

Networks: 1900–39

CHAPTER 5

Academic traffic:
people, objects, information, ideas

On New Year's Day 1937, Grafton Elliot Smith, the retired professor of anatomy at University College London and graduate of the University of Sydney, died at Broadstairs in Kent. Writing to his widow later that year, Robert Broom – a palaeontologist who had spent much of his own career in South Africa – offered his condolences and expressed his gratitude to Elliot Smith for having acted as 'a sort of Ambassador for [him] in London'.[1] Such 'ambassadorial' relationships were common among the scholars and scientists who travelled between the universities of the British settler world in the early twentieth century. Like the agents-general who were employed by organisations and governments to represent colonial interests in Britain, scholars such as Elliot Smith acted on behalf of their absent friends and colleagues, communicating information, co-ordinating publications and brokering opportunities and exchanges.[2] In so far as they helped to mitigate the difficulties of physical distance, such academic relationships were similar to those of the earlier colonial period, in which workers on the periphery served as 'data-gatherers' transmitting valuable specimens back to London in exchange for patronage, goodwill and money, which flowed the other way.[3] In other respects, however, these early twentieth-century 'agents' were significantly different from their nineteenth-century predecessors: they acted both as conduits and as placeholders, facilitating the flows of information, ideas, patronage and publications, which travelled in multiple directions, following scholars as they moved. Such traffic points to social and scholarly communities that were neither exclusively colonial nor exclusively metropolitan, but instead located within the tightly woven and continually shifting networks of the British academic world.

Introductions and admissions

The support of settler professors was crucial for colonial students travelling to Britain. Not only did it help secure them the scholarships that funded their study abroad, but it also gave them access to the disciplinary networks that were so important to a successful academic career. 'If I do not attain something', wrote the young Elliot Smith from London to his Sydney professors in 1896, 'it will not be the fault of my Sydney friends, whose disinterested devotion to my interests has impressed upon me a debt of gratitude which it will be difficult to repay.'[4] Carrying a bundle of introductions, thanks to the connections of his professors in Australia, Elliot Smith was able to form relationships with the most senior figures in British anatomy.

Professors writing from settler institutions were also instrumental in helping their students secure entry to British universities. 'Massey has told me', wrote the physicist, Courtney Mohr, to his Melbourne professor, T. H. Laby, 'of the trouble you went to on my behalf in Cambridge which makes me even more indebted and grateful to you than I thought.'[5] 'It is only out of consideration to you and your Department', wrote Rutherford to Laby in 1934, 'that I am willing to find room for Petrie.'[6] At the start of the century the professor of history at Toronto, G. M. Wrong, had used his connections with former Toronto lecturer, Keith Feiling, and with the New College warden, H. A. L. Fisher, to get his students admitted to Oxford colleges; meanwhile from Auckland the lecturer in Old and Middle English, Philip Sydney Ardern, sent first Kenneth Sisam and then a succession of New Zealanders to Oxford, with each generation extending to the next what Douglas Gray called 'helping hands along the way'.[7] This flow of colonial students into British universities was sufficiently significant for the Irish physicist and professor at University College London, Frederick Trouton, to suggest (in 1914) that there were so many men working in England 'hailing from Australia and New Zealand' that it was 'best nowadays to ask of any young investigator if he comes from the Antipodes.'[8] Like the professors, whose appointments to academic posts were conditioned by the personal ties they possessed, these settler students did not simply 'proceed' to further study in Britain. Rather, their admission depended on the support and connections of their colonial teachers.

At the completion of their studies in Britain some of these settler students returned to take up academic positions in the colonies, but others stayed on, joining the growing number of academics in the United Kingdom who had colonial experience. Such men frequently carried a particular sense of obligation to help settler scholars like themselves: 'it is up to me to do what I can for our Dominion

Students', wrote Rutherford in 1922. Kenneth Sisam and C. J. Martin were among those who shared these sentiments.[9] In Oxford, Sisam appointed so many New Zealanders to Oxford University Press that they later became known as 'the New Zealand mafia', and as director at the Lister Institution in London, Martin made a point of admitting young Australians, particularly those from Melbourne.[10] The presence of these scholars with settler experience in Britain further consolidated and expanded the networks of support that had in the first place enabled the appointment of their former teachers.

Objects, publications, information

During their comings and goings students and their professors corresponded regularly with each other. They shared specimens, artifacts and references; papers, analysis and gossip; and they did so even as they moved. The way in which members of the group of anatomists and embryologists who came together at the University of Sydney in the 1890s trafficked animal specimens is particularly revealing. With intimate personal knowledge of the local area and the ability to adjust their collecting to the annual breeding cycles of the local Australian fauna, this group (which included J. T. Wilson, Elliot Smith, J. P. Hill and C. J. Martin) was able to acquire much better and more useful material than the voracious and aggressive expeditions of visiting British and German naturalists.[11] Although there is no evidence that they relied on assistance from the region's aboriginal population, they did utilise other locally based amateur collectors, of whom Robert Broom was initially one. As a doctor in rural New South Wales, Broom sent various native bat specimens to the group at the University of Sydney.[12] But when Broom travelled to Edinburgh in 1896 he took his large collection of Australian specimens with him and continued to send material, including possum and glider specimens, to Elliot Smith, who was by the end of the year in Cambridge.[13] This line of connection continued following Broom's move to South Africa, with specimens of Cape Golden moles, elephant shrews, lizards and *Insectivora* (a now abandoned classification of insect-eating small mammals) all making their way to Elliot Smith, first in England, and then in Cairo.[14] Broom also sent specimens from South Africa to J. T. Wilson and J. P Hill in Sydney, and Wilson and Hill sent platypus specimens and bat brains to Elliot Smith in Cairo.[15] Smith reciprocated: in 1908 he offered some of his Egyptian material 'quite unofficially' to Wilson, sending on separate occasions three skeletons from Quibell (at Sakkara) for the University Museum, and 'Nubian material' complete with 'full details as to the provenance & date of everything sent you & all references to literature relating to it.'[16] In South Africa, meanwhile, Robert Broom, now at the University of Stellenbosch, also benefited from his connection with Elliot Smith, who was 'only too glad' to offer to send Broom Egyptian human bones in 'exchange for S. African bones of known races'.[17] Although these exchanges masked the complex local relationships involved in collection and entailed the removal of specimens from their place of origin, they did not represent a simple extraction of colonial material to a Latourian 'centre of calculation' in Europe or even Sydney. Rather, such materials moved within and around a circulating social network – following individuals as they undertook what David Lambert and Alan Lester have called 'imperial careering'.[18]

For settler physicists, personal connections were equally important in securing access to the rare commodity of radium. Isolated from pitchblende ore (a uranium-rich material) by Marie and Pierre Curie in 1902, in the first decade of the twentieth-century the mysterious properties of radium fascinated both scientists and the public. But the limited supply of uranium, and the laborious chemical process by which radium was extracted from it, made the substance a rare and expensive item.[19] Rutherford's eminence within the field of atomic and radioactive research gave him considerable influence within this constricted market and it was through personal connection with him that many physicists in settler universities acquired the substance. From Manchester in 1909 he sent 5.2 milligrammes of radium bromide to T. H. Laby, then working in New Zealand, also helping W. H. Bragg acquire 10 mmg for his former student, J. P. V. Madsen in Sydney.[20] A few years later Rutherford procured 0.95 mmg for his former student Ernest Marsden, the professor of physics at Victoria University College in New Zealand, and an unknown quantity for R.W. Boyle, his former McGill assistant, who had moved to the University of Alberta.[21] This flow of 'raw material' from Europe to the colonial 'periphery' inverts the pattern of extraction proposed by Donald Fleming.[22] These anatomists and physicists used their personal connections to acquire access to the materials that in turn enabled them to undertake research in settler locations.

Personal networks were also crucial to bringing settler research to publication in Britain. Until the advent of airmail in the late 1930s, it took at least a month for a letter written in Australia to reach the United Kingdom, and ten days for one to travel between London and Toronto. This meant the process of submission, correction and consultation inherent in the publication of academic articles could be very slow. By presenting the results of their research locally – often to the regional branch of the Royal Society – and then sending an amended copy on to a colleague acting as 'agent' in the United Kingdom who would review it, submit it to a British journal and correct the proofs, colonial research-ers could speed this process significantly. As John Jenkin has shown, this was the means by which W. H. Bragg in Adelaide published his work – usually in the *Philosophical Magazine*.[23] Based in Manchester and then in Cambridge, Rutherford helped Laby in Melbourne, J. P. V Madsen in Sydney, Ernest Marsden in New Zealand and R. W. Boyle in Montreal to bring their colonial research to publication in Britain. Similarly, Elliot Smith and J. P. Hill (in London from 1906 as Jodrell Professor of Zoology and Anatomy) acted as agents for, among others, J. T. Wilson in Sydney, and Broom and Dart in South Africa, seeing their papers through the process of publication in *Nature*, the *Quarterly Journal*, and the *Journal of Anatomy*.[24] Indeed, when it came to pub-lishing in the *Philosophical Transactions* or the *Proceedings* of the Royal Society in London, those working in British universities found themselves in exactly the same positions as their colleagues in the settler colonies. Only Fellows or foreign members of the Society could communicate papers, which meant that all scholars, regardless of their place of residence, needed to know a FRS who was prepared to act in their stead – something that Rutherford, Bragg, Threlfall and others did frequently.[25] As we have seen, these were journals that by the end of the nineteenth century were being acquired by university libraries across the empire and beyond. By facilitating publication in these outlets, the personal networks of settler scholars meant that colonial and provincial research acquired an international audience.

Around these networks flowed various kinds of gossip, speculation and 'soft information'.[26] 'I hear rumours that Sir Carruthers [Beattie] has been ill,' wrote Eric Walker, the Vere Harmsworth Professor of Imperial History in Cambridge, of the vice-chancellor of the University of Cape Town; 'I hear very good reports of [Alan Burns'] work by way of Humphrey Sumner who hears [it] from Cole,' recounted Melbourne's R. W. Crawford of his former student studying in Oxford.[27] Students and scholars in Britain kept their settler colleagues abreast of their own and others' research: 'Curtis an American is attaching y-rays,' wrote former Melbourne student J. S. Rogers in Cambridge to Laby in 1922; 'I understand there is an Indian working on x Ray spectrocapy [*sic*]', and a 'man named White is experimenting on the spectrum of secondary x-rays'.[28] Rutherford, too, wrote to Laby, telling him how his former students were getting along, what was happening at the laboratory, and lending insight into the machinations of the 1851 Exhibition selec-tors.[29] Neither did information only travel from the metropole to the colonies: 'There are various … Toronto people in London now,' wrote George Parkin from Oxford to Wrong, 'so I feel quite in touch with all that you are doing [in Canada].'[30]

Such exchanges were frequently unsanctioned. 'I thought I had better wire to let you know', wrote Wilson's old classmate J. S. Haldane in 1909, 'that the Edinburgh Chair is vacant, in case you hadn't heard of poor Cunningham's death'.[31] Wilson in fact learnt of Cunningham's death from at least three separate sources. On a number of occasions W. H. Bragg took the liberty of sending some of the letters he received from Madsen in Sydney on to Rutherford in Cambridge without Madsen's knowledge.[32]

Reliant on the same networks of personalised trust that were crucial to the making of appointments, unauthorised communications such as these served to strengthen ties between absent colleagues, expedite the process of research and publication, and bring individuals separated by thousands of miles into each others' lives. The archives of settler professors are full of correspondences with former students and colleagues abroad that demonstrate the way personal networks enabled settler scholars to participate in the 'invisible colleges' of informal exchange from which George Basalla has claimed they were excluded.[33] John Jenkin has concluded that, thanks to such connections, although located in Adelaide, '[W. H.] Bragg was not greatly disadvantaged by his distance from London'. Like Frederick Soddy in Glasgow, and Rutherford in Montreal, Jenkin argues, Bragg 'clearly became a center and not a periphery in the evolving science of radioactivity'.[34]

However – as Jenkin also points out – Bragg himself did perceive his distance from London to be a problem, and this perception played a significant role in his decision in 1909 to accept a chair at the University of Leeds.[35] The traffic in objects and information and the use of agents did not always serve to reduce the sense of isolation felt by many settler scholars, or the real obstacles they faced. On the contrary: for G. A. Wood, the professor of history at the University of Sydney, communication with his friends in Britain may even have exacerbated his sense of isolation. At the same time as they brought him accounts of his 'well-beloved Oxford', the letters he received from former students also served to intensify his sense of separation from it.[36] Moreover, the prestige, resources and mutual proximity of institutions in the United Kingdom meant that those who held positions in them often played a central role in any network. But, as Jenkin again suggests, although '[t]he question of isolation is manifestly related to distance ... it is possible to be isolated even when one is close to any center'.[37] Lack of connection to British academic networks could also render scholars in England peripheral. Constructed by individuals as they travelled, these social networks were as crucial as physical location in determining how academic patronage, material and information were trafficked, and how careers were made.

Producing knowledge

G. W. C. Kaye and T. H. Laby's 1911 *Table of Physical and Chemical Constants and some Mathematical Functions* shows how the long-distance networks of the British academic world helped to shape the production of knowledge in British universities. From the first it received favourable reviews. 'The compilation of a book of this kind', wrote a commentator in *Nature* in February 1912, 'must have involved immense labour, and every credit is due both to authors and publishers for the result accomplished ... [w]e have no hesitation in most cordially commending the work to physicists, chemists, and engineers as by far the best small book of its kind, and likely to prove exceedingly useful.'[38] In the years after its publication, Kaye and Laby's text acquired a world-wide circulation, and under their joint editorship it went through nine editions. By 1942 *Nature* was describing it as 'so indispensable in the physics laboratory that every laboratory boy knows what to get when asked for "Kaye and Laby".'[39] In 2013, it is still in print.

In their preface to the first edition, Kaye and Laby alluded to the motives that lay behind the book's creation. Their work at the Cavendish Laboratory, they wrote, had impressed upon them 'the need for a set of up-to-date English physical and chemical tables'.[40] Between 1905 and 1908 both men had been research students at the laboratory under J. J. Thomson, where they were also joined by a third student, the Scottish-born G. A. Carse.[41] All working in the rapidly expanding field of radioactivity, these three young physicists believed there was a particular need for a set of reliable constants. In fact, in 1910 Laby had already published a review article in *Le Radium* that drew attention to this, and the papers he co-authored with Carse and Kaye during this period were similarly characterised by a concern with precise measurement.[42] The first edition of the *Tables* thus grew out of the collective experience and the accumulated data that Laby, Kaye, and Carse had developed during their Cavendish researches.

This research was significantly different from the kind of physics that was contemporaneously being undertaken in continental Europe. At the turn of the century there were broadly two types of physics: the physics of principles and the physics of problems.[43] Writing to W. H. Bragg in 1911, Rutherford identified the former as European: 'the continental people do not seem to be in the least interested in trying to form a physical idea of the basis of Planck's theory'. According to Rutherford, they focused mainly on questions of theory, whereas, by contrast, 'the English point of view [was] much more physical' – concerned with experiment – and, he added, 'much to be preferred'.[44] In this new discipline of nuclear and atomic physics there were no precedents. Experimental tools had to be invented as problems pre-sented themselves. Recalling time spent in the Cavendish in 1911, W. H. Bragg's physicist son, William Lawrence Bragg, spoke of the rudimentary nature of the laboratory's equipment:

> We had to make practically everything for ourselves ... we had to do our own glass-blowing and there was only one foot-pump for the blow-pipe ... J. J. [Thomson] set me on some problem on the variation of ionic mobility with the saturation of water vapour ... but with my self-made, crude set-up [the results] were meaningless.... [M]ost of us were breaking our hearts trying to make bricks without straw.[45]

Instrument-making was the first subject undertaken by young research-ers when they arrived in Cambridge. They were, as J. G. Crowther recalled, sent to the 'nursery' – 'an attic above Rutherford's room, just under the roof' where 'it could be oppressively hot or draughtily cold' – to learn equipment-making and glass-blowing.[46]

In this environment, broad practical skills were highly sought after. Originally established to provide experimental experience to graduates of the prestigious Cambridge Mathematical Tripos, under J. J. Thomson (director, 1884–1919) the Cavendish Laboratory continued to fill this role.[47] But Thomson also recognised the need for graduates with a much broader training than was provided by the Tripos. As Katrina Dean has argued, Thomson 'was open to [the] external recruitment of these skills because the graduates of the University [of Cambridge] often had no experience in experimental research, due to the emphasis on examination performance'.[48] The diverse social backgrounds and practical experience of colonial students made them particularly suited to this kind of work. The early career of Thomas Laby is a case in point. While completing his science degree in the evenings, he had worked as an assistant in the chemical laboratory of the New South Wales Agricultural Department and served as junior demonstrator in chemistry at the University of Sydney, where he acquired practical skills of a kind not taught in Cambridge. 'I have been greatly impressed by Mr Laby's skill as an experimenter,' wrote J. J. Thomson in 1907:

> in fact I do not remember after a long experience anyone who has excelled him in this respect. He has a wide and accurate knowledge of physics and is in addition a good chemist. This enables him to undertake success-fully researches which would be impossible for anyone who knew only one of these subjects.[49]

Rutherford, too, had first learnt his experimental skills in a colonial context. 'I learnt more of research methods', he wrote in 1909, 'in those first investigations under somewhat difficult conditions [in New Zealand] than in any work I have done since.'[50] Similarly, arriving in

Adelaide as a young professor, W. H. Bragg supplemented his mathematical training by receiving 'instruction from a firm of instrument makers, [where he] learned to use the lathe and [make] the apparatus for his classes'.[51] Heavily influenced by his father-in-law Charles Todd, astronomer and superintendent of telegraphs for the South Australian government, in Adelaide Bragg also worked on new technologies such as wireless telegraphy, the telephone, radio and electricity.[52] Knowledge and skills acquired in colonial universities were thus valuable in the rapidly developing field of experimental physics.

Kaye and Laby's *Tables* provided indispensable assistance to this new breed of physicist. Not only did they serve a scholarly community in which 'colonial knowledge' played a fundamental role, but the volume was itself produced along the expansive routes of British physics. Although – as the acknowledgments in Kaye and Laby's preface attest – the Cavendish Laboratory was clearly a crucial site in the story of the text's creation, when the first edition was published Kaye was working at the National Physical Laboratory (NPL) in Teddington, England, and Laby at Victoria College in Wellington, New Zealand. The project continued following Laby's move to the University of Melbourne, and the eight subsequent editions Kaye and Laby brought to publication were produced in the context of this distance. Laby himself presented the project as a consequence of the restrictions settler life imposed upon him. 'When I first came to New Zealand,' he later wrote, 'being unable to undertake experimental research for want of apparatus, I gave my time to the compilation of this book'.[53] Yet paradoxically, this 'lack of apparatus' may have been exactly what had initially led him, as it led Rutherford and Bragg, to develop the very practical skills that would later be so important to his research.

At Melbourne Laby expressly sought to cultivate in his students these experimental skills. He oversaw researches into heat, especially into thermal conductivity (k) and the mechanical equivalent (J), with a particular focus on achieving precise measurement.[54] The latter project became his personal concern and, together with Cavendish graduate and Melbourne lecturer E. O. Hercus, between 1918 and 1929 he engaged in researches that built on the principles initially developed by another Melbourne student, J. K. Roberts, before his own departure for Cambridge in 1920.[55] Laby also continued with research on the nature and application of x-rays, investigating the measurement of line intensities, while with another Melbourne and Cavendish graduate, C. E. Eddy, he worked on quantitative atomic analysis.[56] Equipping his students to work in the developing field of experimental physics, the work in precise measurement that Laby's laboratory pursued in Melbourne fed directly into the successive editions of the *Tables*. They were, wrote his obituarist, D. K. Picken, 'typical of the method and thoroughness of [all Laby's] work'.[57]

As a consequence, when Laby's students were admitted to the Cavendish, they already possessed many of the skills needed for research. Not only had they usually undertaken courses in chemistry and physics as part of their Melbourne science degree, but they had often also spent a year or more working as junior demonstrators. In fact, L. H. Martin was able to obtain a Cambridge PhD in two years because he could show he had in Melbourne 'done research work of a certain standard for at least 12 months before [going] to Cambridge'.[58] Moreover, these colonial students fitted easily into the social environment of the laboratory. Crowther believed the 'independent attitude' encouraged under both Thomson and Rutherford was 'specially attractive to [Commonwealth] students', as they 'tended to be self-standing people, who found the regime congenial'.[59] Sharing Rutherford's informal manner, they readily won the affection of the director: he 'had a tendency', wrote Crowther, 'to fix a lot of attention on particular men, especially those from the British Dominions'.[60] Katrina Dean has called this the 'colonization' by colonial students of the Cavendish. Not only, she argues, did colonial and overseas students provide a research labour force and help define and determine 'a coherent research program that [was] ... later dubbed "modern physics"', but they also 'created a new career model in Cambridge physics, replacing wranglers with researchers'.[61]

Like Laby's relationship with Rutherford, his collaboration with Kaye also opened a space into which his Melbourne students could step. Throughout the 1920s and 1930s Kaye welcomed to Teddington several of those who went to Cambridge. At the NPL during the war was the Melbourne lecturer, Walter Morrell Holmes, and he was later followed by J. K. Roberts who worked in the heat section between 1922 and 1924.[62] Newly arrived Melbourne students would call in on Kaye at Teddington, with Massey reporting to Laby that he had seen 'Dr Kaye who went to a great deal of trouble in showing me around'.[63] These students formed an important channel of communication between the two laboratories. Indeed, in 1923, when the 'whole question of the determination of J was being considered' at the NPL, Roberts ensured Laby's Melbourne interests were protected by suggesting to Kaye that the Teddington group '[do] the electrical equivalent first as [Laby was] determining the mechanical equivalent.' 'I am glad to say', Roberts reported, 'that the question of doing J has been shelved for the moment'.[64]

While such practical skills were not unique to settler graduates, the forms of knowledge they developed in colonial contexts proved especially well adapted to the field of modern physics, while the expansive structures of the British academic world facilitated their passage to Britain. The combination of these forces worked – as the case of the Kaye and Laby *Tables* shows – to embed 'colonial knowledge' deep within 'metropolitan' expertise and 'metropolitan' centres of scholarship. In the process they also linked physicists working in Australia into an expansive and circulating network that was itself productive of knowledge and ideas.

Like all intellectual products, Kaye and Laby's book did not exist outside the field of power relations. Academic networks and the ideas produced by those who belonged to them could be and were harnessed to the cause of career progression, disciplinary formation, nationalisation and racial ideology alike. As detailed by Saul Dubow, the relationship between archaeology, physical anthropology and racial theory in South Africa provides a case in point.[65] It is not possible, Dubow suggests, to understand the history of racial science in South Africa, Britain and abroad without paying attention to the 'simultaneously ... greater independence from, and integration into, the imperial patronage network' that the interwar expansion of the South African university system initiated.[66] Picking apart the relationship between power and academic knowledge in this period means attending to the expansive disciplinary networks that penetrated British universities. The story of Kaye and Laby's *Tables* points to the new intellectual histories that such an approach might make possible.[67]

—◆—

The expansive academic networks to which Elliot Smith and T. H. Laby belonged are in many ways analogous to what economic geographers have in more recent years called the 'buzz-and-pipeline' effect. It is the 'combination of local interaction or "buzz"', argues Harald Bathelt, that together 'with interaction conducted through trans-local linkages or "pipelines"' creates the 'dynamic process of knowledge creation'.[68] Indeed, it is striking that, when describing the way Rutherford's 'personal contacts ... sometimes replaced the slower, formal communications', the historian Lawrence Badash framed the British physics network in just this way, suggesting that 'anyone wishing to pursue radioactivity seriously found it advisable to tap into the [Rutherford] pipeline'.[69] Yet according to the urban theorist, Meric Gertler, 'buzz and pipeline' are not on their own enough to produce innovation: technologies of communication create various kinds of friction that inhibit collaboration at a distance. '[G]eographical proximity', argues Gertler, 'should not be confused with relational proximity'. The latter, he contends, 'is more important': the 'buzz-and-pipeline' effect only really works when all parties belong to 'communities of practice' that share common languages and norms, common codes of civility and sociability, and common referent points.[70]

The connective mechanisms established by settler universities in the late nineteenth century, together with the personalised systems of trust they employed, created just such 'communities of practice'. British scholars did not stop travelling to European universities, reading French and German publications or corresponding with continental colleagues, and academics in Canadian universities continued to build relationships with their American colleagues that influenced their intellectual production. However, the intimate and personal ties that linked individuals working in settler universities with those in Britain, and the ways these scholars utilised such ties for the exchange of all kinds of academic goods, need to be set alongside European and American connections and contrasted to them. Although traffic between British and settler scholars frequently ran along axes that extended to and from Britain, it nonetheless traced an academic landscape that accords neither with the geo-political concepts of 'metropole' and 'colony' traditionally favoured by imperial historians nor with the notion of 'spaces of generation which are local, and spaces of diffusion or circulation', that Kapil Raj has identified as implicit in recent attempts to understand the history of science.[71] Instead, it points to a world in which experiences of study and travel, and the strong personal connections academics forged during them, created shifting social landscapes of intellectual production and exchange.[72] Extending along the routes of empire, yet not to all its parts and places, it was in this limited yet expansive space of connection that academic ideas were also made.

Notes

1 BL *Warren Dawson Papers*, Add 56303/70-71/Broom to Lady Elliot Smith, 12 Jan. 1937.

2 'Agents-general' promoted emigration, placed government orders, floated loans, paid bills, and negotiated contracts and concessions. See Lillian M. Penson, 'The Origin of the Crown Agency Office', *English Historical Review*, 40, no. 158 (1925): 196–206; Raewyn Dalziel, *The Origins of New Zealand Diplomacy: The Agent-General in London, 1870–1905* (Wellington: Victoria University Press, 1975); Bernard Attard, *The Australian High Commissioners* (London: Menzies Centre for Australian Studies, 1991), p. 3; H. Gordon Skilling, *Canadian Representation Abroad* (Toronto: Ryerson Press, 1945), pp. 107–9; Roy McNab, *The Story of South Africa House* (Johannesburg: Jonathan Bell, 1983), pp. 64–8. See also John Darwin, 'Imperialism and the Victorians: The Dynamics of Territorial Expansion', *English Historical Review*, 112, no. 447 (1997): 614–42.

3 Zoë Laidlaw, 'Networks, Patronage and Information in Colonial Governance: Britain, New South Wales and the Cape Colony, 1826–1843' (DPhil., University of Oxford, 2001), p. 179. Works that examine scientific networks in the early nineteenth century include: Roderick Weir Home (ed.), *Australian Science in the Making*

(Cambridge: Cambridge University Press, 1988); R. W. Home and S. G. Kohlstedt (eds), *International Science and National Scientific Identity* (Dordrecht: Kluwer Academic, 1991); H. MacDonald, 'A Scandalous Act: Regulating Anatomy in a British Settler Colony, Tasmania 1869', *Social History of Medicine*, 20, no. 1 (2007): 39–56.

4 Australian Academy of Science, Basser Library (AAS), *Grafton Elliot Smith Papers,* MS56/387/Elliot Smith to Wilson, Apr. 1896.

5 UMA, *T. H. Laby Papers,* UM85/144/2/1/2/1929, Mohr to Laby, 8 Oct. 1930.

6 *Ibid.*, UM85/144/3/7a/Rutherford to Laby, 7 June 1934.

7 UTA, *G. M. Wrong Papers,* B2004-2005/box 002/76/Feiling to Wrong, 21 Mar. 1910; Fisher to Wrong, 30 Jan. 1930; James McNeish, *Dance of the Peacocks: New Zealanders in Exile in the Time of Hitler and Mao Tse-Tung* (Auckland: Vintage, 2003), pp. 83, 356–7.

8 *Report of the Eighty-Fourth Meeting of the British Association for the Advancement of Science, Australia 1914* (London: John Murray, 1915), p. 285.

9 These include but are by no means limited to: Thomas Mackie (South Africa – bacteriology); George Parkin (Canada – various disciplines); Arthur Dendy (Australia, New Zealand, South Africa – zoology); Alfred Radcliffe-Brown (Australia, South Africa, United States – anthropology); Eric Walker (South Africa – history); Kenneth Bell (Canada – history); Lance Hogborn (Canada, South Africa – zoology); C. K. Allen (New Zealand – classics); Ronald Syme (New Zealand – Roman history); Zelman Cowan (Australia – law); Dan Davin (New Zealand – Oxford University Press editor).

10 Janet Wilson, 'Post-Colonial Relocations: Australia, New Zealand and the Study of the Early European Past', *British Review of New Zealand Studies*, 16 (2006–7): 179–206, pp. 191–2; McNeish, *Dance of the Peacocks: New Zealanders in Exile in the Time of Hitler and Mao Tse-Tung*, pp. 82–4, 356–8. Alice M. Copping, counted herself 'lucky that [she] came from New Zealand and it was near enough to Australia to give [her] a chance to work first as a research assistant in the Lister Institute', Copping, 'Sir Charles James Martin – A Biographical Sketch (1866–1955)', *The Journal of Nutrition*, 101:1 (January, 1971), found in AAS, *C. J. Martin Papers,* MS11 /1/1/A.M. For the Melbourne connection see F. C. Courtice, 'Research in the Medical Sciences: The Road to National Independence', in R. W. Home (ed.), *Australian Science in the Making* (Cambridge: Cambridge University Press, 1988).

11 Tamson Pietsch, 'Between the Nation and the World: J.T. Wilson and Scientific Networks in the Early Twentieth Century', in Brett M. Bennett and Joseph Morgan Hodge (eds), *Science and Empire: Knowledge and Networks of Science across the British Empire, 1800–1970* (New York: Palgrave Macmillan, 2011), p. 147.

12 AAS, *Grafton Elliot Smith Papers,* MS56/1/20/Elliot Smith to Broom requesting *miniopterus,* 10 Mar. 1896; 1/21/Elliot Smith to Broom regarding bats' heads, 23 Mar. 1896.

13 *Ibid.*, MS56/1/26/Elliot Smith to Broom regarding *foetal Phalangista,* 2 Sept. 1896; BL, *Warren Dawson Papers,* Add 56303/XLVI/Elliot Smith to Broom, 11 Dec. 1896.

14 AAS, *Grafton Elliot Smith Papers,* MS56/1/31/Elliot Smith to Broom regarding *Chrysochloris,* from Montreal, 3 Sept. 1897 (Elliot Smith was in Canada for the British Association meeting); AAS, *Grafton Elliot Smith Papers,* MS56/1/42/Elliot Smith to Broom regarding Macroscelides, from Cairo, 25 Dec. 1901; BL, *Warren Dawson Papers,* Add 56303/XLVI/Elliot Smith to Broom regarding lizards, 5 Nov. 1902; regarding Insectivora, 2 Mar. 1903.

15 USA, *J.T. Wilson Papers,* P162/1/97/Elliot Smith to Wilson, 21 Nov. 1902; AAS, *Grafton Elliot Smith Papers,* MS56/1/97/Elliot Smith to Wilson, 27 May 1897.

16 AAS, *Grafton Elliot Smith Papers,* MS56/433/Elliot Smith to Wilson, 12 Apr. 1908; 1/431/Elliot Smith to Wilson, from Cairo, 26 Mar. 1907; 1/432/Elliot Smith to Wilson, from Belfast, 27 July 1907.

17 *Ibid.*, MS56/1/47/Elliot Smith to Broom, Cairo, 4 Mar. 1903

18 Bruno Latour, *Science in Action: How to Follow Scientists and Engineers through Society* (Milton Keynes: Open University Press, 1987), p. 215; D. Lambert and A. Lester, *Colonial Lives across the British Empire: Imperial Careering in the Long Nineteenth Century* (Cambridge: Cambridge University Press, 2006).

19 D. I. Harvie, *Deadly Sunshine: The History and Fatal Legacy of Radium* (Stroud, Glos.: The History Press, 2005); B. Goldschmidt, 'Uranium's Scientific History, 1789–1939' (paper presented at the Fourteenth International Symposium, London, 1989), accessed 7 Dec. 2007, http://socrates.berkeley.edu/~rochlin/ushista.html; J. R. Morgan, 'A History of Pitchblade', *Atom*, 329, no. March (1984): 63–8. Uranium was also discovered in South Australia in 1906 and was treated in New South Wales, though production was haphazard until after the First World War.

20 UMA, *T. H. Laby Papers*, UM85/144/3/3a/Rutherford to Laby, 1 July 1909.

21 SMLA, *Rutherford Correspondence*, vol. 7, Marsden to Rutherford, 18 Sept. 1915. Boyle thought the hot springs near Edmonton might be radioactive and wanted to test them against a pure sample that Rutherford sent him. SMLA, *Rutherford Correspondence*, vol. 3, Boyle to Rutherford, 30 Sept. 1912 and 17 Aug. 1915.

22 Fleming, 'Science in Australia, Canada and the United States: Some Comparative Remarks', p. 181.

23 See Jenkin, 'William Henry Bragg in Adelaide', pp. 87–8.

24 UMA, *T. H. Laby Papers*, UM85/144/3/Rutherford to Laby, 13 Dec. 1929; Laby to Rutherford 15 Nov. 1929; Laby to Rutherford, 29 Dec. 1928; Rutherford to Laby, 26 Apr. 1928; Laby to Rutherford, 1 Apr. 1927; Rutherford to Laby 21 Feb. 1927; SMLA, *Rutherford Correspondence*, vol. 7, Madsen to Rutherford, 8 Nov. 1935; 6 Apr. 1936; 20 May 1937; 14 May 1915; vol. 3, Boyle to Rutherford, 17 Nov. 1908. For Elliot Smith and J. P. Hill, see USA, *J. T. Wilson Papers*, P162/1/Elliot Smith to Broom, 11 Dec. 1896, 5 June 1897, 12 Nov. 1897, 26 Aug. 1899, 15 May 1899, 2 Mar. 1903, 8 June 1920, 22 May 1930; Elliot Smith to Arthur Keith, the editor of *Journal of Anatomy*, 26 Nov. 1924; Elliot Smith to Wilson, 27 Jan. 1897; P162/3/5/Hill to Wilson, 18 Jan. 1907.

25 USA, *J. T. Wilson Papers*, P162/3/5/Hill to Wilson, 21 Jan. 1903; AAS, *Grafton Elliot Smith Papers*, MS56/1/397/Elliot Smith to Wilson, 27 May 1897.

26 Soft information is considered to be essentially qualitative in nature (such as suggestion, opinion, rumour, anecdote and speculation), unlike hard information, which is quantitative.

27 UCTA, *Mandelbrote Papers*, BC576/181/Walker to Mandelbrote, 21 Dec. 1938; UMA, *R. M. Crawford Papers*, series 6, box 21/6/3/1/Crawford to McBriar[?] 17 July 1947 – probably the political theorist and Reader in Economics at University College, Oxford, G. D. H. Cole.

28 UMA, *T. H. Laby Papers*, 1/2/1922/J.S. Rogers to Laby, 18 Oct. 1922.

29 *Ibid.*, Rutherford to Laby, 20 July 1931.

30 UTA, *G. M. Wrong Papers*, box 003/Parkin to Wrong, 22 May 1907.

31 *Ibid.*, P162/3/2/Haldane to Wilson, 1 July 1909.

32 AAS, *J. P. V. Madsen Papers*, MS72/1/3–4/Bragg to Madsen, 18 May 1909; SMLA, *Rutherford Correspondence*, vol. 7, Madsen to Bragg, 7 Nov. 1911.

33 George Basalla, 'The Spread of Western Science', *Science*, 156, no. 3775 (1967): 611–22, p. 614.

34 Jenkin, 'William Henry Bragg in Adelaide', pp. 87, 90.

35 *Ibid.*, 87–8.

36 USA, *J. T. Wilson Papers*, P13/3/Letters Received, A. W. Wheare to Wood, 16 Oct. 1921; J. F. Bruce to Wood, 29 Apr. 1915.

37 Jenkin, 'William Henry Bragg in Adelaide', p. 88.

38 J. A. Harker, '(1) Tables of Physical and Chemical Constants, and Some Mathematical Functions (2) Smithsonian Miscellaneous Collections', *Nature*, 8 Feb. (1912): 477.

39 W. H. G., '[Short Notices]', *Nature*, 25 April 1942, p. 453.

40 G. W. C. Kaye and T. H. Laby, 'Preface', *Table of Physical and Chemical Constants and Some Mathematical Functions* (London: 1911), p. v.

41 Kaye had studied physics at Liverpool College before transferring to the Royal College of Science and graduating with a first-class degree. After a short period as a demonstrator he went up to Trinity College, Cambridge, as a research student from 1905 to 1908. From 1908 to 1910 he was personal assistant to the director, J. J. Thomson. He left the Cavendish in 1910 for the National Physics Laboratory, where he worked

until his death in 1941. George Alexander Carse was born in Edinburgh in 1880 and studied mathematics, physics and chemistry at the University of Edinburgh. After undertaking research in physics and working as an assistant in the Edinburgh department of physics he went to the Cavendish (1904–7), before being appointed lecturer in natural philosophy at his old university where he worked until his retirement in 1948. J. J. O'Connor and E. F. Robertson, 'George Alexander Carse', *The MacTutor History of Mathematics Archive* (University of St Andrews, 2008), accessed 1 May 2008, www-history.mcs.st-andrews.ac.uk/Biographies/Carse.html. Laby was also at the Cavendish between 1905 and 1909.

42 T. H. Laby, 'Tables des Constants de l'Ionisation et de la Radioactivité', *Le Radium*, 7, no. 7 (1910): 189–96; G. A. Carse and T. H. Laby, 'On a Relation between the Velocity and the Volume of the Ions of Certain Organic Acids and Bases', *Proceedings Cambridge Philosophical Society*, 13 (1906): 288–95; G. A. Carse and T. H. Laby, 'A Relation between the Velocity and Volume of Organic Ions in Aqueous Solutions', *Proceedings Cambridge Philosophical Society*, 14 (1906): 1–12; T. H. Laby and G. W. C. Kaye, 'Gaseous Ionization and Pressure', *Philosophical Magazine, Series 6*, 16 (1908): 879–89.

43 Roy MacLeod, 'Leverhulme Lectures' delivered at Oxford, 2007.

44 SMLA, *Rutherford Correspondence*, vol. 3, Rutherford to Bragg, 20 Dec. 1911.

45 W. L. Bragg, Autobiographical notes, 28, quoted in Jenkin, *William and Lawrence Bragg, Father and Son*, p. 326.

46 J. G. Crowther, *The Cavendish Laboratory, 1874–1974* (London: Science History Publications, 1974), p. 212.

47 Thomson strongly held the view that 'most of the students ... who are studying applied mathematics would be much better equipped for research in [physics] if they came into touch with the actual phenomena in the Laboratory', See Jenkin, *William and Lawrence Bragg, Father and Son*, pp. 51, 59.

48 Dean, 'Inscribing Settler Science', p. 228.

49 Quoted in *Ibid*.

50 Ernest Rutherford reminiscing in 1909 about his work at Canterbury College, quoted in J. Campbell, *Rutherford: Scientist Supreme* (Christchurch, NZ: AAS Publications, 1999), pp. 160–71, 119.

51 W. L. Bragg quoted in Jenkin, 'William Henry Bragg in Adelaide', p. 83.

52 Jenkin, *William and Lawrence Bragg, Father and Son*, pp. 133–157, 155.

53 Laby quoted in D. K. Picken, 'Thomas Howell Laby, 1880–1946', *Obituary Notices of Fellows of the Royal Society*, 5, no. 16 (1948): 739.

54 Walter George Kannuluik, a researcher in Laby's department, was associated with the measurements for (k), a programme initiated by Hercus while still a student under Laby in New Zealand. See W. G. Kannuluik and L. H. Martin, 'The Thermal Conductivity of Some Gases at 0°C', *Proceedings of the Royal Society of London*, A144 (1934): 496–513; E. O. Hercus and D. M. Sutherland, 'Thermal Conductivity of Air', *Proceedings of the Royal Society of London*, A145 (1934): 599–611.

55 The definitive paper is T. H. Laby and E. O. Hercus, 'The Mechanical Equivalent of Heat', *Philosophical Transactions of the Royal Society*, A227 (1927–28): 63–91; J. K. Roberts and A. R. Miller, *Heat and Thermodynamics* (London: 1960); J. K. Roberts, 'The Design of an Induction Motor with Large Air Gap and Rotating Field Magnets', *Proceedings of the Royal Society of Victoria*, 32 (1919–20): 156–63.

56 Ed Muirhead, *A Man Ahead of His Times: T. H. Laby's Contributions to Australian Science* (Melbourne: Spectrum Publications, 1996), p. 24; T. H. Laby and G. E. Eddy, 'Quantitative Analysis by X-Ray Spectroscopy', *Proceedings of the Royal Society of London*, A127 (1930): 20–42.

57 Picken, 'Thomas Howell Laby, 1880–1946', p. 739.

58 UMA, *T. H. Laby Papers*, UM85/144/2/1924/L.H. Martin to Laby, 2 Apr. 1924

59 Crowther, *The Cavendish Laboratory, 1874–1974*, p, 234.

60 *Ibid.*, p. 194.

61 Dean, 'Inscribing Settler Science', p. 232.

62 'Holmes, Walter Morrell (1883–1955)', *Encyclopaedia of Australian Science*, accessed 21 Oct. 2011, www.eoas.info/biogs/P001694b.htm.

63 UMA, *T.H. Laby Papers*, UM85/2/1/2/1929/Massey, in Cambridge, to Laby, 1929, date unknown; H. S. W. Massey, 'T. H. Laby, F.R.S.', *The Australian Physicist*, (Dec. 1980): 183.

64 UMA, *T. H. Laby Papers*, UM85/2/1/2/1923/Roberts, National Physical Laboratory, Teddington to Laby, 19 May 1923.

65 Saul Dubow, *Scientific Racism in Modern South Africa* (Cambridge: Cambridge University Press, 1995); Saul Dubow, 'Human Origins, Race Typology and the Other Raymond Dart', *African Studies*, 55, no. 1 (1996): 1–30; Saul Dubow, 'Opération Coup de Poing', *Archaeological Dialogues*, 10, no. 1 (2003): 26–32, pp. 28–9.

66 Dubow, *Scientific Racism in Modern South Africa*, p. 13.

67 In fact, by paying attention to Laby's network, Katrina Dean has charted an alternative 'Australian' history of the neutron. Katrina Dean, 'Settler Physics in Australia and Cambridge, 1850–1950' (PhD, Cambridge, 2004), pp. 226–7.

68 Harald Bathelt, 'Buzz-and-Pipeline Dynamics: Towards a Knowledge-Based Multiplier Model of Clusters', *Geography Compass*, 1, no. 6 (2007): 1282–98, p. 1290; Jason Owen-Smith and Walter W. Powell, 'Knowledge Networks as Channels and Conduits: The Effects of Formal Structure in the Boston Biotechnology Community', *Organization Science*, 15, no. 1 (2004): 5–21.

69 Lawrence Badash, 'The Origins of Big Science: Rutherford at McGill', in M. Bunge and W.R. Shea (eds), *Rutherford and Physics at the Turn of the Century* (Folkestone: Dawson Publishing, 1979), p. 33.

70 Meric S. Gertler, 'Buzz without Being There? Communities of Practice in Context', *Community, Economic Creativity, and Organization*, 2008 (September 2008): 203–27; Meric S. Gertler, *Manufacturing Culture: The Institutional Geography of Industrial Practice* (Oxford: Oxford University Press, 2004).

71 Raj, 'Introduction', p. 515.

72 W. K. Hancock, 'The Moving Metropolis', in A. R. Lewis and T. F. McGann (eds), *The New World Looks at Its History* (Austin: University of Texas Press, 1963); Roy MacLeod, 'On Visiting the "Moving Metropolis": Reflections on the Architecture of Imperial Science', *Historical Records of Australian Science*, 5 (1982): 1–16.

CHAPTER SIX

The Great War:
mobilising colonial knowledge and connections

When on 4 August 1914 Britain declared war on Germany, much of the British scientific establishment was stepping off a boat in Australia. Over three hundred scholars from across the British Isles, Canada, India, New Zealand and South Africa, as well as several from Europe and the United States, had travelled there to attend the first Australasian meeting of the British Association for the Advancement of Science. This was an initiative of the Australian universities, organised largely under the direction of the Tasmanian-born, Oxford-educated lecturer in chemistry at Melbourne, A. C. D. Rivett.[1] Virtually all of Australia's scientific associations participated, and over the course of several weeks, lectures were delivered, papers presented and honorary degrees conferred at universities across the country. In the context of the recently declared hostilities, the German scholars in the party might have feared a hostile reception. But walking onto the Union Jack-bedecked stage at the University of Adelaide a week after the declaration of war, they were instead greeted with cheers that 'were warmer than those for their British confrères': 'science knows no nationalities, no enmities' was the conclusion of the Melbourne *Argus*.[2]

Yet with two empires at war, science was not to remain above politics for long. The publication in September 1914 of the infamous 'Professors' Manifesto', in which ninety-three German professors pledged their support for their country's war aims, ended talk of scientific internationalism. As Norman Lockyer – the British astronomer, chemist and founder of the journal *Nature* – wrote in response:

> Many of us have been great admirers of Germany and German achievements along many lines, but we have now learned that her 'culture' and admirable organization have not been acquired ... for the purpose of advancing knowledge and civilisation, but, in continuation of a settled policy, they have been fostered and used in order that a military caste in Germany, with the Kaiser at its head, shall ride roughshod over Europe.[3]

In both Britain and the settler colonies there were calls for the dismissal of German-born university staff. Although resolutely opposed by some, at the University of Melbourne demands both from inside and outside the institution led the council to decide in December 1914 not to renew the contracts of Eduard Scharf, the lecturer in music, and Walter von Dechend, the lecturer in German. Under similar pressure in Toronto, President Falconer tried to work out exchanges with American universities for three of his lecturers, but to no avail: they too were forced to resign.[4] And in New Zealand, despite opposition from the Victoria College council, the government introduced legislation to remove the German-born George William von Zedlitz from his position as professor of modern languages.[5] British academics in Germany received similar treatment. The South Australian Rhodes scholar, H. H. L. A. Brose, who had been visiting his relatives in Hamburg following his first year at Oxford, was interned in Ruhleben Prisoner of War Camp near Berlin along with around 370 British academics and undergraduates, including the physicists James Chadwick and Charles Ellis, the historian John C. Masterman, the Canadian bacteriologist Allan Lochead, and several English and Scottish footballers.[6] By the start of 1915 it was clear that the outbreak of war had closed off the previously porous borders of the British academic world.[7]

However, while it curtailed academic relations with Germany, the war also served to intensify the expansive scholarly networks with colonial scholars that had been built up over the course of the previous three decades. It marshalled the intellectual resources dispersed across the universities of the settler world and in doing so fostered new connections that would go on to shape the nature of British and settler universities into the 1930s. As we saw in Part II, these were all processes that had begun in the 1880s when the settler universities began more consciously to connect themselves with the wider world of British academia. The war drew upon these linkages and turned them to practical purposes. In the process it solidified the boundaries of the British academic world and provided new opportunities for settler and British scholars to connect with each other.

The universities go to war

At the declaration of hostilities, the universities in Britain immediately threw themselves behind the war campaign. However, neither they nor the military leadership initially saw their contribution as primarily intellectual. Rather than minds, it was manpower that the universities offered up, with students streaming in to enlist in large numbers and professors ardently encouraging them. When the new academic year commenced in October 1914 the extent of their response was apparent. Numbers at Manchester had dropped by a third, and at University College in London they had more than halved.[8] At Bangor the intermediate chemistry class disappeared, while at Glasgow the number of fell by fifty per cent.[9] But perhaps no university was more changed than Oxford. A total of 3,097 students had left for their summer vacations in July 1914, but six months later the city was like a ghost town, with just under 369 mainly women and foreign students still in residence. At colleges such as King's in Cambridge and Balliol in Oxford, mortality rates were twice the national average: 29.3 per cent of those who matriculated at Oxford in the years between 1910 and 1914 never returned.[10] For a time there was talk of temporarily closing the university, but instead it was made over as a military camp – its colleges billeting soldiers and its Examinations Schools turned into a hospital. While fully in support of the war effort, the principal of Magdalen College, T. Herbert Warren, grieved over these changes. Writing in 1917, he remembered the 'Oxford of yore': 'her ancient walls crowded with young life, her study and sport jostling each other in happy, gay confusion', and contrasted it to '[Oxford] as she is now, her buildings tenantless or turned to strange uses, her true life reduced to a memory, a dream, a hope!'[11]

In the settler world, too, the universities responded by doing all they could. In the months that followed the August declaration, special regulations were passed to allow male students – particularly those studying medicine – to complete their courses quickly; recruiting events were organised; rifle clubs and officers' training corps were convened or established and classes set aside for compulsory drill, ambulance, and signal practice; patriotic lectures were delivered; and 'honour rolls' were published listing the names of those who had enlisted. At Toronto a special convocation was held in February to award degrees to the students about to leave for the front; at Cape Town concessions were granted to serving members; and, although in French-speaking Quebec the wider response was more muted than in Anglophone Ontario, at McGill the Graduate Society had organised a provisional battalion before the recruiting offices even opened. Although figures are problematic – not least because war was declared during the northern hemispheres' summer break, making it difficult to tell who should be counted as a university student – they indicate that the response from settler universities was enthusiastic. Within the first eight months, 160 undergraduates from Melbourne, nearly 500 from Toronto and 'practically all the third year students who were fit' at New Zealand's Victoria University College had joined up, with more than one-third of the entire alumni body of Rhodes University

College at Grahamstown also enlisting.[12] These were numbers that, although not as large as in Britain, were nonetheless significant. Roy MacLeod has estimated that perhaps thirty-five per cent of Australian university students enlisted, as compared with over fifty per cent from the British universities. According to Stanley Frost, at McGill it was sixty-five per cent.[13] And these figures do not account for the many women students who worked in official and unofficial capacities: as nurses and ambulance drivers, and as organisers for bodies such as the Canadian Patriotic Fund. Although the reality of the conflict was made brutally clear in April and May of 1915, when casualty lists bearing the names of Australians and New Zealanders killed at Gallipoli, tales from the Canadians of the trenches at Ypres, and news of the sinking of the Lusitania all appeared in the newspapers, the settler universities remained resolutely supportive of the conflict.

Faculty members, too, sought to contribute.[14] By the end of 1915, forty-seven members of the staff at the University of Melbourne and thirty-six from Sydney were on active military service abroad with a good number of others undertaking war work at home. According to the universities' *Yearbook* for 1919–20, during the war 165 members of staff had enlisted from Toronto, forty-nine from the University of Manitoba and its constituent colleges, and twenty-one from Queen's in Kingston. In total twenty-one staff joined up from Otago, and, even though support for the war was more mixed at the Cape, by the middle of 1915 eight members of the staff of the South African College and five from Transvaal College in Pretoria were already on active service, with many more waiting to be called up.[15]

But the attempt to utilise the expertise of these academic volunteers was, as in Britain, initially very limited. Medical and engineering training was valued, and some professors were enlisted in administrative or strategic capacities, while others such as Adelaide's professor of history, G. C. Henderson, occupied themselves by giving patriotic lectures.[16] For the most part, however, the early stages of the war saw university personnel enrolling in the forces alongside everyone else. Toronto history lecturers Vincent Massey and E. J. Kylie led companies of the Canadian Officers Training Corps, and Arnold Wynne, a lecturer in English at the South African College, joined the King's Regiment in the British Army as a second lieutenant. As the Melbourne professor of physiology, W. A. Osborne, later recalled, the only thing 'the military authorities could think of in the way of utlising [the] exceptional gifts [of Australia's first lecturer in biochemistry, A. C. Rothera] was to give him the task of inspecting latrines'.[17] Such policies could have tragic consequences. The death at Gallipoli of H. G. J. Moseley, a brilliant young physicist who had been undertaking pioneering work at Manchester with Ernest Rutherford, was just the most prominent. Kylie, Wynne, and Rothera also died in the course of their duties, as did many of their contemporaries in Britain.[18] As H. A. L. Fisher noted in 1919, 'at the beginning of the War there was a most inadequate apprehension of the results which might be derived from the laboratories and brains of the universities'.[19] Although in November 1914 the Royal Society had formed a war committee to offer scientific advice, no one in government or the armed services seemed to be listening.

However, as the first waves of mustard gas wafted over the French and Algerian trenches in April 1915, it became rapidly apparent that the conflict was, as J. A. Fleming would a few months later tell the students at University College in London, to be 'a war quite as much of chemists and engineers as of soldiers and sailors'.[20] The British government and the War Office finally began to heed pre-war calls for better state support of scientific and industrial research. In July 1915 a committee of the Privy Council established the Scientific Advisory Council that twelve months later would became the Department of Scientific and Industrial Research (DSIR) and the same month the Admiralty set up the Board of Invention and Research (BIR).[21] But the real changes for the universities had come a few weeks earlier when the Ministry of Munitions was established. Intended initially to address the shortage of shells, it quickly realised that the expertise and the laboratories of the universities and their employees constituted vital assets and began actively enlisting them for war-related research.

These changes marked the transformation of the nature of the universities' involvement in the war. By early 1916 *The Times* was approvingly referring to Leeds, Liverpool, Manchester and Sheffield universities as 'branches of the country's defensive forces'.[22] Chemists in particular were needed for the production of dyes, explosives, drugs and poison gas; physicists and mathematicians for submarine detection, sound-ranging and aircraft design; geographers for making maps; and bacteriologists for sanitation and the treatment of wounds. Across the country professors joined engineers, industrialists and businessmen on the committees of the Ministry of Munitions, Board of Trade, and Board of Agriculture and Fisheries responsible for the supervision of wartime production.[23]

But rather than displacing pre-war academic networks, these new organisational initiatives worked by appropriating them. For example, established in October 1917, the Ministry of Munitions' Chemical Warfare Committee absorbed the anti-gas departments of the Royal Army Medical College and the Ministry's own Chemical Advisory Committee, both of which were staffed by the members of the various war committees of the Royal Society. Moreover, the informal academic connections and spaces of scientific sociability that had characterised British research before 1914 continued to play a crucial role in the functioning of science during the war. The Royal Society Club served as a particularly important hub, especially for those who came from the settler universities and from America.[24] As Marion Girard has pointed out, 'this form of war service asked men who normally exchanged professional information to continue to do so; the war, in effect, adapted to their way of working together collegially.'[25]

Mobilising settler talent

This mobilisation of British scientific networks extended to the Dominions, where settler universities (together with those in Scotland) had since the turn of the century fostered the kind of expertise that the war now demanded. As Toronto's principal, Robert Falconer, explained in 1921, from the 1880s and 1890s settler universities had been forced 'to '[adjust] themselves to the emergent needs of their own localities'. They had developed schools of engineering, applied science, mining and medicine, and learned 'new methods of instruction and add[ed] new departments' that he thought probably seemed strange in England.[26] The war created many opportunities for academics with such experience. Fashioned in the face of limited resources and through engagement with industry and agriculture, in the context of the scientific war their 'colonial knowledge' became highly valued.

As the nature of the conflict became clearer, scientists in settler universities also began to petition their governments for greater state support of scientific and industrial research. Acting on their pre-war sense of themselves as part of an expansive British academic community, colonial academics pressed for the extension of the British DSIR to the Dominions. In August 1915 a copy of the white paper proposing the establishment of the department reached Frederick Hagelthorn, the Minister of Public Works in Victoria, Australia. He showed it to William Osborne at Melbourne University, and together the governments of Victoria and New South Wales and the universities of Melbourne and Sydney urged London to establish an organisation that would enable the 'pooling or consolidation of the resources of the Empire for the purposes of scientific research'.[27] The British Prime Minister, Lloyd George, was enthusiastic. However, much to the chagrin of the Australian universities, their own Prime Minister, Billy Hughes, did not want to co-operate: in January 1916 he instead set up an independent Australian Advisory Council of Science and Industry (later the Council for Scientific and Industrial Research, or CSIR). Similarly, in Canada the foundation of the DSIR in Britain led

the local universities and scientific societies to lobby for a commission on industrial research.[28] But, as in Australia, the federal government proved unwilling to support imperial scientific co-operation and
was slow to respond. Only when the British Minister of Munitions
issued a circular letter to the Canadian as well as the UK universities
requesting help with military research did the Canadian government
– alarmed at the prospect of its universities' independent action – see
fit to take steps of its own, finally establishing in November 1916 an
Honorary Canadian Advisory Council for Scientific and Industrial
Research (later the National Research Council, or NRC).[29] Thus, while
settler academics and universities sought integrated forms of scientific
co-operation, Dominion governments asserted their control over what
they were beginning to see as their own national intellectual assets.

Yet in the end these Dominion research councils played little role in
co-ordinating the wartime involvement of scientists in the settler universities. More important were the various local munitions committees that worked in concert with the Ministry of Munitions in London.
In Canada the administrative incompetence of the 'Shell Committee',
formed in late 1914, led the British government in November 1915 to
set up its own 'Imperial Munitions Board' (IMB), which operated under
the direction of the Canadian banker and member of the University of
Toronto's board of governors, Joseph W. Flavelle. It purchased munitions in Canada on Britain's behalf, co-ordinated the diffuse lines of
production, and established its own factories to fill the gaps. The
Dominion government therefore had little role to play in the supply
of munitions, which was instead carried out through private arrangements between Canadian businesses and the IMB. The work of chemists in Canadian universities fed into this local production. At McGill,
H. W. Matheson and H. S. Reid worked on the catalytic manufacture
of acetone, and Professor Alfred Stansfield researched magnesium; at
Toronto, J. Watson Bain investigated picric acid and Clara Benson the
chemistry of explosives.[30]

In Australia federal and state munitions committees were set up
by governments eager to support the war effort. They oversaw the
production of cordite at Maribynong in Victoria, and rifles at Lithgow
in New South Wales. A number of academics served on these committees, providing a conduit for some university laboratories to adapt their
research to war needs. However, the efforts of these Australia-based
researchers were hampered by both the difficulties of standardising
weapons across large distances and the departure of skilled labourers
either in the Australian Imperial Force (AIF) or to work in chemical
factories in Britain.[31] Although there were others who attempted to
undertake war-related research in the Dominions, as Katrina Dean has

pointed out, the decentralisation of the scientific war effort, combined with slow and bureaucratic communication networks and a lack of access to the systems of technological testing and design, made this difficult.[32] Instead, it would be in Britain that settler scientists made their contribution to the war.

A good number of scientists with settler experience were already in Britain when war broke out. Working as research students or in university posts, they were recruited into service via the professional and associational networks that Marion Girard has argued were so central to wartime research.[33] In fact, several scientists with close ties to settler universities took up prominent positions on the various bodies that were given responsibility for guiding wartime research. The New Zealand physicist Ernest Rutherford was chair of the Admiralty's Board of Invention, on which William Bragg (previously professor of mathematics at Adelaide and, since 1909, at Leeds) and Richard Threlfall (until 1898 professor of physics at Sydney) also served. Threlfall additionally worked on the Scientific Advisory Committee, while McGill's former professor of anatomy, Auckland Geddes, was director of recruiting at the British War Office, and the Cambridge-educated South African Afrikaaner Prime Minister, Jan Smuts, sat on the War Cabinet. Others filled less executive but equally significant roles – the Canadian Regius Professor at Oxford, William Osler, gave consultancy to many military hospitals; the one-time demonstrator at the University of Sydney, Almroth Wright, was director of biological research at the Medical Research Council; the South African Basil Schonland was scientific adviser to Field Marshal Montgomery; and the Melbourne graduate and superintendant of metallurgy and chemistry at the National Physical Laboratory (NPL), Walter Rosenhain, directed its war research. Close to the centre of this world sat the former professor of chemistry at the University of Sydney, Archibald Liversidge. As vice-president of the Chemical Society, member of the Overseas Branches Committee of the Institute of Chemistry, and researcher at the Royal Institution's Davy Faraday Laboratories, he dominated British chemistry networks and helped recruit British and settler chemists for war work, while also providing advice to the Admiralty's BIR.[34] These and other individuals acted as nodal points within networks of connection that drew upon forms of trust, sociability and mutual interest reaching back into the pre-war period.

The wartime career of Richard Threlfall provides a good example of the way expansive academic connections underpinned war work. After his return from the University of Sydney to England in 1898, Threlfall had become director of the Birmingham chemical manufacturing firm Albright and Wilson. Suggesting early in the war that helium could be used instead of the flammable hydrogen in airships, Threlfall was asked to locate a source of the substance through the American branch of his firm. Utilising old academic networks to enlist the help of the Toronto professor of physics John MacLennan (whom Threlfall had met via J. J. Thomson, during MacLennan's time at the Cavendish Laboratory in 1898–99), they enacted a scheme to produce helium in Canada on an industrial scale.[35] It was J. J. Thomson who in July 1915 recruited Threlfall to serve on the Admiralty's BIR, following which he later became a founding member of the Advisory Council on Scientific and Industrial Research and chairman of two DSIR research boards.[36] Described as 'one of the most sociable and "clubbable" of men', Threlfall drew heavily in his work upon the overlapping academic circles to which he belonged: in addition to the Cavendish network, there were his fellow members of the Royal Society, and old Sydney and Australian colleagues such as Bragg, Liversidge, Masson and Pollock. This interlocking world of academic connection underwrote not just Threlfall's work but the entire scientific war project.[37] The extent to which these networks reached out and drew in academics from the settler colonies is evident in a number of key aspects of wartime science: in particular, chemistry, geology and physics.

Chemistry

The outbreak of war exposed the dependence of British industries on imports – either from hostile states in Europe or from countries such as Spain and the United States, with whom trading routes were threatened.[38] Britain faced a crisis in the supply of a number of chemical products crucial to the war effort: synthetic dyes, pharmaceutical products, optical glass, and chemicals necessary for the manufacture of explosives. Moreover, it also found itself facing a serious shortage of qualified personnel. To fill its laboratories and factories, Britain appealed not only to United States but also to its empire where there were many men with chemical training already working in what Roy MacLeod has called 'frontier' industrial occupations'.[39] In fact, at the beginning of the war, one-seventh of the members of the British Institute of Chemistry were living abroad.[40] In 1915 they flocked back to Britain to swell the meagre ranks of British chemists.

Central to this story was the Australian munitions expert Arthur Edgar Leighton. Born in Surrey and educated at the Birkbeck Literary and Scientific Institution in London, in the 1890s Leighton had worked for the consulting firm of the explosives expert William Macnab. In this capacity he had helped Fletcher Moulton on the landmark Nobel and Abel cordite patent case (1892–95).[41] Appointed in 1903 to run the Aravunkadu explosives factory in India, during his leave in England in

1907 he was recruited by C. Napier Hake, chief inspector of explosives in Victoria, to manage the cordite factory in Australia.[42] Based there until the outbreak of war, in April 1915 Leighton was sent by the Australian government to collect information from India and Britain on arsenal design. He arrived in London only six weeks after the foundation of the Ministry of Munitions where he found his old employers Macnab and Moulton running the Department of Explosives and Supply. They had already recruited the American-born South African engineer, Kenneth Bingham Quinan from De Beer's Explosive Works in Cape Town, and he had brought across several other South African engineers to help design factories in Britain. In fact, the official *History of the Ministry of Munitions* produced after the war records that Quinan's staff at the Ministry were 'drawn mostly from South Africa'. But the Ministry desperately needed trained chemists to assist with the making of the chemicals needed for explosives, and skilled engineers to help with production on an industrial scale.[43] This kind of experience was limited only to a handful of people in Britain, but Australia had perhaps two hundred or more appropriately qualified men. To assist Quinan, Moulton recruited Leighton who remained in London with the dual task of helping the Ministry and organising an arsenal for Australia.

On his appointment, Leighton contacted the academics in Australia who were involved in the state munitions committees – David Orme Masson, the professor of chemistry at Melbourne; S. H. Barraclough, the professor of mechanical engineering at Sydney; and A. J. Gibson, the professor of engineering at Brisbane – and asked them to 'get every chemist who could be spared from Australia to England'.[44] Coming from across Australia and New Zealand, these men were placed in key positions in the factories at Queensferry, Gretna and Avonmouth. Others were employed in research – Melbourne graduates R. E. Summers, Charles Stubbs and Masson's son Irvine worked under Robert Robertson in the research department at the Woolwich arsenal; another Masson student, A. C. Cummings, was with James Walker at Edinburgh; Bertram Steele, the University of Queensland's professor of chemistry, worked at University College London; Adelaide's J. C. Earl assisted James Irvine at St Andrews; another Melbourne graduate, William Jewell, went to Sheffield. They were followed in September 1916 by Sydney's Professor S. H. E. Barraclough, in command of a volunteer army of seven thousand skilled Australian munitions workers.[45]

Of the approximately 250 chemists working for the Factories Branch of the Ministry of Munitions' Department of Explosives Supply during the war, Roy MacLeod has estimated that 130 were from Australia, with some sixty or eighty running whole sections of this key British industry.[46] As graduates and often also employees of Australian universities, these settler chemists were closely linked to what H. A. L. Fisher called 'the chemist's shop in Cockspur Street' – otherwise known as the Board of Invention and Research, whose members included Rutherford, W. H. Bragg and Threlfall.[47] They brought to Britain much-needed skills in practical science. But bound to British scholarship by dense ties of affection, connection and personal experience, they also had a familiarity with British practice that meant they could be absorbed seamlessly into the chemical munitions project – so seamlessly, in fact, that their contribution to British wartime science has too often been obscured.[48]

Geology and mining

If chemical research was fundamental to the war above ground, geology was crucial to the war waged beneath it. The Germans were quick to realise this and mobilised their geological experts in early 1915, utilising the seized resources of the Institut de Géologie at Lille and appointing *Kriegsgeologen* to each of the German army corps.[49] By contrast, the British Expeditionary Force (BEF) arrived in France with little knowledge of the landscape. They therefore initially prioritised surveying and map-making. However, although a mining branch of the Royal Engineers was created early in 1915, it was not until June that a geological adviser – the recently graduated William B. R. King, who was a former member of the Geological Survey and serving as a lieutenant in the Welsh Fusiliers – was seconded to the Western Front.[50] With some assistance from his French and Belgian colleagues, he worked virtually alone, until the arrival in mid-1916 of T. W. Edgeworth David and his troops of colonial miners and geologists.

Born in Wales and educated at Oxford and the Royal School of Mines in London, Edgeworth David had served on the New South Wales Geological Survey before being appointed to the chair of geology at the University of Sydney.[51] As a Fellow of the Royal Society and a member of Shackleton's 1907–9 British Antarctic Expedition, and heavily involved in the organisation of the British Association meeting in Australia in 1914, Edgeworth David remained intimately connected to the world of British science throughout his long tenure at Sydney. At the outbreak of the war he had thrown himself into patriotic work, but on receiving news that mining was being undertaken at Gallipoli, in early 1915 he joined forces with his Melbourne colleague Ernest Skeats and with the Victorian government geologist Hyman Herman to convince the Australian government that it should raise a special mining corps for service with the Australian Imperial Force (AIF).

Enlisting despite his age (he was fifty-eight), Edgeworth David was commissioned as a major and left Australia in February 1916 with the AIF Mining Battalion, which consisted of miners and engineers, as well as a good number of his and Skeats's own students. The battalion was intended for Turkey, but following the withdrawal of the AIF from the Dardanelles in January 1916 it was diverted instead to France where it was divided into three tunnelling companies.

Initially, Edgeworth David served as the chief geological advisor to the First, Second and Third Armies in France, but following an injury incurred whilst inspecting a mining shaft, in 1916 he was posted to the Inspector of Mines' office at General Head Quarters, advising all the controllers of mines in Britain's three armies. From June 1918 he was chief geologist of the entire British Expeditionary Force. At General Head Quarters Edgeworth David was close to William King, and together they were assisted by his Sydney colleague James Pollock, who later directed the Mining School at Proven near Poperinghe. In September 1916 the group was joined by another Australian, Clive Loftus Hills, and then in the last months of the war by an additional two lieutenants from the Australian tunnelling companies (G. A Cook and C. S. Honman). This small, tight-knit and largely Australian group was responsible for all of the British geological work on the Western Front – for securing drinking water, supervising military mining, organising dugout construction, and managing the work of the 25,000 men who by mid-1916 were engaged in active underground warfare.[52] Their officers were frequently mining graduates from the settler universities or the Royal School of Mines where Edgeworth David had himself been a student. More than one-third of the tunnellers were also from the settler colonies: in addition to the three Australian, there was one New Zealand and three Canadian companies, while miners from South Africa were allocated to the twenty-five British and French companies in which settler officers also served.[53] Moving between all these units and linking them together was the special Australian Electrical and Mechanical, Mining and Boring Company.

At a disadvantage because of his lack of knowledge of Belgium's geology, Edgeworth David adapted techniques he had developed in the New South Wales survey and used drilled bores to identify soils and strata. This enabled the compilation of detailed scientific maps that were invaluable in the context of trench warfare. From 1916 he began lecturing to the First Army School of Mines and by 1917 he was using coloured geological maps in order to prepare the controllers of mines and chief engineers in a wholly new way. As Roy Macleod has suggested, it was '[t]hanks in large part to the Australians, [that] the British gradually recognized military mining as a science'.[54] Indeed, it was largely Australian expertise and largely settler labour that was responsible for directing and executing the biggest mining operation of the war: the tunnelling under and exploding of the German fortifications on the Messines and Wytschaete ridges in Belgium on 7 June 1917. With skills fostered in the geology departments and mining schools of the settler colonies, Australian geologists, alongside Canadian, New Zealand and South African tunnellers, led the underground war on the Western Front.

Physics

While chemists and geologists helped fight the war in France, at sea it was the physicists who were called to arms. In 1914 Admiral Percy Scott's prediction that German submarines would threaten Britain's wartime trade had been dismissed by the *Manchester Guardian* as 'imaginative ... fancy picture making'.[55] But following the German announcement in early February 1915 that all merchant ships in the waters around the UK and Ireland would be sunk on sight, the effect on vital lines of supply was felt immediately. Between February and April, thirty-nine merchant ships were destroyed. The most dramatic event occurred in May when the passenger liner RMS *Lusitania* was torpedoed by a German U-boat, with the loss of 1,198 lives, including 128 Americans. Complaints from Washington led Germany temporarily to modify its unrestricted policy, but by the summer of 1915 it was nonetheless clear that submarine attack would be a major feature of the war – one for which the British Admiralty were wholly unprepared.[56] In July the Admiralty consequently charged the BIR's Section II with the responsibility of co-ordinating the scattered research being done in its various experimental stations, at Portsmouth, Hawkcraig in Scotland, and at Woolwich.

Leading this work was Professor W. H. Bragg. In many ways he was uniquely fitted for the task. As we have seen, during his time at the University of Adelaide, he had developed the experimental skills so important to wartime science, working with his father-in-law, the South Australian superintendent of telegraphs, on radio and wireless telegraphy.[57] But moving to Leeds in 1909, Bragg was also intimately connected to the wider world of British science. At the BIR he was collaborating with colleagues he knew well: his old friends Rutherford and Threlfall, and his former Cavendish teacher, now director of the NPL, Richard Glazebrook.[58] Moreover, he was also in close contact with his son W. L. Bragg (Lawrence), who had studied physics with him in Adelaide and with whom he was jointly to share the 1915 Nobel Prize. Elected to a fellowship at Trinity College, Cambridge, in 1914, Lawrence had signed up and been seconded to the Royal

Engineers where he too was put to work on sound research, working alongside two of Rutherford's former Manchester students – Harold Robinson and the Melbourne-born McGill lecturer J. A. Gray – using microphones to detect the position of enemy guns in France.[59]

In September 1915 Bragg sent a number of academic scientists to the Admiralty's experimental station at Hawkcraig on the Firth of Forth, including two of Rutherford's other students, Albert Wood and Harold Gerrard. Tensions soon emerged between the academics and the Navy researchers, however, and Bragg was appointed there as resident director of research.[60] Rutherford (who was working with a team in Manchester), kept up close correspondence with the group, first at Hawkcraig and then at Harwich following their relocation at the end of 1916. Together they used their networks to recruit a number of settler physicists: from McGill in Canada came Rutherford's former colleagues A. S. Eve and Louis V. King, L. A. Herdit and R. B. Owen; from the University of Toronto came his Cavendish contemporary John McLennan; and from the University of Alberta came another of Rutherford's former McGill students, Robert W. Boyle. In the Manchester group was also the one-time Adelaide professor, Horace Lamb, while Melbourne's W. M. Holmes, the University of Tasmania's Professor Alexander MacAulay, and Laby's former student, the New Zealander E. O. Hercus, were placed in other units across the country. From his son Lawrence in France, Bragg learnt about sound-ranging and adapted it to underwater conditions with great success; and in Manchester, Rutherford and Boyle developed the work of the French physicist Paul Langevin that at the end of the war led to the invention of ASDIC (Sonar).[61] Together their research embraced all aspects of submarine warfare, including hydrophones, acoustic mines and loop-detectors. With experimental skills fostered in universities in Canada, Australia and New Zealand, this expansive physics network underpinned Britain's anti-submarine wartime research.

These chemists, physicists and geologists were not the only academics with settler experience to contribute to the scientific war. The No. 4 General Hospital – first located in Salonika and then at Basingstoke – was staffed by thirty-eight officers (including one woman, Dr Harriet Cockburn) and seventy-three nurses, almost all of whom were drawn from hospitals connected to the University of Toronto. McGill University equipped and staffed the No. 3 Canadian General Hospital that sailed for Britain in May 1915, while Otago's Medical School signed-up for the Medical Corps almost *en masse*.[62] Soldiers who had gained engineering degrees in settler universities were also highly valued, with Melbourne's John Monash and Saskatchewan's C. J. Mackenzie perhaps the most prominent among the many who served.[63] In lower numbers, academics from the smaller South African and New Zealand colleges also served as doctors and engineers. The military understood the value of these disciplines and had well-established ways of incorporating such expertise, but it was less able to adjust to the new forms of knowledge demanded by the scientific war. Without accepted structures for the state support of science, the existing organisational forms of the British academic world underpinned the scientific war effort.

Laboratory and common room

By bringing settler scholars into close collaboration with colleagues in Britain, the war created opportunities for new sorts of academic and intellectual connection.[64] Drawing men in to Britain, the war placed them in working relationships with English, Scottish, French and American colleagues and gave them resources and a field of enquiry replete with urgent problems. In short, the war functioned as both an exceptional laboratory and an enormous common room, at once drawing upon and intensifying the processes and networks that had held the British academic world together since the 1880s. As Roy MacLeod has written of wartime chemistry: in a 'huge laboratory of deadly trial and error' skills were 'either born of necessity or borrowed from overseas'.[65] In the process, relationships were formed that would last beyond the conflict and into the peace.

Writing in the 1930s, C. H. Foulkes, director of gas services, described, 'the theatre of war itself [as] a vast experimental ground … [in which] Human beings provided the material for these experiments on both sides of No Man's Land'.[66] In the context of the stalemate of trench warfare, innovation and adaptation were crucial to military success. Industrialists worked with academics, civilian doctors and scientists with the Army and Navy, and physiologists with chemists, in ways they had not previously. The process was not always without friction, but it resulted in much pioneering work – some of which was undertaken by settler academics. Edgeworth David's innovation in environmental geological mapping resulted in the birth of the new discipline of 'military geology'; A. C. D. Rivett discovered the 'wet process' for producing ammonium nitrate; Boyle's work with Rutherford on ASDIC would later transform submarine navigation.[67] Meanwhile, at the University of Toronto's No. 4 General Hospital, Professors Mackenzie and FitzGerald, together with the bacteriology lecturer Duncan Graham and in close connection with Osler in Oxford and T. G. Brodie back in Toronto, made significant advances in blood transfusions and anti-tetanus toxins. Indeed, the war saw medical research take great leaps forward, particularly in the fields of surgery and hygiene.

The close connections that settler academics developed with their colleagues in Britain reinforced but also extended the very ties that had brought them to Britain in the first place. The importance of the Royal Society Club has already been noted, but the numerous other sites and spaces of wartime science functioned in similar ways. The hospital tents of the Western Front and the laboratories of Harwich fostered a male sociability that was not dissimilar to that of the university common room. In these spaces were born connections – both social and intellectual – that bridged the divides between professional and academic workers, junior men and senior professors, and the various parts of the empire.[68] The laboratory of war made settler scientists instant members of a great and powerful academic society – one whose members came from across the entire British academic world. As H. A. L. Fisher said at the 1919 Imperial Education Conference:

> Here we have all the different parts of the Empire collected together and mixed up for the first time. The Australian can get to know the New Zealander, the Canadian the Scotchman, the Welshman, Irishman and Englishman, and all can compare notes and establish contact one with another.[69]

For many settler scientists, wartime links translated into peacetime employment. The example of Charles Kellaway is a case in point. While serving as a captain in the Australian Army Medical Corps, Kellaway met the former Sydney demonstrator, C. J. Martin, who since 1903 had been director of the Lister Institute of Preventative Medicine in London. When Kellaway was severely gassed in 1917, Martin took him in as a researcher, and it was there that he met the pharmacologist and physiologist H. H. Dale. Repatriated at the end of the war back to his position as acting professor of physiology at the University of Adelaide, Kellaway had his return to England in 1920 sponsored by Martin and Dale, and for three years he worked in the National Institute for Medical Research's new laboratories in Hampstead, where Dale was head of the department of biochemistry and pharmacology. Thus, when Kellaway went back to Australia in 1923 to become director of the Walter and Eliza Hall Institute of Medical Research, he took with him close ties to Martin and the Lister Institute, and to Dale and the Institute for Medical Research, that would shape the careers of a generation of Australian medical researchers.[70] Similarly, the contacts that B. D. Steele, the University of Queensland's professor of chemistry, made during his wartime work at University College London helped secure him the Fellowship of the Royal Society in 1919, to which Sydney's

James Pollock, Toronto's John MacLennan and McGill's A.S. Eve were all also admitted during or shortly after the war.[71]

However, the wartime common room was not open to everyone. By equating academic networks with masculine cultures of heroic endeavour, it in many ways reinscribed the gendered nature of academic sociability. Michael Bliss conveys this well in his biography of Frederick Banting, the Canadian inventor of insulin who during the war served in the Canadian Army Medical Corps: 'He liked to drink and smoke and swap stories with his medical or army buddies ... [i]t was a way of belonging that filled an intense need in Banting and countless men of his and most other generations.' And then, identifying, perhaps, with these 'countless men', Bliss continues: 'A little frightened of the complexities of life, not at all sure how to behave in the presence of women, a little lonely, you found security and acceptance and could come out of your shell when you got together with the fellows, the boys, the old gang.'[72] As comforting as the 'gang' may have been to its male members, it reinforced the peripheral place of women in the peacetime academy.

But even as it connected them to British scholars, the war also helped consolidate emerging national scientific communities in the Dominions. After 1919, Australian chemists who had worked together in Britain formed the Australian Chemical Institute, and in Melbourne T. H. Laby used the failure of the University of Melbourne respirator to push for the local development of scientific research.[73] Both Toronto and McGill successfully capitalised on their wartime work to secure large grants from the Rockefeller Foundation, while McGill received one from the Carnegie Corporation as well.[74] Moreover, despite their somewhat reluctant birth, in the interwar period the state-funded research councils established in both Australia and Canada grew rapidly. In South Africa, too, an Office of Census and Statistics was established in 1917, followed by a Research Grants Board within the Department of Mines and Industries in 1918. However, although the ideology of what Saul Dubow has called Dominion 'South Africanism' dominated the organisation of knowledge in South Africa between the wars, tensions within this project remained.[75] The war intensified divisions between Afrikaaner and English, and the development of three new universities during the conflict reflected this politics. At the end of years of bitter wrangling, in 1918 Victoria College became the Afrikaans-speaking Stellenbosch University, the South African College became the English-speaking University of Cape Town, and the various other colleges continued to prepare students for the (English-language) examinations of the new University of South Africa.[76]

The foundation of state-based knowledge institutions both reflected and advanced the sense of independence engendered by colonial service during the war. But for the most part their development was framed within a context of continuing imperial co-operation.[77] Academics such as Laby saw national research institutions as means of enabling settler scholars to participate as equal partners in a wider project of imperial science: it was through the co-operation of independent colonial communities that both the nation and the empire would be built. In fact, the men appointed to lead the various Dominion councils of scientific and industrial research had without exception participated in the scientific war effort: in Canada, Archibald Macallum; in Australia, A. C. D. Rivett; and in New Zealand, Ernest Marsden. Even in South Africa it was Basil Schonland – student under Rutherford at Cambridge, scientific advisor to Field Marshal Montgomery, professor at University College Toronto, head of the Bernard Price Institute at Wits University, Fellow of the Royal Society, and well connected to wider networks of British science – who in 1944 became the first director of the country's CSIR. As the example of Kellaway shows, those who worked in the new state-supported research institutions in the Dominions remained deeply connected to the dense networks of the British academic world.

The Khaki University

Scientists dominated the universities' contribution to the war, but they were not the only academics who benefitted from wartime sociability. When the conflict ended, hundreds of young men from the settler colonies who had seen active service in France and the Mediterranean also found their way into British universities. This process was aided by what H. A. L. Fisher in 1919 called the war's 'most surprising invention of all, the invention of education in the Army'.[78] As he outlined, the 'Canadians started the Khaki University and the Australians and New Zealanders forwarded their own educational movement ... [and then] there was a pioneer movement led by the Y.M.C.A. in the British Army'.[79] All three endeavours grew from a concern that the troops should, as a 1918 article in the *Christian Science Monitor* explained, 'utilize their spare time in improving their education and in fitting themselves to occupy ... more important and lucrative positions in civil life'.[80] It was the mind and discipline of the soldier during the war, together with his role as a national and imperial citizen after it, that these various programmes sought to build.

The British and the Canadian schemes were initially linked to the activities of the YMCA, which provided entertainment and supplies as well as classes to soldiers at bases in various theatres of war.[81] The man in charge of the Canadian Overseas YCMA was Colonel Gerald Birks, a McGill graduate who would go on to be a fighter ace in the Royal Flying Corps. Noting the popularity of its classes, in 1917 Birks wrote to Henry Marshall Tory, president of the University of Alberta and formerly professor at McGill, asking him to visit the Canadian troops in England and assess what else might be done for the soldiers. The report Tory wrote contained two recommendations. First, he advised that existing classes should be co-ordinated to provide a curriculum that, on the one hand, would relate to the war (including subjects such as geography, economics and the history of the British Empire), and, on the other hand, would aid the soldiers after it (agriculture, electrical engineering, telegraphy, etc). Second, Tory suggested that at the close of the war a 'Khaki University' should be set up at a central camp in England to enable soldiers to take courses that would receive credit in Canada. Instead of waiting at a loose end for months in Britain, soldiers could work towards a university degree.[82] Tory convinced Canada's university presidents to endorse his plan, and together with McGill's vice-principal, Frank Adams, and several staff from the country's universities, he travelled to England in March 1918 to put it into action.

On arrival Tory strove to co-ordinate all the classes being provided for Canadian soldiers in various locations: by army chaplains and the YMCA; by the Dalhousie professor of Hebrew, H.A. Kent, for the 17th Reserve Battalion camped in Witley; and by Lieutenant-General Arthur Currie at what was dubbed the 'University of Vimy Ridge' in France. These diverse activities were eventually incorporated as constituent 'colleges' of the 'Khaki University', and by May 1918 there were an estimated eleven such colleges active in England. They provided instruction directed as much to 'middle-aged men who read ordinary English with difficulty' as to the 'keen young fellows looking ahead to the days when they w[ould] have to resume civilian employment'.[83] This education was seen by military officials as key to maintaining discipline, but it was understood by Tory and his fellow university presidents as something that would help build the emerging Canadian nation. In total more than fifty thousand Canadian soldiers are estimated to have attended Khaki college classes. Meanwhile, Canadian soldiers taking university-level courses were encouraged to pursue subjects examined by the University of London. When the Armistice was declared, these dispersed activities were consolidated into a central 'university' at the Khaki College in Ripon, Yorkshire, and professors from Canada – the historians George Wrong (Toronto) and Frank Underhill (Saskatchewan) among them – were brought over to provide the teaching. The final report of the Khaki University recorded that 682 students had enrolled on university-level courses, with another 290 men placed in British universities.[84]

Similarly, the Australian universities' venture was conceived along-side the mobilisation in June 1918 of the Sydney University Company, as a means of providing instruction to students while they were on active service abroad. But recognising that the repatriation process would in all likelihood be a long one, the Sydney Senate banded to-gether with the University of Melbourne to propose to the Australian government a plan for the continuing education of soldier-students following demobilisation in Britain. The scheme enabled matriculated Australian university students to attend classes in British universities, with the federal government paying both their fees and a living allow-ance.[85] It proposed that British universities might recognise classes previously attended in Australia, permitting Australian students to obtain British degrees. Nominated to run the whole programme was the University of Sydney's assistant professor of English, Ernest Holme.

The declaration of the Armistice brought these plans forward, and in February 1919 Holme sailed for England along with the classicist H. W. Allen, the vice-master of Ormond College at the University of Melbourne, and E. V. Clark, lecturer in engineering at the University of Adelaide. On his arrival in England, Holme found that much work had already been done by the Anglican Bishop of Bathurst and director of education at the Australian Corps Headquarters, George Merrick Long. Securing the co-operation of both the universities and a range of other technical and commercial bodies including the Worker's Educational Association, Long had already placed members of the Army Medical Corps, the Dental Corps, the Veterinary Service, and the Engineers in various British universities. Nevertheless, by April 1919 Holme's committee had charge of 275 Australian soldier-students studying in universities across England and Scotland, and by June the number had risen to five hundred.[86]

Although not on the same scale, the South African and New Zealand overseas forces also organised educational services and appointed aca-demics to run them. The New Zealanders were able to benefit from some of the provisions organised by Long and Holme, but the South Africans did not fare so well. As Major E. B. Walker, the demonstra-tor in physics at the University of Cape Town, explained, 'inspite [sic] of their war service and in spite of their having matriculated, [South African students] have not been accepted straight away into British Universities'. Instead they were frequently asked to undertake certain additional subjects. 'Well,' continued Walker, 'there are two Universities, Glasgow and Edinburgh, which do not insist on that, and the result is that all our students go there.'[87] Walker regretted this policy and wished his students could be better distributed across the universities in Britain. His comments point to the tensions within the British academic world that remained just below the surface of wartime collaborations. At the 1919 Imperial Education Conference convened by the Imperial General Staff, Holme spoke of the British universities' generosity in relaxing their previous entrance criteria. Nevertheless, he went on to explain: 'except in the case of a great Scottish University, it was not our matriculations but our war-service that usually qualified us for entrance to a United Kingdom University; not our previous University record, but our war-service, that enabled us to push on to graduation, by favour of a United Kingdom University.'[88] The old questions about the mutual recognition of degrees remained. Yet the war enabled many settler students to enter British universities who otherwise would not have had the opportunity. In this sense it was similar to the travelling scholarship schemes that had been bringing settler graduates to Britain since the late nineteenth century.

In supporting khaki programmes, the universities were clear that their role was at once national and imperial. The senate of the University of Sydney noted in 1919: '[t]he experience gained by our students in the well-equipped laboratories of the home country, and their association with distinguished professors, will be of great advantage to them personally as well as to Australia.'[89] As with so many other aspects of the Dominions' involvement in the war, the settler universities saw the conflict both as an occasion for loyalty and as an opportunity to promote their own interests. For the most part, they did not consider these two impulses to be contradictory. As the University of British Columbia's report of its war service read, 'in the opportunities for service and sacrifice for which the Great War gave abundant scope, the young institutions found opportunities for the establishment of traditions which in future years w[ould] be a precious and imperishable heritage.'[90]

—◆—

During the Great War the work of the universities was, as Michael Sanderson wrote in 1972, 'absolutely indispensable to national survival': without their services 'the prosecution of the war, let alone its winning, would have been quite impossible'.[91] However, Sanderson and the historians who have followed him have too often failed to acknowledge that the mobilisation of British universities extended to the settler colonies. Already in Britain or working in settler institutions, settler scientists were absorbed into the war effort through their pre-existing networks of informal academic connection. In committee rooms, field stations and underground tunnels, they laboured alongside

British and later American researchers, bringing knowledge framed in colonial locations to bear upon common problems. Although missing from many historical accounts, the expansive networks of the British academic world are inscribed in wartime science.

The Great War therefore reveals both the importance and the ordinariness of the scholarly networks that criss-crossed the British academic world. It both shows how productive these networks could be, and how much they were part of the routine workings of British universities. For although it drew men into the armed services and into state and military research units, the war neither destroyed the existing academic system, nor created a new apparatus of imperial academic connection. Rather, it appropriated the expansive academic structures that had been in operation since the end of the nineteenth century. In the process, and as the settler universities were quick to perceive, the conflict at once expanded the opportunities for mobility within the British academic world and solidified its previously more porous borders. As both an enormous common room and a bloody laboratory, it enabled settler scholars to forge connections that renewed the very networks that had carried them to war in the first place. Thus, far from breaking the foundations of the old academic order, the Great War extended into the interwar period the intimate scholarly connections that, since the end of the nineteenth century, had tied the British and settler universities to each other.

Notes

1 Roy MacLeod and Peter Collins (eds), *The Parliament of Science: The British Association for the Advancement of Science, 1831–1981* (Northwood: Science Reviews, 1981); Roy MacLeod (ed.), *The Commonwealth of Science: ANZAAS and the Scientific Enterprise in Australasia, 1888–1988* (Melbourne: Oxford University Press, 1988).
2 'British Association: Members Reach Adelaide', *The Argus*, 10 August 1914, p. 5.
3 Norman Lockyer, 'The War – and After', *Nature*, 64, no. 2341 (1914): 29–30, p. 29. On the Professors' Manifesto, see John Heilbron, *Dilemmas of an Upright Man: Max Planck as Spokesman for German Science* (Berkeley, CA: University of California Press, 1986), pp. 66–71.
4 Selleck, *The Shop*, pp. 530–42; UTA, *Office of the President*, A1967-0007/box 46a; Falconer to Penton (President University Vermont), 12 Mar. 1917.
5 J. C. Beaglehole, *Victoria University College: An Essay Towards a History* (Wellington: New Zealand University Press, 1949), pp. 164–9.
6 John Jenkin, 'Henry Herman Leopold Adolph Brose: Vagaries of an Extraordinary Australian Scientist', *Historical Records of Australian Science*, 3 (1999): 287–312; J. Davidson Ketchum, *Ruhleben: A Prison Camp Society* (Toronto: University of Toronto Press, 1965), pp. ix–x, xiii.
7 Daniel Kevles, 'Into Hostile Political Camps: The Reorganisation of International Science in World War One', *Isis*, 62 (1979): 47–60. Work in progress by Heather Ellis suggests some connections were able to continue during the war: 'Intercourse with Foreign Philosophers': Transnational Collaboration and the British Association for the Advancement of Science, 1870–1914' (paper presented at the 'International values

and global science' workshop, University of Exeter, August 2012).

8 Falling from 2,200 in 1913–14 to 1,000 in 1914–15. Michael Sanderson, *Universities and British Industry, 1850–1970* (London: Routledge and Kegan Paul, 1972), p. 217.

9 *Yearbook of the Universities of the British Empire, 1918–19* (London: G. Bell and Sons, 1918), p. 440.

10 W. T. S. Stallybrass, 'Oxford in 1914–18', *Oxford Magazine*, winter (1939): 41; J. M. Winter, 'Oxford and the First World War', in T. H. Aston and Brian Harrison (eds), *The History of the University of Oxford: Vol. 8, the Twentieth Century* (Oxford: Oxford University Press, 1994), pp. 3–26.

11 T. H. Warren in H. A. L. Fisher (ed.), *British Universities and the War: A Record and Its Meaning* (London: The Field and Queen, 1917), p. 3.

12 Selleck, *The Shop*, pp. 528–9.

13 MacLeod, *Archibald Liversidge, FRS*, p. 404. Stanley Brice Frost, *McGill University for the Advancement of Learning: Vol. 2, 1895–1971* (Montreal: McGill-Queen's University Press, 1980), p. 99.

14 The War Rolls published in the 1915 Universities' *Yearbook* records the early response of universities across Britain and the Empire. *The Yearbook of the Universities of the Empire, 1915*, pp. 606–72.

15 'Report of the Senate, 1914', *Calendar of the University of Sydney, 1915* (Sydney: University of Sydney, 1914), p. 580; Friedland, *The University of Toronto*, pp. 253–54; *Yearbook of the Universities of the Empire, 1918–19*, pp. 451–2; G. E. Thompson, *A History of the University of Otago, 1869–1919* (Dunedin: J. Wilke and Co., 1919), p. 277; *Yearbook of the Universities of the Empire, 1915*, pp. 666–7.

16 These were later published as George C. Henderson, *Reflections on the War* (Adelaide: G. Hassell and Son, 1916).

17 Friedland, *The University of Toronto*, pp. 253–4; Dubow, *A Commonwealth of Knowledge*, fn. 23, p. 164. See also W. A. Osborne, 'Remembrance of Things Past: How Biochemistry Came to Melbourne', *Meanjin*, 20, no. 2 (1961): 209–14.

18 Ernest Rutherford, 'Henry Gwyn Jeffreys Moseley', *Nature*, 96, no. 2393 (1915): 33–4; 'The Waste of Brains: Young Scientists in the Fighting Line', *The Times*, 24 Dec. 1915, p. 3. As Roy MacLeod points out, during 1915 alone, Sherrington's laboratory at Oxford lost five men, A.V. Hill's at Cambridge lost two, and Haldane's at University College London, another two. Roy MacLeod, 'The Chemists Go to War: The Mobilization of Civilian Chemists and the British War Effort, 1914–1918', *Annals of Science*, 50, no. 5 (1993): 455–81, p. 473.

19 H. A. L. Fisher, *The Place of the University in National Life* (Oxford: Oxford University Press, 1919), p. 6.

20 Lecture reprinted as J. A. Fleming, 'Science in the War and after the War', *Nature*, 96, no. 2398 (1915): 181–5. For an account of science in the war see Guy Hartcup, *The War of Invention: Scientific Developments, 1914–18* (London: Brassey's Defence Publishers, 1988); Sanderson, *Universities and British Industry*, pp. 214–42.

21 Roy MacLeod and E. Kay Andrews, 'The Origins of the DSIR: Reflections on Ideas and Men, 1915–1916', *Public Administration*, 48, no. 1 (1970): 23–48.

22 'Science for War: The Work of Modern Universities', *The Times*, 9 February 1916, p. 5.

23 Sanderson, *Universities and British Industry*, pp. 230–2.

24 MacLeod, *Archibald Liversidge, FRS*, 406; Roy MacLeod, 'The Royal Society and the Commonwealth: Old Friendships, New Frontiers', *Notes and Records of the Royal Society of London*, 64, Supplement 1 (2010): 137–49, p. 3; Roy MacLeod, 'The Scientists Go to War: Revisiting Precept and Practice, 1914–1919', *Journal of War and Culture Studies*, 2, no. 1 (2009): 37–51; T. E. Allibone, *The Royal Society and Its Dining Clubs* (Oxford: Pergamon Press, 1976), pp. 291–6.

25 Marion Girard, *A Strange and Formidable Weapon: British Responses to World War I Poison Gas* (Lincoln, NE: University of Nebraska Press, 2008), p. 83.

26 *Second Congress Proceedings*, p. xxiii.

27 George A. Currie and John L. Graham, *The Origins of the CSIRO: Science and the Commonwealth Government, 1901–1926* (Melbourne: CSIRO Publishing, 1966), pp. 11–42.

28 *Ibid.*

29 Rod Millard, 'The Crusade for Science: Science and Technology on the Home Front, 1914–1918', in David MacKenzie (ed.), *Canada and the First World War: Essays in Honour of Robert Craig Brown* (Toronto: University of Toronto Press, 2005), p. 306. In South Africa a Council for Scientific and Industrial Research (CSIR) did not come into existence until 1945, but in New Zealand a Department of Scientific and Industrial Research (DSIR) was constituted in 1926. See Dubow, *A Commonwealth of Knowledge*, pp. 241–6; D. G. Kingwill, *The CSIR: The First 40 Years* (Pretoria: CSIR, 1990); Ross Galbreath, *DSIR: Making Science Work for New Zealand* (Wellington, NZ: Victoria University Press, 1998).

30 *History of the Ministry of Munitions*, vol. 2 (London: Ministry of Munitions, 1918–23), part 5 (India); part 4 (Canada), ch. 6, p. 49; Friedland, *The University of Toronto*, p. 262; 'Clara Cynthia Benson', *Fond Listings* (University of Toronto Archives and Records, 2011), accessed 29 Mar. 2011, http://utarms.library.utoronto.ca/researchers/fond-listings/clara-cynthia-benson; Frost, *McGill University for the Advancement of Learning: Vol. 2*, pp. 104–5.

31 *History of the Ministry of Munitions*, vol. 2, part 6, pp. 3, 9, 15. Melbourne's professor of natural philosophy, Thomas R. Lyle, sat on the Federal Munitions Committee and the Scientific Advisory Council, and also on the Naval Board, which had been founded before the war in 1911; the professor of engineering, Henry Payne, who had moved to Melbourne from the South African College in 1910, sat on the Australian Arsenal Committee; and the Engineering and Chemistry laboratory at the University of Sydney undertook chemical and physical tests on shells. In the end the production of munitions in Australia would prove limited.

32 For example, in Melbourne Frederick William Wheatley helped uncover the cypher key used in the German Pacific Squadron's encryptions, and W. A. Osborne and T. H. Laby designed a respirator (though it was never actually used). Robert Hyslop, 'Wheatley, Frederick William (1871–1955)', *Australian Dictionary of Biography* (Melbourne University Press, 1990) accessed 29 Mar. 2011, http://adbonline.anu.edu.au/biogs/A120507b.htm; Katrina Dean, 'Demonstrating the Melbourne University Respirator (Lessons Australia Learned from World War I)', *Australian Journal of Politics and History*, 53, no. 3 (2007): 392–406, pp. 397–402.

33 Girard, *A Strange and Formidable Weapon*, p. 83.

34 MacLeod, *Archibald Liversidge, FRS*, pp. 404–7.

35 R. W. Home, 'First Physicist of Australia: Richard Threlfall at the University of Sydney, 1886–1898', *Historical Records of Australian Science*, 6, no. 3 (1984): 333–357; R. W. Home, 'Threlfall, Sir Richard (1861–1932)', *Australian Dictionary of Biography*, accessed, http://adb.anu.edu.au/biography/threlfall-sir-richard-8802/text15437.

36 MacLeod, *Archibald Liversidge, FRS*, p. 404.

37 J. J. Thompson, 'Sir Richard Threlfall: 1861–1932', *Obituary Notices of Fellows of the Royal Society*, 1, no. 1 (1932): 45–53, p. 52.

38 For accounts of the chemical war see L.F. Haber, *The Poisonous Cloud: Chemical Warfare in the First World War* (Oxford: Clarendon Press, 1986); Roger Cooter, Mark Harrison and Steve Sturdy (eds), *War, Medicine and Modernity* (Phoenix Mill: Sutton Publishing, 1998); Trevor Williams, *The Chemical Industry in the First World War* (London: Penguin, 1953), pp. 69–87.

39 MacLeod, 'The Chemists Go to War', pp. 472–3.

40 James J. Dobbie, 'The Address of the Retiring President', *Proceedings of the Institute of Chemistry of Great Britain and Ireland*, no. 2 (1918): 25–42, p. 33.

41 For the cordite case see Henrik Schück and Ragnar Sohlman, *The Life of Alfred Nobel* (London: W. Heinemann, 1929), pp. 136–44. See also Appendix I: Alfred Nobel's English lawsuit. Mr Justice Romer's judgment in the "Cordite Case".

42 L. W. Weickhardt, "Leighton, Arthur Edgar (1873–1961)", *Australian Dictionary of Biography* (Melbourne University Press, 1986), accessed 2 Apr. 2012, http://adb.anu.edu.au/biography/leighton-arthur-edgar-7165/text12377.

43 *History of the Ministry of Munitions*, vol. 8, part 2, p. 74; C.S. Robinson, 'Kenneth

Bingham Quinan', *The Chemical Engineer*, no. 203 (1966): 290–7; Dick Dent, 'Famous Men Remembered', *The Chemical Engineer*, no. 431 (1986): 56–7. In 1915, J. A. Pease told the House of Commons there were no more than 225 graduate chemists working in British Industry, though these figures seem to have come from 1903. See Roy MacLeod, 'The "Arsenal" in the Strand: Australian Chemists and the British Munitions Effort 1916–1919', *Annals of Science*, 46, no. 1 (1989): 45–67, p. 55.

44 Leighton quoted in MacLeod, 'The "Arsenal" in the Strand', p. 57.

45 *Ibid.*, p. 55.

46 *Ibid.*, p. 48.

47 Fisher quoted in 'Science and Munitions of War', *Nature*, 95, no. 2386 (1915): 562–4.

48 Roy MacLeod, upon whose work this chapter draws heavily, has done the most to highlight the contribution of settler scientists to the war effort. His work over a number of decades has focused on the contributions, particularly of Australian scientists, to both the war effort and international science more broadly. See particularly MacLeod, 'The "Arsenal" in the Strand'; 'The Chemists Go to War'; 'The Scientists Go to War'.

49 For a general overview of the work on military geology in the First World War, see Peter Doyle, Matthew R. Bennett and Fiona M. Cocks, 'Geology and Warfare on the British Sector of the Western Front 1914–18', in Edward P. F. Rose and C. Paul Nathanail (eds), *Geology and Warfare: Examples of the Influence of Terrain and Geologists on Military Operations* (Bath: Geological Society, 2000).

50 Roy MacLeod, '"Kriegsgeologen and Practical Men": Military Geology and Modern Memory, 1914–18', *British Journal for the History of Science*, 28, no. 4 (1995): 427–50, pp. 429–30; F. W. Shotton, 'William Bernard Robinson King', *Biographical Memoirs of Fellows of the Royal Society*, 9 (1963): 171–82. As MacLeod points out, in April three geologists had be seconded from the Geological Survey to help find drinking water in Gallipoli, and at the same time R. W. Brock of the Canadian Geological Survey had been appointed to the Army in Palestine. See E. P. F. Rose and M. S. Rosenbaum, 'British Military Geologists: The Formative Years to the End of the First World War', *Proceedings of the Geologists' Association*, 104 (1993): 41–9.

51 David Branagan, 'David, Sir (Tannatt William) Edgeworth (1858–1934)', *Oxford Dictionary of National Biography* (Oxford University Press, 2004), accessed 25 Mar. 2011, http://217.169.56.137/view/article/32725.

52 Rose and Rosenbaum, 'British Military Geologists', p. 45; Doyle, Bennett and Cocks, 'Geology and Warfare', p. 114.

53 Rose and Rosenbaum, 'British Military Geologists', p. 45; David Branagan, *T. W. Edgeworth David: A Life* (Canberra: National Library of Canberra, 2005); Roy MacLeod, 'Phantom Soldiers: Australian Tunnellers on the Western Front, 1916–17', *Journal of the Australian War Memorial*, 13 (1988): 31–43; J. C. Neill (ed.), *The New Zealand Tunnelling Company 1915–1919* (Auckland: Whitcombe and Tombs, 1922). See also Anthony Byledbal, 'New Zealand Tunnellers Website' (2009), accessed 25 Mar. 2011, www.nztunnellers.com.

54 MacLeod, 'Phantom Soldiers', p. 34; W. Grant Grieve and Bernard Newman, *Tunnellers: The Story of the Tunnelling Companies, Royal Engineers During the World War* (London: H. Jenkins, 1936), pp. 6–7. For the story of the war underground see Peter Barton, Peter Doyle and Johan Vandewalle, *Beneath Flanders Fields: The Tunnellers War 1914–1918* (Staplehurst: Spellmount, 2004).

55 David Hannay, 'The Submarine – Menace or Bogey?', *Manchester Guardian*, 6 June 1914, p. 8.

56 Roy MacLeod and E. Kay Andrews, 'Scientific Advice in the War at Sea, 1915–1917: The Board of Invention and Research', *Journal of Contemporary History*, 6, no. 3 (1971): 3–40, pp. 18–19; Glen O'Hara, *Britain and the Sea since 1600* (Basingstoke: Palgrave Macmillan, 2010), p. 142.

57 Jenkin, *William and Lawrence Bragg, Father and Son*, pp. 153–5.

58 For accounts of anti-submarine research during the war see Willem Hackmann, *Seek and Strike: Sonar, Anti-Submarine Warfare and the Royal Navy, 1914–1954* (London: Her Majesty's Stationary Office, 1984); Willem Hackmann, 'Underwater Acoustics and the Royal Navy, 1893–1930', *Annals of Science*, 36, no. 3 (1979): 255–78;

J. Terraine, *Business in Great Waters: The U-Boat Wars, 1916–1945* (London: Cooper, 1989); J. K. Gusewelle, 'Science and the Admiralty During World War I: The Case of the BIR', in G. Jordan (ed.), *Naval Warfare in the Twentieth Century, 1900–1945: Essays in Honour of Arthur Marder* (London: Croom Helm, 1977).

59 Jenkin, *William and Lawrence Bragg, Father and Son*, p. 370.

60 MacLeod and Andrews, 'Scientific Advice in the War at Sea', pp. 21, 35.

61 Millard, 'The Crusade for Science', p. 303; Hackmann, *Seek and Strike*, p. xxv; Hackmann, 'Underwater Acoustics and the Royal Navy, 1893–1930', pp. 272–6.

62 Friedland, *The University of Toronto*, p. 259; Frost, *McGill University for the Advancement of Learning: Vol. 2*, p. 101; Hanaway, Cruess and Darragh, *McGill Medicine: 1885–1936*; Ian McGibbon and Paul Goldstone (eds), *The Oxford Companion to New Zealand Military History* (Auckland: Oxford University Press, 2000); W. P. Morrell, *The University of Otago, a Centennial History* (Dunedin: University of Otago Press, 1969), pp. 119–20. For medicine in the war, see Mark Harrison, *The Medical War: British Military Medicine in the First World War* (Oxford: Oxford University Press, 2010); Cooter, Harrison and Sturdy (eds), *War, Medicine and Modernity*.

63 Geoffrey Serle, 'Monash, Sir John (1865–1937)', *Australian Dictionary of Biography* (Melbourne University Press, 1986), accessed 29 Mar. 2011; R. F. Legget, 'Chalmers Jack Mackenzie: 10 July 1888 – 26 February 1984', *Biographical Memoirs of Fellows of the Royal Society*, 31 (1985): 410–34. For more on the settler academics' contribution, see *Yearbook of the Universities of the Empire, 1918–19*; Friedland, *The University of Toronto*, pp. 261–8; Wilfrid Egglestone, *Scientists at War* (Toronto: Oxford University Press, 1950); Selleck, *The Shop*, pp. 503–10.

64 On the importance of colonial encounter and exchange to the development of knowledge in Europe, see Mark Harrison, *Medicine in an Age of Commerce and Empire* (Oxford: Oxford University Press, 2010); Kapil Raj, *Relocating Modern Science: Circulation and the Construction of Knowledge in South Asia and Europe, 1650–1900* (Basingstoke: Palgrave Macmillan, 2007).

65 MacLeod, 'The Chemists Go to War', pp. 456, 455.

66 Charles Howard Foulkes, *Gas! The Story of the Special Brigade* (Edinburgh: W. Blackwood and Sons, 1934), p. 274. For discussion of the war as laboratory, see also Roy MacLeod, 'Sight and Sound on the Western Front: Surveyors, Scientists, and the Battlefield Laboratory: 1915–1918', *War and Society*, 18, no. 1 (2000): 26–46; Steve Sturdy, 'War as Experiment: Physiology, Innovation and Administration in Britain, 1914–1918: The Case of Chemical Warfare', in Roger Cooter, Mark Harrison, and Steve Sturdy (eds), *War, Medicine and Modernity* (Phoenix Mill: Sutton Publishing, 1998), p. 74.

67 Indeed, when the American geologists from Columbia arrived in 1918, they came as much to learn as to lend their expertise. MacLeod, 'Kriegsgeologen and Practical Men', pp. 440–1; MacLeod, 'Phantom Soldiers', p. 33; Doyle, Bennett and Cocks, 'Geology and Warfare', p. 114; Rose and Rosenbaum, 'British Military Geologists'; MacLeod, 'The "Arsenal" in the Strand', p. 61; Sturdy, 'War as Experiment', p. 72; Hanaway, Cruess and Darragh, *McGill Medicine: 1885–1936*, p. 235.

68 Peter Alter, *The Reluctant Patron: Science and the State in Britain, 1850–1920* (Oxford: Berg, 1987), pp. 221–31.

69 *Imperial Education Conference: Convened by the Chief of the Imperial General Staff, June 11–12, 1919* (London: His Majesty's Stationary Office, 1919), p. 4.

70 Courtice, 'Research in the Medical Sciences', pp. 290–1.

71 R. W. Home, 'The Royal Society and the Empire: The Colonial and Commonwealth Fellowship, Part 2: After 1847', *Notes and Records of the Royal Society of London*, 57, no. 1 (2003): 47–84, p. 60.

72 From Michael Bliss, *Banting: A Biography* (Toronto: McClelland and Stewart, 1984). Quoted in Donald Avery, *The Science of War: Canadian Scientists and Allied Military Technology* (Toronto: University of Toronto Press, 1998), p. 7, fn. 22.

73 MacLeod, 'The 'Arsenal' in the Strand', pp. 65–7. For the history of the University of Melbourne respirator – a largely unsuccessful gas mask developed by Laby among others – see Dean, 'Demonstrating the Melbourne University Respirator'.

74 Frost, *McGill University for the Advancement of Learning: Vol. 2*, p. 108. See also Chapter 8.

75 Dubow, *A Commonwealth of Knowledge*, pp. 199–202, 245–6.

76 Boucher, *The University of the Cape of Good Hope*, pp. 149–51, 177–8.

77 For other examples of the imperial vision of scientific and economic co-ordination in the interwar period, see Dean, 'Demonstrating the Melbourne University Respirator', 405–6; Barry Butcher, 'Science and the Imperial Vision: The Imperial Geophysical Experimental Survey, 1928–1930', *Historical Records of Australian Science*, 6, no. 1 (1984): 31–43; Ian M. Drummond, 'The Imperial Vision: Dream and Action in the Nineteen-Twenties', *British Economic Policy and the Empire, 1919–1939* (London: Allen and Unwin, 1972), pp. 36–88.

78 *Imperial Education Conference, 1919*, pp. 2–3.

79 *Ibid.*, p. 3.

80 UTA, *Office of the President*, A1967-0007/ box 62/'Canadians start Khaki University', *The Christian Science Monitor*, 2 May 1918.

81 The Carnegie Corporation funded the building and stocking of libraries at various camps, including that at Ruhleben enabling internees to work towards examinations of the University of London's external degree programme. Theodore Wesley Koch, *War Libraries and Allied Studies* (New York: G. E. Stechert and Co., 1918), pp. 7–9.

82 Tim Cook, 'From Destruction to Construction: The Khaki University of Canada, 1917–1919', *Journal of Canadian Studies*, 37, no. 1 (2002): 109–43; Frost, *McGill University for the Advancement of Learning: Vol. 2*, pp. 105–6.

83 A May 1918 report from the Khaki College at Shorncliffe, quoted in Cook, 'From Destruction to Construction', pp. 117–19.

84 *Ibid.* Frost puts the number placed in British universities at between four hundred and five hundred. Frost, *McGill University for the Advancement of Learning: Vol. 2*, 107. See also UTA, *Office of the President*, A1967-0007/62/329/'Khaki University of Canada, Report for the Rt Hon Sir Robert L Borden, Prime Minister of Canada, prepared by HM Tory'.

85 Turney, Bygott and Chippendale, *Australia's First*, p. 427.

86 *Ibid.*, p. 428.

87 *Imperial Education Conference, 1919*, p. 26.

88 *Ibid.*, pp. 13; 14.

89 'Report of the Senate, 1918', *Calendar of the University of Sydney* (Sydney: University of Sydney, 1919), p. 651.

90 *Yearbook of the Universities of the Empire, 1918–19*, p. 44.

91 Sanderson, *Universities and British Industry*, p. 239.

CHAPTER SEVEN

After the peace:
the Universities' Bureau and the
expansive nation

On 4 July 1921, the chancellors and rectors of the universities of the United Kingdom, together with delegates from their sister institutions across the empire, sat down to lunch at the Savoy Hotel. They were gathered in London to attend the second Congress of the Universities of the British Empire, scheduled to begin the following day in Oxford. Proposing the toast on behalf of the government, Arthur Balfour, the former Conservative Prime Minister and Foreign Secretary, reflected on the dramatic events that had elapsed in the nine years since the first congress had taken place in 1912:

> [There] have been crowded and compressed changes the magnitude of which no man living – none even of the learned thinkers whom it is my privilege to address – can as yet estimate ... The work of estimating its magnitude falls, and must fall inevitably, to the historian, and to him alone. But we can see quite plainly each one of us, within our own experience, how the world has been shaken by the vast catastrophe of the Great War.[1]

For the delegates, the universities seemed especially changed. In his opening address, Lord Curzon – at the time chancellor of the University of Oxford and British Foreign Secretary – went so far as to assert that no institutions had been 'more profoundly affected [by the war] than the older universities'. During the conflict they had been emptied; Oxford had become a 'quasi-military camp' and a hospital for the wounded; the pens of its writers turned to 'informing the public mind' and the brains of its 'men of science' directed to research. 'Can it be imagined,' asked Curzon, 'that four years of this experience did not leave an enduring impression both upon the life of the University and upon the mind of the State?'[2]

Yet at the same time as they noted the war's influence on Britain's universities, those who attended the 1921 Congress also argued that these were institutions that had a vital role to play in rebuilding the society the war had ravaged. In Curzon's words, it was 'not so much on paper conventions or signed documents, or even on political combinations', that they thought the future peace of the world would depend, but rather on the 'growing commerce of knowledge and ideas … the drawing together of the minds and consciences of educated and thoughtful men'.[3] Thus at the same time as the delegates struggled to come to terms with the immense social and cultural transformations wrought upon their own institutions, they also strove to find ways to heal the ruptures of the recent past. Exhausted by the conflict, to meet the challenges of the new era, they turned to structures and processes they had inherited from the old.

A changed academic landscape?

Even as the guns were still firing, commentators, politicians and university leaders alike were predicting that the war would reshape the world of British universities.[4] First, they anticipated that science would grow in importance; and second, they expected British networks to swing towards the United States. In the latter part of the war *Nature* magazine published several articles about the American system, and a number of academics and university administrators undertook investigative and promotional missions there.[5] The Great War did, as Peter Alter submits, make 'British science planners aware of the high standard of science in the United States and of its exemplary organisational forms'; and it did instigate a new and significant investment in scientific research. However, the war did not herald the unbridled turn to science and to America that both contemporaries and some historical accounts tend to suggest.[6]

Although the war had very much been a war of science, it had also been hugely destructive. In this context, the congress delegates saw the universities and the liberal education they traditionally offered as holding a renewed importance. At the 1921 meeting several speakers reasserted the value of the humanities and of a 'balanced education' in the face of the mechanised annihilation of so much human life. As the chancellor of the University of St Andrews suggested, 'all young men standing on the threshold of their careers in life', and especially those who would specialise in science or in business, needed the 'humanizing life of a University with its variety of individuals and interests and its broadening influence on the formation of character'.[7] In addition to 'pure classicism … knowingly utilized', a broad education that included economics, civics and politics was advocated by the Université de Montréal's Edouard Montpetit as that which would best 'produce educated citizens of an imperial democracy, fit for the duties of leadership in public life'.[8] Despite the significant expansion of scientific education and research, history and the social sciences also emerged as disciplines that, alongside those of the traditional liberal education, were seen as important for shaping citizens of both the nation and the empire.

Similarly, although closer relations between British, Dominion and United States universities did begin to be forged in the aftermath of the war, the universities in Britain also renewed their ties with the Dominions. As we have seen, the period witnessed not the redirection but instead the expansion of travelling scholarship schemes designed to carry settler graduates to the United Kingdom. The changing career profiles of professors appointed to the University of Manchester further illustrates the growing importance of the empire to universities in Great Britain in this period. As the oldest of the provincial universities in England, by 1919 Manchester was also one of the largest and, founded in the 1850s, it is broadly comparable to its contemporaries in the settler colonies. In the last two decades of the nineteenth century there was a significant European presence at Manchester and several European-born professors were appointed, particularly to teach language and science subjects. However, between 1900 and 1918 no European professors were recruited to Manchester's staff. Instead, several empire-born candidates were selected, and although Europeans began to appear again in the 1920s, they only came to outnumber the empire-born in the 1930s. Only one American professor was appointed across this whole period. Similarly, Manchester professors elected between 1900 and 1930 were more likely to have had imperial experience than they were to have had European or American experience. Although over thirty per cent of professorial appointments at the university had undertaken some study or work in the British Empire, only twenty per cent of Manchester professors appointed between 1919 and 1930 had European experience, and only ten per cent had experience in the United States.[9] These figures suggest that the decade after the Great War was one in which universities such as Manchester resumed the pre-war patterns and practices that linked them to the settler world. For many British academics the United States remained an alien land. Although the war piqued interest in its universities, the deep channels of affection and interest that linked universities in Britain with those in the settler colonies would not swiftly be abandoned.

The Bureau and the interwar congresses

This interwar regeneration of academic ties between Britain and the Dominions is reflected in the activities of the Universities' Bureau of the British Empire. It was the only existing association of universities in Britain at the end of the war, and both the government and the universities turned to it when they came together to plan for the peace. But central to the Bureau's activities in the 1920s and 1930s was an expansive understanding of the nation, carried over from the period of its Edwardian foundation. When the universities looked to the Bureau, they therefore looked to an organisation that understood itself in imperial terms. With its archives destroyed during Second World War bombing, the story of the Bureau has been neglected.[10] But its history is an important one because it highlights universities' expansive framing of the nation in this period: the Bureau and the universities believed that their contribution to rebuilding the war-torn nation lay not so much in improving access to higher education vertically among the people (student numbers in the UK rose by only 0.2 per cent between 1919 and 1939), but rather in extending it horizontally across the empire.[11]

The Bureau in the 1920s

The outbreak of war in 1914 seriously curtailed the Bureau's promising early growth. It limped through, however, sustained largely by the efforts of its honorary secretary, Alex Hill, who was also principal of the University College of Southampton. Seeing the opportunity presented by the universities' service during the war, in 1918 Donald MacAlister led the Bureau's committee in lobbying the government for funding. His efforts were successful, and in early 1919 the Board of Education made a one-off grant of £5,000 to the Bureau, subject to two conditions: first, that it become a corporation capable of holding property; and second, that it pay for its maintenance out of its own funds. With this much-needed financial injection, the Bureau sprang to new life. It was incorporated under the Companies Act and gained a constitution, established and then administered the UK Committee of Vice-Chancellors and Principals, purchased a ten-year lease on 50 Russell Square, and looked to its members – both in Britain and overseas – to fund its operational costs.[12] By 1919 Alex Hill could write, '[i]n a very much larger sense than heretofore the Bureau is now recognized by the Board of Education, the Treasury, the Foreign Office, and the other Government Departments as their medium of communication with the Universities.'[13] But despite this new role at home, the organisation's horizon continued to extend to the settler universities abroad.[14]

In fact, it was under the imperial auspices of the Bureau that the first official conference of universities in the United Kingdom took place. Held in May 1917, the meeting was concerned with a subject that had long been dear to settler universities – the British PhD.

Adjourning for a year to allow representatives to ascertain the views of their respective governing bodies, on the day before the conference was scheduled to reconvene, the delegates were summoned to see the Foreign Secretary, A. J. Balfour. As Renate Simpson has pointed out, at this meeting Balfour pressed upon British universities the need for the 'strengthening of post-graduate work and the institution of a PhD degree in order to divert to Britain the traffic in scholars and scientists [from the USA] which before the war had gone to Germany'.[15] But it is less often noted that when Balfour made this request, he also called for the establishment of a mechanism by which the universities could speak with one voice: he wanted to see extended 'the tentative efforts at common expression, which began in 1912 with the foundation of the Bureau'.[16] Thus, Balfour's attempt to forge closer relations with the United States through a British PhD was intimately tied to his desire to institutionalise imperial academic links at home.

When it came to formal co-operation, however, the universities were less than enthusiastic. They remained highly sceptical of anything that seemed to threaten their independence and this had significant consequences for the Bureau. Constrained by the universities' refusal to let it act on their behalf, the Bureau had little option but to resume its relatively uncontroversial pre-war task of distributing information. During the 1920s, in increasing quantities, it produced a steady flow of reports, booklets, surveys, programmes and circulars designed to facilitate unofficial rather than official co-ordination. These included 'lists of Students from abroad studying in the Home Universities', statements of the Bureau's accounts and minutes of its meetings, titles of theses approved for research degrees, proposals for graduate tours, and various agitations about ways to foster student exchange.[17] A large amount of data was procured for the annual *Yearbooks* and a flurry of consultative correspondence took place in the lead up to the congresses, which the Bureau continued to organise every five years.

Yet despite its best efforts, during the 1920s the Bureau struggled to win the confidence of many of its members. Its focus on fostering informal connections meant that the older settler universities in particular did not see it as essential. Replying in 1925 to a letter from the Bureau advertising its services as an employment and introduction agency, information centre and a 'firstrate club', the registrar of the University of Melbourne was clear about this.[18] After acknowledging that some of the members of his university 'from time to time call[ed] upon [the Bureau]', the registrar explained:

> This country [Australia] and this University in particular is not yet (and I hope never will be) very rigidly cut off from the Old country. Most of our Professors come from British Universities and have Home connections

so that when they go to England they do not go as strangers in a strange country.[19]

Indeed, in 1926, following a request from the Bureau for the university to increase its annual grant, the Melbourne registrar responded on behalf of the university council by reducing it to only £20 per year![20] Oxford and Cambridge, too, remained sceptical of the organisation's value: although the Bureau collated and disseminated information about admission, in 1928 Oxford still insisted on communicating directly with Dominion universities regarding entrance requirements.[21] Both in the United Kingdom and abroad, the more established universities preferred to continue with the informal practices they knew well. For them, the Bureau had been grafted onto an already existing system of personal exchange that was largely independent of its efforts and offices.

Moreover, the informal operational structure that had been the precondition for the Bureau's pre-war existence continued to influence its development after it. Administered by the proprietorial Alex Hill, throughout the 1920s the organisation laboured with too few employees in a dilapidated building at the Imperial Institute and struggled to manage the one task that was clearly its own: the dissemination of information.[22] Between 1921 and 1925 the Bureau only just broke even, and in 1926 it lost £400 on the distribution of the *Yearbooks* alone. Universities began to withdraw their support, with subscriptions declining from £2,776 in 1924–25, to between £2,169 and £2,483 in the years before 1929. As the Report for 1931 outlined, '[t]hese defects caused congestion and delays, discouraged initiative and rendered impossible the development of a coherent and purposeful policy'.[23]

The chaotic nature of the Bureau's operations was reflected in its organisational design. Although it had been incorporated under the Companies Act in 1919, the sub-committee convened that year to report on its aims and objectives had immediately became mired in conflict. Noting that the 'present machinery for managing the Bureau would be inadequate for the functions it would be called upon to perform', Ramsay Muir (a member of Sadler's Commission on Calcutta University) and Gregory Foster (the provost of University College London) recommended the establishment of a formally elected representative council to oversee its work and appoint its officers annually. But Alex Hill objected to these moves, accusing Muir of exceeding the terms of the sub-committee's reference. As Eric Ashby pointed out in 1963, 'one cannot help feeling that the technical objection covered a disinclination on Hill's part to see the Bureau become more formal and professionalized'.[24] For a time in 1920 there was suggestion that the Bureau should seek a Royal Charter, but this was resoundingly rejected by the member universities, and in the end the Articles of Association remained, although in amended form. Hill retained his ongoing role as secretary and the Bureau its loose and disordered character.[25]

The interwar period is sometimes seen as a time when British social and political life underwent various forms of bureaucratisation, rationalisation and professional organisation. But for the universities and for the Bureau, the decade after the Great War was one in which the informal, affective and de-centralised relationships of the pre-war period retained their primary importance. These relations were those of the generation of university men whose lives linked the Edwardian period with the 1920s. Shaken by the war, the universities and those who worked in them believed they could best contribute to the re-building of society by resuming the practices and the philosophy that had represented stability before it.

Reorganisation

It was only in the 1930s that the Bureau began to function effectively as a professional association that rationalised relations between universities. The death in 1929 of Alex Hill created an opportunity for reform, and Frank Heath, formerly secretary of the (British) DSIR, was appointed to review the Bureau's workings. Increasing the staff and doubling the annual expenditure, Heath also proposed constitutional changes that substituted the old Articles of Association under which the Bureau operated as an association of persons, with new ones that defined it as a 'world-wide association of corporate bodies – of Universities'.[26] He also put in place measures that ensured greater security of income, requiring a minimum subscription rate from each member institution. These reforms revived the organisation, and from the early 1930s universities and colleges from various parts of the Commonwealth began increasingly to use its services.

Scorned by the Melbourne registrar in 1925, the Bureau's appointments service witnessed particular growth. Initially it was the newer and smaller universities – some in the settler colonies but mostly those in India and the new University Colleges growing up in East Asia – who were the keenest. Without the connections to informal British academic world networks, they looked to more formal processes. For example, in 1932 the Bureau acted for Adelaide, Andhra, Bombay and Hong Kong universities, Auckland College, Canterbury College, and the Egyptian University in Cairo.[27] But increasingly the older settler institutions were also persuaded to use its appointments service. Although in 1932 Melbourne was still sceptical – 'I am afraid that we do not look upon our membership of the Bureau as being of very much practical use', wrote the Registrar – by 1933 both it and

Sydney were employing Heath on a trial basis to chair their selection committees.[28] From the mid-1930s the Bureau offered a more professional – and cheaper – appointments service than could committees of selection constituted through individual university networks. By 1933 it could report that '[u]niversities overseas are enlisting the services of the Bureau more and more in filling vacant appointments'.[29]

The growing popularity of the Bureau's formal structures did not, however, diminish the importance of informal connections to settler universities. If the Bureau served to centralise some of these networks, it did not displace them. Canadian institutions continued to rely on personal correspondence, and the Australian universities remained convinced of their need to, in the words of Melbourne's vice-chancellor, Raymond Priestley, 'keep close touch ... with the right sort of Heads of Departments at Oxford, Cambridge or London, who have some personal interest in our own University'.[30] Better run and better resourced, it was under Heath in the 1930s that the Bureau came to function much more effectively as the central 'clearing house' it had always aspired to be.

The Bureau's standing with its member universities was also enhanced by its management of the grant made by the Carnegie Corporation of New York in 1930, the terms of which stipulated only that the sum of $40,000 should 'be expended for the benefit of Empire Universities Overseas'.[31] After spending some of this money to enable settler and Indian delegates to attend the 1931 Congress, the Bureau determined that the balance should be used to permit 'selected members of the teaching and administrative staffs of oversea universities' to visit the United Kingdom for the purpose of advanced study or research work. Bringing such individuals 'into personal contact with each other' would, the Bureau felt, 'promote closer cooperation between the oversea and the home universities'.[32]

Leaving universities to choose their own candidates, and regional conferences to put forward a handful of nominees, the executive committee of the Bureau selected a final three scholars from the total nominations they received. The scheme was repeated annually between 1932 and 1936 and proved hugely attractive to academics working in the Dominions. In fact, the Australian Conference found having to make a selection from among their own number 'a very awkward and invidious task' and sought to divest themselves of this responsibility: 'it is rather like throwing a bone amongst a lot of hungry dogs', wrote the University of Western Australia's Hubert Whitfeld to the Melbourne Registrar in 1933.[33] They wished instead for a system of *greater* centralisation – proposing that each university should forward its first choice to the Bureau, which would then choose among these institutional nominations. Together with Heath's reforms, the management of the Carnegie Grants helped raise the Bureau's profile in the eyes of its member institutions. In offering the possibility of tangible benefits it provided an incentive for universities abroad to begin to utilise the Bureau's other services as well, marking a significant shift in its character.

Specialisation and interchange

Yet even as it professionalised, the Bureau remained faithful to its original mission of fostering the informal and personal connections that underwrote the British academic world. This is evident in its focus throughout the 1920s and 1930s on the entwined issues of specialisation and interchange.

Although 'specialisation' had been discussed at both conferences held before the war, it received a renewed impetus afterwards. The Bureau's stance on the subject was articulated clearly by Robert Stout, the vice-chancellor of the University of New Zealand: 'if you desire economy you must specialize in education. You cannot expect each University to undertake to teach all the subjects required for professional and industrial training.'[34] Public money and post-war austerity, so the argument went, meant that each university needed to maximise its 'efficiency' – a word that rebounded in discussions throughout the period – by specialising in a particular set of subjects which built upon what Lord Crewe called 'its local advantages': the natural, industrial or professional character of the region in which it was located.[35] H. A. L. Fisher argued in 1922,

> [t]he expense of University education has become so great and the development of applied science ... has now reached such a point that I feel it is quite impossible for the nation, as a whole, to advance unless there is a much higher degree of co-operation between Universities in respect to the distribution of studies.[36]

These arguments were not just taken up by scientists. They also proved a boon to men like L. R. Farnell who wanted to protect the classical curriculum and privileges of Oxford and Cambridge. 'Must there not be some distribution of functions,' he asked, 'not only as between the old Universities and the new, but between the one or two old Universities and many of the new?'[37]

As far as the Bureau was concerned, the 'nation, as a whole' included the British settler colonies, and therefore the 'distribution of studies' should encompass colonial universities as well. '[T]he overseas Universities', wrote Alex Hill to Bureau members in 1922, quoting the Liberal politician and historian James Bryce's comments at the 1912

Congress, 'offer special opportunities of studying certain branches of applied science, such, for example, as mining and forestry.'[38] Repeatedly placing specialisation on the agendas of the newly instituted annual conferences of the universities of Great Britain and Ireland, as well as on the programmes of the congress meetings, the Bureau also attempted to push the issue via an empire-wide information campaign. Beginning in 1922, it prepared annually a detailed report on the 'Distribution of Subjects of Study to which exceptional attention is given in certain of the Universities and University Colleges of the United Kingdom'.[39] From 1926 this summary was expanded to include the specialist studies of the 'Universities in the Dominions Overseas'.[40] It was by using the dispersed educational resources of the British universities abroad as well as those in the United Kingdom that the Universities' Bureau thought the nation might most efficiently be served.

Yet for all its seeming virtues, this idea of institutional specialisation raised two major stumbling blocks. The first had been identified long before the war, when the issue had initially been raised at the 1903 Allied Colonial Universities Conference. It concerned the problems of co-ordination between autonomous universities. Despite Bryce's protestations that there was 'no idea present to the mind of any one of us of attempting in any way to circumscribe or to override the independence of each university', a rationalised system of specialisation nonetheless implied an erosion of sovereignty that the universities were not prepared to countenance.[41] The second problem involved the mutual recognition of matriculation examinations; something was needed to facilitate the movement of undergraduates from one institution to another. The debate split between the empire-wide standard desired by settler universities and the older system of bilateral accreditation preferred by universities such as Oxford and Cambridge. But as the 1920s progressed, and the newly instituted British PhD began to take hold, the issue of student interchange increasingly came to be seen in terms of graduate rather than undergraduate study. Sir Thomas Holland, principal of the University of Edinburgh, gave expression to this at the 1931 Congress:

> I feel sure that undergraduates ought not come [to Britain] at all except from those areas in which there are no existing native Universities. The position of the post-graduate student creates a wholly different picture. His movement from one University to another, whether within or without Great Britain, is an advantage to him and an advantage to us, and that has nothing to do with the University but with the individual specialist of repute under whom he goes to study.[42]

Therefore, while 'specialisation' never dropped off the congresses' programmes or the Bureau's radar, the meaning of the term changed significantly. By the late 1920s the emphasis had shifted from the institution to the individual: 'specialisation' was used to refer less to the institutional 'distribution of studies', and more to the newly valued specialised knowledge of individual researchers.

The Bureau's commitment to specialisation in both these forms complemented its long-held aim of fostering bonds of connection by facilitating the movement of staff and students. As the University of London's representative at the 1936 Congress, Lord MacMillan, argued, as 'a man' moved from one university to another seeking specialised teaching, 'he would acquire new loyalties [and] ... he would form new friendships'.[43] And while scholarships were thought to enable student 'interchange', various schemes were proposed to improve the mobility of staff. In 1921 Sydney's H. S. Carslaw suggested the institution of an imperial system of sabbatical leave; in 1926 Sheffield's W. M. Gibbons focused on an empire-wide Federated Superannuation Scheme; and in 1936 the Bureau established a special committee 'to inquire into the possibility of effecting the exchange of members of University Teaching Staffs'.[44] Neither was the Bureau inactive between congresses: in 1922 it appointed 'interchange correspondents' in each university, and by 1927 it could report that it had 'arranged for the temporary exchange of junior posts between teachers in Great Britain and teachers in the Dominions'.[45]

Indeed, the quinquennial congresses themselves were as much occasions at which senior academics from across the empire could come together as they were opportunities for the formal exchange of ideas. As A. C. Seward, the vice-chancellor of the University of Cambridge, noted in the closing session of the 1926 meeting, 'the great advantage of a congress is not so much what one gets from listening to discussions but from the personal contact between the members'.[46] Each event was accompanied by social events, official dinners, honorary degree ceremonies, train journeys and university tours that afforded every opportunity for delegates to forge and foster relations with each other. Therefore, at the same time as they sought to formalise and describe the personal connections that wrapped up the British academic world, through their emphasis upon interchange and as events in themselves the congresses also worked to reinscribe and extend these ties.

Internationalism

At the 1921 Congress, Curzon had thought that the Bureau would help draw 'closer the bonds of the British Empire,' but he also hoped it might 'aspire to a wider and more cosmopolitan range of influence'. As it drew 'within its orbit the educated intelligence of other countries, and notably of America', Curzon hoped the Bureau and the congress meeting might 'exercise an appreciable influence on the peace of the world'.[47] Lord Robert Cecil, the chancellor of the University of Birmingham and one of the architects of the League of Nations, was similarly minded: 'Learning has no territorial boundaries; ... Learning is one of the great unifying forces of the world, and we have now, more than at any other time in our lives, a further opportunity to demonstrate this.'[48] The interwar congresses and the Bureau embraced this new language of internationalism. Delegates discussed the need to extend interchange programmes to France and the United States as well as Dominions (though notably not to Germany). American as well as French representatives attended the quinquennial meetings, and throughout the 1920s the Bureau rented rooms in its premises at 50 Russell Square to the American University Union in Europe, the Harkness Foundation, the Office National des Universités et Ecoles Françaises, and the British Bureau of the Danish Student's International Committee.[49]

Yet despite this engagement, delegates were clear that the Bureau's internationalism remained underpinned by the notion of an expansive British community. McGill's Ira McKay made this clear in 1926, when he proclaimed that although he had 'never known two nations to love one another', the British Empire was in his opinion an exception:

> because, after all, there is a great mass weight of friendship between the people of the overseas Dominions and the people of the Motherland, and between the people of the Motherland and those of the Dominions.... Here, then, is a great mass weight of human material out of which we may carve a new contribution to human history if only we have the courage, the knowledge, and the skill to do it.[50]

As far as the Bureau was concerned, it was as an embodiment of a unique kind of political and educational community – one that stretched between Britain and the Dominions – that the British universities' contribution to the new international world order would be made. Indeed, when the League of Nations' Committee on Intellectual Co-operation was established in 1922, it was the imperially framed Bureau rather than associations from the various Dominions that represented British and settler universities.[51] Many of the delegates who attended the interwar congresses preached a version of the 'imperial internationalism' that Mark Mazower has argued underpinned the early history of the League.[52] For them, the new internationalism grew out of – and complemented – the expansive British community that had preceded it.

Moreover, the interwar congresses were underpinned by chauvinist conceptions of civilisational and race difference that Mazower suggests were foundational for the League. At the congresses the place of the Indian delegates in particular was a fraught one. The official rhetoric of the meetings extended to all the universities of the British Empire. As Sir Deva Prasad Sarvadhikari from Benares noted, the 1921 Congress 'differ[ed] from the last,' because at it the Indian universities for the first time enjoyed 'all the advantage of corporate life'.[53] Congress discussions after 1926 were characterised less by overt references to 'racial unity' and more by coded celebrations of apparently 'shared' cultural norms such as law and literature, history, 'common ideals' and mutual loyalty. This discursive shift, however, is indicative of the extent to which the Indian universities were merely grafted onto an older imagining of a socially and racially circumscribed British academic world. The words of the Rev. Dr Scott Lidgett, vice-chancellor of the University of London, in 1931 are revealing. In hoping that 'the friendly and intimate conversations which we shall be privileged to hold during the coming days [with the Indian delegates] may do something real, if not startling, to bring us together in a common mind and a common purpose', Lidgett at once highlighted the sociable character of the imperial academic community, and the Indian universities' exclusion from it.[54]

This marginalisation was reinforced by congress programmes that did little to address the experience or issues of Indians. As Professor J. Mitter from Allahabad noted in 1936, 'it was the Dominions which were chiefly referred to and ... India unfortunately seemed to take a very back place'.[55] The 1931 plea of Aligarh's representative, Fakhruddin Ahmad, that the Bureau should give 'greater attention to the discussion of the Indian University problems and their solution, so that the much desired end of closer co-operation and understanding with Indians may be more rapidly and surely attained', went unheeded.[56] The interwar congresses therefore exhibited the contradictory language and the 'durability of British ideas of "racial" hierarchy' that Daniel Stephen has argued were similarly evident in other aspects of British imperial culture in this period.[57] Although the professional activities of the Bureau were officially extended to India, in this period the 'British' character of the community the Bureau had originally been designed to foster was not fundamentally reimagined.

In fact, even as committees of vice-chancellors and principals met with increasing frequency in Britain, and even as national conferences in the Dominions assumed more active roles, universities and those who worked in them asserted the ongoing importance of the expansive British academic community. Cherishing the links that bound universities together would only become more desirable, argued Donald MacAlister at the 1931 Congress, '[a]s the nations of the British Commonwealth bec[a]me more and more politically autonomous'.[58] Indeed, for many at the 1936 Congress, in the shadow of another war, the unity of the British academic world seemed an urgent necessity. 'In these days of peril,' contended the University of Sydney's Percival Halse Rogers, 'the co-operation of various parts of the Empire is more than ever essential': '[d]angers threaten on every hand, and unity is our only safeguard.'[59]

—◆—

Despite the appearance of alternative political currents that were beginning to frame new national and international alliances in the years between the wars, it was an older vision of the British academic world that remained central to the Bureau's sense of itself and its role in this period. This vision was at once centrifugal and centripetal. It looked out to the universities of the settler world and sought to foster de-centralised and informal connections between them, while at the same time it also strove to incorporate the various strengths of these institutions and to systematise their relations with each other. The tension the Bureau maintained between these two impulses suited most of its members. It enabled the older English universities to maintain their privileged positions as institutions that had long cultivated their own relationships with Whitehall, and it permitted the more established settler universities to continue to rely on the long-distance informal ties that had, if anything, been strengthened by the conflict.

For historians attempting to estimate the 'magnitude' of the changes the Great War brought to British society, the history of the Bureau is revealing. It complicates the story of the interwar period as a time in which British culture was steadily Americanised; it points to the imperial framings that conditioned contemporary languages of internationalism; and it highlights the older forms of informal association that persisted within new organisational structures.[60] But above all, the history of the Bureau shows that it was not a local and democratised conception of the British nation that animated universities in this period, but rather an expansive and affective one that stretched out to include the Dominions. Offering familiarity in times of uncertainty, this broad national framing was a means by which the Bureau and its member universities reproduced in the 1920s and 1930s the structures and orientations that had shaped British and settler academia since the 1880s.

Notes

1 *Second Congress Proceedings, 1921*, p. xviii. Sections of this chapter were previously published in Tamson Pietsch, '"Mending a Broken World": The Universities and the Nation, 1918–36', in L. Beers and G. Thomas (eds), *Brave New World: Imperial and Democratic Nation–Building in Britain between the Wars* (London: Institute of Historical Research, 2012), pp. 161–80.

2 *Second Congress Proceedings, 1921*, p. 4.

3 *Ibid.*, p. 6.

4 See Lawrence Badash, 'British and American Views of the German Menace in World War I', *Notes and Records of the Royal Society of London*, 34 (1979–80): 91–121.

5 For example, see 'Research Institutions in the United States', *Nature*, 99, no. 2483 (1917); 'Industrial Research in the United States', *Nature*, 97, no. 4727 (1916); 'The National Research Council of the United States', *Nature*, 97, no. 2440 (1916). An official British 'universities mission' to America was undertaken in the winter of 1918 by Bryce, Rutherford, Balfour and Holme, among others.

6 Alter, *The Reluctant Patron*, p. 200. See also Joseph Ben-David, *The Scientist's Role in Society: A Comparative Study* (Edgewood Cliffs, NJ: Prentice-Hall, 1971); Kevles, 'Into Hostile Political Camps', pp. 47–60; Schroeder-Gudehus, 'Challenge to Transnational Loyalties: International Scientific Organisation after the First World War', *Science Studies*, 3 (1973): 93–118; Zuoyue Wang, 'The First World War, Academic Science, and The "Two Cultures": Educational Reforms at the University of Cambridge', *Minerva*, 33 (1995): 107–27.

7 Lord Balfour of Burleigh in *Second Congress Proceedings, 1921*, p. 239.

8 Edouard Montpetit in *Ibid.*, pp. 78–9.

9 Pietsch, 'Wandering Scholars?', p. 384.

10 For an analysis of the Bureau between the wars see Pietsch, 'Mending a Broken World', pp. 161–80.

11 McKibbin, *Classes and Cultures*, p. 248; see also A. H. Halsey, 'Oxford and the British universities' in Harrison, *History of the University of Oxford, Vol. 8*, pp. 577–606.

12 Ashby, *Community of Universities*, pp. 10–16, 23–6.

13 UMA, *Registrar's Correspondence*, UM312 UM312/1920/444/Hill to the Melbourne Registrar, 22 Nov. 1919.

14 USA, *Registrar's General Subject Files*, G3/13/723/'The Universities of the British Empire Memorandum and Articles of Association, 1921'.

15 Renate Simpson, *How the PhD Came to Britain* (Guildford: Society for Research into Higher Education, 1983).

16 Balfour quoted in Ashby, *Community of Universities*, pp. 21–2. See also *Yearbook of the Universities of the British Empire, 1918–19*, p. 6.

17 UMA, *Registrar's Correspondence*, UMA312/1921/482/Hill to the Melbourne Registrar, 19 July 1921; UM312/1927/557/Hill to the Melbourne Registrar, 11 Nov. 1926; UM312/1927/557/'Secretary's report of a meeting of the Standing Committee of Vice-Chancellors and Principals held at Russell Square, Sat 24th 1927'.

18 *Ibid.*, UM312/1924/503/Letter from Alex Hill to the Registrar, 30 July 1925.

19 *Ibid.*, UM312/1925/503/Melbourne Registrar to Alex Hill at the British Empire Universities' Bureau, 9 Oct. 1925.

20 *Ibid.*, UM312/1926/535/Melbourne Registrar to Bureau Treasurer, 29 Oct. 1926.

21 *Ibid.*, UM312/1928/176/Conference of Australian Universities, Aug. 1928.

22 Ashby, *Community of Universities*, p. 32.

23 *Ibid.*, p. 103; UMA, *Registrar's Correspondence*, UM312/1926/535/Melbourne Registrar to Bureau Treasurer, 29 Oct. 1926; *Fourth Congress of the Universities of the Empire, 1931: Report of Proceedings* (London: G. Bell and Sons, 1931), pp. 261, 251.

24 Ashby, *Community of Universities*, pp. 28–9.

25 USA, *Registrar's General Subject Files*, G3/13/723/'The Universities of the British Empire Memorandum and Articles of Association, 1921'; *Second Congress Proceedings, 1921*, p. 434.

26 Ashby, *Community of Universities*, pp. 34–5; *Fourth Congress Proceedings, 1931*,

p. 213.
27 UMA, *Registrar's Correspondence*, UM312/1933/403/'Report of the Executive Council and Accounts of the Bureau for the year 1 August 1932 – 31 Jul. 1933.
28 *Ibid.*, UM312/1933/403/Melbourne Registrar to the Bureau, 15 Nov. 1933
29 *Ibid.*, UM312/1933/403/'Report of the Executive Council and Accounts of the Bureau for the year 1 Aug. 1932 – 31 Jul. 1933.
30 *Ibid.*, UM312/1935/415/Universities Bureau General matters, Bainbridge to Priestley, 22 Aug. 1934; Priestley (in Cambridge) to Bainbridge (Melbourne Registrar), 25 Sept. 1934.
31 'Empire Universities Carnegie Research Grants', *The Times*, 6 June, 1932, p. 7.
32 *Ibid.*
33 UMA, *Registrar's Correspondence*, UM312/1933/403/Registrar, University of Western Australia, to Melbourne Registrar, 1 Dec. 1933.
34 *Second Congress Proceedings, 1921*, p. 292.
35 *Ibid.*, p. 187.
36 USA, *Registrar's General Subject Files*, G3/13/723/'Annual Conference of the Universities of Great Britain & Ireland 1922 Abridged Report of Proceedings'
37 *Second Congress Proceedings, 1921*, p. 329.
38 USA, *Registrar's General Subject Files*, G3/13/723/'Minutes of a Meeting of the Interchange Committee of the Bureau held May 12, 1922'.
39 *Ibid.*, G3/13/723/'Copy of Draft report listing the Distribution of Groups of Subjects in the Universities and University Colleges of the United Kingdom'.
40 UMA, *Registrar's Correspondence*, UM312/1927/556/Hill to the Melbourne Registrar, 5 Mar. 1926.
41 'Official Report of the Allied Colonial Universities Conference', p. 77.
42 Holland in *Fourth Congress Proceedings, 1931*, p. 181.
43 *Ibid.*, p. 43.
44 *Second Congress Proceedings, 1921*, pp. 388–92; W. M. Gibbons (University of Sheffield, Secretary to the Federated Superannuation Scheme for Universities) in *Third Congress of the Universities of the Empire, 1926: Report of Proceedings*, ed. Alex Hill (London: G. Bell and Sons, 1926), p. 244; *Fifth Quinquennial Congress of the Universities of the British Empire, 1936: Report of Proceedings* (London: G. Bell and Sons, 1936), p. 230.
45 UMA, *Registrar's Correspondence*, UM312/1927/558/'Bureau Committee's Report to the recent Congress'.
46 *Third Congress Proceedings, 1926*, p. 261.
47 Curzon in *Ibid.*, p. 6.
48 *Ibid.*, p. 336.
49 Ashby, *Community of Universities*, p. 33.
50 *Third Congress Proceedings, 1926*, p. 36.
51 *Ibid.*, p. 270. For the Committee on Intellectual Co-operation and other international organisations, see Daniel Laqua, 'Transnational Intellectual Cooperation, the League of Nations, and the Problem of Order', *Journal of Global History*, 6, no. 2 (2011): 226–47; Christophe Charle, Jürgen Schriewer and Peter Wagner, *Transnational Intellectual Networks: Forms of Academic Knowledge and the Search for Cultural Identities* (Frankfurt: Campus, 2004); Emma Rothschild, 'Arcs of Ideas: International History and Intellectual History', in Gunilla Budde, Sebastian Conrad and Oliver Janz (eds), *Transnationale Geschichte: Themen, Tendenzen Und Theorien* (Göttingen: Vandenhoeck and Ruprecht, 2006), pp. 217–26.
52 Mark Mazower, *No Enchanted Palace: The End of Empire and the Ideological Origins of the United Nations* (Princeton, NJ: Princeton University Press, 2009).
53 *Second Congress Proceedings, 1921*, p. 420.
54 *Fourth Congress Proceedings, 1931*, p. 4.
55 *Fifth Congress Proceedings, 1936*, p. 64.
56 *Fourth Congress Proceedings, 1931*, p. 212.
57 Daniel M. Stephen, '"Brothers of the Empire?": India and the British Empire Exhibition of 1924–25', *Twentieth Century British History*, 22, no. 2 (2011): 164–88, p. 167. For race relations in the interwar period see also Frank Füredi, *The Silent*

War: Imperialism and the Changing Perception of Race (London: Pluto, 1998); Laura Tabili, *We Ask for British Justice: Workers and Racial Difference in Late Imperial Britain* (Ithaca: Cornell University Press, 1994).

58 *Fourth Congress Proceedings, 1931*, p. 154.

59 Halse Rogers (Judge of the Supreme Court of New South Wales and Chancellor of the University of Sydney) in *Ibid.*, p. 255.

60 *Second Congress Proceedings, 1921*, p. xviii.

PART IV

Erosions, 1919–60s

CHAPTER EIGHT

Alternative ties:
national and international forces

In August 1944, Ernest Holme, the retired professor of English at the University of Sydney, wrote to his old friend, J. T. Wilson, emeritus professor of anatomy at Cambridge. Wilson and Holme had been colleagues at Sydney between 1880 and 1920 and they had corresponded with each other for most of their lives. At the end of his career, Holme lamented the changes he perceived to be at play in their old university:

> Development can proceed too quickly. Money can be provided too lavishly. Educational change can be too comprehensive. That is what has happened under the new system of control and under political influence, also under the excitements and special necessities of war time. An American influence is also operating and the whole complex is not likely to be helpful. People like yourself and [Edgeworth] David and [Mungo] MacCallum and [Frederick Augustus] Todd belong to a period of our history that has closed and will never recur.[1]

Tinged with nostalgia, Holme's letter nonetheless points to the changes – complex new forms of administration, the expanding interest of the state, a growing American influence, and a shift in the nature of appointments – that by the 1940s were reshaping the universities of the British academic world. Although they gathered pace in the post-war period, many of these changes began in the decades between the wars. This was a time in which academics continued to tread the scholarly routes laid down in the late nineteenth century, but it was also a period which witnessed the appearance of alternative academic ties that first supplemented, and then supplanted, the networks on which the British academic world depended. The old connections did not disappear, but increasingly they came to be set in the context of national and international forces that altered their meanings and tempered their influence.

American encroachment

The networks that mapped the British academic world largely excluded Americans. As we have seen, academics born in the United States were only rarely appointed to university posts in the United Kingdom and the Dominions. Although the Australian universities began to bring out visiting American lecturers in the early 1920s and in the same decade South Africans began to go to the United States on funded visits, settler graduates from Australia, New Zealand and South Africa still predominantly used travelling scholarships to study in Britain, and professors also overwhelmingly took their leave of absence there.[2] Canada was the exception. Since the end of the nineteenth century Canadian scholars had been going to the United States in significant numbers to undertake research degrees, and a good number had been recruited back as professors: from the 1880s, approximately thirty per cent of the Toronto professoriate had had some kind of study or work experience in the United States.[3] Closer to the United States, Canadian professors caught the train south to New York and Boston to work in libraries and attend American academic conferences. In fact, from 1912, Toronto began to award small grants to cover the expenses of senior faculty members wishing to conduct academic business in the United States.[4] These movements opened up an alternative axis of connection for Canadian academics and universities.

But it was not only Canadians who drifted south. In the first decade of the twentieth-century, American institutions also began to reach north. As early as 1906, the Trustees of the Carnegie Foundation for the Advancement of Teaching in New York considered admitting the Universities of Toronto and McGill to the list of accredited institutions entitled to share in the Foundation's pension scheme, and two years later both were incorporated, to the 'great relief' of many Canadian professors thinking about retirement with additional Canadian educational institutions following in 1915.[5] This move stimulated other kinds of engagement between Canadian and American universities, one of which was the proposal of the Canadian-born president of Cornell, J. G. Schurman, that both Toronto and McGill should be admitted into the Association of American Universities.[6]

But with this incorporation of Canadian universities into aspects of American academic organisation also came American attempts to rationalise, professionalise and influence the development of Canadian university practice. To some extent Canadian university leaders found this convenient. The need to provide the Carnegie Foundation with extensive information about his university's practices spurred Toronto's president, Robert Falconer, to begin his own data-gathering exercises. He commissioned committees to source information and wrote personally to the presidents of the major American universities, soliciting details of their policies and gathering data on issues including sabbatical leave, state funding, alumni relations and student fees.[7] Falconer compiled this information into tables that placed Canadian institutions alongside those in the United States. Not only did he submit these to the Carnegie Foundation, but he also used them as tools in his drive to reform the University of Toronto and renegotiate its relationship with the Provincial Ontario government.

In other ways, however, Canadian universities resisted the Carnegie Foundation's early attempts to influence them. The long-running debate between Falconer and the Foundation over academic 'terminology' provides a good example.[8] At the start of the century Canada shared the British system of academic nomenclature, whereas American universities employed an entirely different system adapted from the German one. If academics from Canadian universities were to be incorporated into the American pension scheme, the Foundation would have to work out how to equate the two. But this was not as easy as it at first seemed. Falconer claimed that the British position of 'lecturer' was equivalent to the American position of 'assistant professor', but the Foundation's president, Henry S. Pritchett, was reluctant to accept this argument because in the United States a 'lecturer's' duties were similar to those undertaken in Britain by demonstrators or instructors.[9] However Falconer could not assent to a simple equation between the US 'lecturer' and the British 'demonstrator' because in some subjects in the British system the term 'demonstrator' was used synonymously with that of 'lecturer': 'two of our staff in Physics are called demonstrators,' he explained, 'but have drawn salaries that run up as far as two thousand dollars'. Refusing to accept Falconer's assurances about the seniority of his own staff, Pritchett wanted to establish a framework rigidly defined by the degree standard, age and salary designations of academics in the United States.[10] Indeed, in 1917 he even went so far as to suggest that, in the interests of 'a uniform system of designating the instructing staff', the Canadian Universities should 'discontinue the use of the term [lecturer]' altogether.[11] His dispute with Falconer was not just a difference of opinion about terminology. Rather, it was a fight about to which academic system the Canadian universities were to belong. This was a question that in this period was never really officially settled. Although attracted to the resources, opportunities and some aspects of the professionalism of universities in the United States, throughout the interwar period universities in Canada remained wary of American encroachment and consciously strove to preserve their 'British' character.[12]

These early American efforts to influence Canadian universities were extended to other parts of the British world in the period after the Great War. For at the same time as the conflict brought British universities into contact with the United States, it also made Americans and American organisations much more aware of the British scene. If Arthur Balfour's 1917 British university delegation to the United States in one sense signalled the British discovery of American universities, then it also highlighted what Balfour described as the *American* desire for the 'British Universities to take a more active share in the postgraduate work of American students'.[13] In the interwar period, American institutions and organisations can be seen exploiting the avenues opened up by the conflict and making inroads into an academic world that had previously been closed to them.

The new language of 'internationalism' provided one conduit for American educationalists. During the war, American bodies had developed a number of initiatives that – much like the Khaki University of Canada – aimed 'to minister to the College men in the American Expeditionary Force'.[14] During the war these various agencies were grouped together in Paris as the 'American University Union in Europe', and in 1920 it reorganised and shifted to London. The American University Union brought under its umbrella the American Council of Education, the Institute of International Education, the Association of American Colleges, and the American Association of University Professors. Renting premises from the Universities' Bureau at 50 Russell Square in London, it undertook the task of co-ordinating the 'between twenty and thirty great agencies in the United States … engaged in the work of interchange of students and interchange of professors'. This was an undertaking that the director of the Union, George E. MacLean, saw as intimately tied up with 'the new era of internationalism'.[15] To him, the 'labour of uniting into still closer unity and understanding the English-speaking peoples' represented 'the anchor to the windward for the storm-tossed League of Nations'.[16] In the name of internationalism, American academics and institutions sought to renegotiate the relationship between their universities and those in the British sphere. Professional bodies played some role in this: in 1929, for example, at exactly the same time as the Bureau was refashioning its appointments service, the American Association of University Professors wrote to Canadian universities also offering to help in the making of academic appointments.[17] However, it was American philanthropy that most explicitly sought to infiltrate and reform British academic practices.[18]

Two philanthropic foundations were particularly important: the Carnegie Corporation and the Rockefeller Foundation. Believing that 'the duty of the man of Wealth' was to create opportunities for 'those who will help themselves' by providing 'the ladders upon which the aspiring can rise', from the 1870s until 1914 the Scottish-born American industrialist Andrew Carnegie had made numerous endowments to support education.[19] Among the largest of these was the Carnegie Foundation for the Advancement of Teaching (1905), mentioned above, and the Carnegie Corporation of New York (1911). Other benefactions dedicated funds to the promotion of international co-operation and world peace, and this agenda often dovetailed – both implicitly and explicitly – with Carnegie's educational one. Following Carnegie, and influenced by his 1889 essay on philanthropy, in 1909 the American oil magnate John D. Rockefeller also established a foundation, giving 50 million dollars' worth of Standard Oil shares 'to promote the well-being of mankind throughout the world'. Granted a charter in 1913, the Rockefeller Foundation had an overtly global focus and directed its energies to the support of education and research in fields that included medicine, the social sciences and international relations.[20] Through conditional grant-making, and by emphasising efficiency, sustainability and governance, these American philanthropic organisations sought to 'modernise' the practices and the proclivities of universities and academics in the English-speaking world.[21]

The Rockefeller bequest to support medical research at the University of Toronto is a case in point.[22] At the end of 1919, Rockefeller made a large gift to his Foundation for the promotion of medical education and public health, expressing the desire that the medical schools in Canada should receive some support and highlighting in particular their wartime work.[23] Influenced by the 1910 report of Abraham Flexner into medical education in North America, and following the investigative tour of two Foundation representatives in 1919 (one of whom – the Foundation's new president George Edgar Vincent – was the cousin of prominent Torontonian Vincent Massey), six Canadian medical schools were selected to receive aid, with Toronto and McGill each promised one million dollars.[24] However, as with all Rockefeller bequests, the money was conditional – both upon additional funds being found, and a set of criteria determined by the Foundation being met. Although the Foundation consciously avoided the appearance of imposing an inflexible system from abroad, the re-evaluation of curricula, infrastructure and methods their grant necessitated, together with the subsequent efforts to attract private and public donors, exerted a major influence on the reformation of medical education in Canada.[25] Many of these changes had been advocated in Canada before the war, but it was the Rockefeller money that provided the spur to their full-scale implementation. It cemented the kind of scientific and laboratory-based medicine that had been established in Germany and the United States since the 1870s, pushed Canadian institutions towards the American system of full-time clinical teaching and post-graduate degrees, and thereby facilitated the development of Canadian careers in medical research (as opposed to practice). These processes were accompanied by significant tensions and negotiations between Canadian universities and the Rockefeller Foundation: Toronto in particular disputed the Foundation's criteria right up until 1923, when the Foundation itself began to alter its focus and means of operation. But they nonetheless reshaped Canadian universities, drawing them into closer connection with their southern neighbours. Moreover, on the back of this involvement in Canada, in the 1920s the Rockefeller Foundation also began to send representatives to investigate universities in the other Dominions as well.[26]

This was an interest that, by the mid-1920s the Carnegie Corporation was also pursuing. In 1917 it had allocated $10 million of its original endowment to the support of projects abroad, predominately in Canada, and in 1926 this fund was remodelled as the Dominions and Colonies Fund. Building on its interest in race relations, citing the principle of trusteeship established by the League of Nations, and motivated by connections with the Phelps Stokes Fund and a number of South African educationalists who had come to the Columbia Teachers College in search of formal training not available in Britain, in 1926 the Corporation sent James E. Russell on an investigative trip to East and South Africa.[27] The following year the Corporation's president, Frederick P. Keppel, made the same journey, a visit that led to the controversial Carnegie-funded *Poor Whites Commission*. This interest in South Africa in turn led to reconnaissance trips by Corporation representatives to Australia and New Zealand – first by Russell in 1928, then by others in 1932, 1933 and 1934, with Keppel himself travelling out in 1935. The Carnegie visitors viewed the Dominions in strategic terms. Russell called them 'experiment stations for all English speaking peoples' 'trying out problems in democracy' that were crucial to American interests in the Pacific.[28] But as Julia Horne has shown, in these modern democracies the Carnegie visitors found institutions that seemed to them still to be cemented in the antiquated traditions and practices of the British Empire: 'Their chairs have been filled with graduates of Oxford, Cambridge and the Scotch universities,' read Russell's 1928 report, 'who have brought with them the standards and ideals of the past'. Indeed, he judged some Australian university 'pundits' positively hostile to America, and his successors found institutions that held fast to their British connections.[29]

Believing education to be central to successful democracies and seeing these older British traditions as ill-suited to the realities of the modern world, the Carnegie Corporation sought to spread modern American educational theories and practices by building new kinds of connections with settler universities.[30] 'The time is ripe for closer contacts,' wrote Russell to Keppel in 1928, 'and the safest way is through educational agencies.'[31] From the late 1920s on, the Corporation attempted to establish systems very similar to those that held together the British academic world. It fostered and utilised an informal network of 'key men' who served as agents and ambassadors in each of the Dominions, and these men in turn gave advice about which ventures and individuals should receive support.[32] It looked sympathetically on applications that focused on research or aimed to contribute to national policy, and helped support both the professional study of education and new forms of association, through organisations for Educational Research established in South Africa, Australia and New Zealand, and through the New Educational Fellowship conferences (held in South Africa in 1934, and New Zealand and Australia in 1937).

Central to Carnegie efforts to influence settler academics was the provision of travel grants designed to pull them away from Britain and bring them into contact with the United States and Canada. Eight Carnegie Fellowships were established for the Dominions in 1935, and in the 1930s the vice-chancellors of Melbourne, Sydney and Western Australia all travelled to the United States on funded fact-finding tours.[33] These Carnegie grants became part of a suite of American travelling fellowships that were beginning to open up new routes for Dominion scholars. From 1925 the Commonwealth Fund (later Harkness) Fellowships enabled British academics to study in the United States, with the scheme widened in 1927 to include academics from Australia, Canada, New Zealand and South Africa. Rockefeller Foundation Fellowships were offered from 1933 and Carnegie Fellowships in International Law from the same period. These combined with British-based schemes – such as the Leverhulme Trust (established in 1925) – that took small but increasing numbers of British and settler academics to the United States.[34] Similarly, American institutions provided a growing number of scholarships for graduate students. From the late 1920s, scholarships from the Rockefeller Foundation, National Science Foundation, Spelman Foundation, Harkness, and Phelps Stokes Fund, among others, began to take students from the British sphere to the United States, though it would not be until the foundation of the Fulbright scholarships in 1946 that a large-scale scheme was established.

With such initiatives, American educational institutions began to look abroad, seeking to penetrate the routes and routines that tied up the British academic world.[35] Traditionally, scholars have understood the rise of American philanthropic institutions such as the Carnegie Corporation and Rockefeller Foundation in terms of American cultural imperialism, and certainly their activities in the field of higher education carried such an agenda.[36] To some extent this intrusion was welcomed: in the difficult economic climate of the late 1920s and early 1930s, American philanthropic organisations offered sources of support that were eagerly received by British and settler universities which, influenced by the new educationalist and progressive outlook of the period, were themselves beginning to lift their gaze to new horizons. But at the same time, and as the Canadian contention with the Carnegie Foundation over terminology shows, settler universities remained deeply committed to the intimate social ties that connected them to British academia. Interwar engagement with the United States did not displace the wider networks that connected the settler universities to Britain, but it did supplement and alter these older practices, offering alternative models and bringing intellectual influences that would only become more important as the century progressed.

Anti-colonial activism

Just as American universities and philanthropic bodies began to alter the traditional patterns of the British academic world, so too did a growing number of graduates from India, the Caribbean, Africa and elsewhere. According to the Colonial Office there were 1,421 Indians, 793 Africans (although this probably included South Africans) and 351 Egyptians studying in Britain in 1925, while the Bureau's *Yearbook* estimated that by 1936 there were 5,534 overseas students, with 2,488 of these coming from the non-settler empire.[37] Associated with the emerging anti-colonial movements of the 1920s and 1930s, these students pushed for access to and reform of the exclusive university system they encountered in Britain. As Susan Pennybacker has written, 1930s London was 'an unofficial center of colonial and antifascist exile', in which not just Indians and Africans, but also American radicals featured heavily.[38] Studying in London had a transformative effect upon many of these students, and, although they remained largely excluded from the dense ties that helped to constitute the racially exclusive British academic world, they forged their own parallel networks that succeeded in challenging and disturbing many of its assumptions.[39]

Many of those students who came to British universities from the Indian and dependent empire arrived as what the Trinidadian historian C. L. R. James described as self-identified 'British intellectuals'.[40] In Britain, however, they came face to face with racism and racial exclusion, confronting considerable obstacles in their quest for advanced degrees, university appointments and professional recognition. Only a handful of Indian teachers found employment in British universities, and black scholars were even less likely to find work. For example, despite the unanimous support of the 1947 selection committee for the chair of economics at the University of Liverpool, the application of the Caribbean lecturer W. Arthur Lewis was rejected by the vice-chancellor because of 'other considerations than high academic standing'.[41] As Marc Matera has shown, black students too often lacked outlets for their analytical work which, when it appeared, was frequently reviewed negatively and accused of subjectivity and bias.[42] Treatment such as this furthered the alienation and fostered the politicisation of Indian and black intellectuals alike. From the 1920s on, in the context of internationalism and the emergence of the new social sciences, Indian and black students and activists in Britain began to challenge the racial structures of European knowledge and forge new opportunities for themselves both inside and outside the academy.

Indians and Africans faced different kinds of challenges. As numerous scholars have recently shown, India was central to the production of knowledge in – and indeed the creation of – a variety of disciplinary fields that in the late nineteenth century had begun to stake their claim on the British academy.[43] Yet the ability of Indian scholars to secure teaching posts in British universities was limited. The British Raj had created opportunities – mostly as language teachers – for a small number of Indians: in the years before 1823 a handful were appointed to the schools of the East India Company in England, while in the latter part of the century, the opening of the Indian Civil Service to competitive examination again created some posts.[44] In 1867 Dadabhai Naoroji was appointed as the first Indian professor at a British University, teaching Gujarati at University College London (despite having held the chair of mathematics and natural philosophy in Bombay) and, towards the end of the century, the rise of theosophy and the European interest in eastern mysticism also created publishing opportunities. The establishment of the Indian universities in the 1850s opened up additional channels for the movement of people. Appointed by the India Office and by the Christian missions, British graduates travelled to work in Indian universities, while select Indian students came to Britain for the university education that served both as a marker of prestige and the condition for entry to the professions. They returned to India to find employment in law and medicine, in the lower rungs of the government services and in the colleges that proliferated under the umbrella of the Indian examining universities. But these Indian graduates were paid on a different salary scale from that of their European colleagues, and posts at the better-remunerated and more prestigious Indian Civil and Education Services remained closed to them. Therefore, although there was a measure of British respect for 'Oriental' studies, Indians were for the most part consigned to being custodians of indigenous knowledge; and although there was a developed university sector along Western lines in India that sent graduates on to Britain for further study, advancement within the British academic world remained all but impossible for those of Indian origin.

Initially Indians focused their protest on the local university system. Sanjay Seth has argued that from the very first 'the Indian student had bent the [Western] system to his own strengths, finding loopholes which resulted in the pedagogic process being shaped by Indian students (and teachers), rather than the students reshaped by pedagogy'.[45] This remodelling of Western forms of knowledge continued throughout the first half of the twentieth century, institutionalised in the educational experiments of Rabindranath Tagore and embodied in the practices of Gandhi.[46] But by the 1880s Indians were also pressing for inclusion within the British-run Indian university hierarchy. This pressure led to the opening up of senior teaching posts to 'native' appointments, and from the turn of the century on, these British-trained Indian professors began to push for entry into the higher ranks of the Indian Education Service (IES) as well. Recruitment was opened up during the war, and then in 1924 the service itself was dissolved. Meanwhile, as Sumita Mukherjee has argued, the experiences of Indians as students in Britain continued to foster a sense not of imperial loyalty but rather imperial alienation – something that stood in stark contrast to the experience of students from the settler colonies.[47] Coming together in associations such as the London-based pro-independence India League, begun in the 1920s by Krishna Menon, Indian students in Britain began to agitate for political as well as educational independence.

Yet even as they pressed for these changes, Indian scholars found new roles for themselves within the empire.[48] In the province of Natal in South Africa a handful of Indian university graduates as well as Indian graduates from British universities found roles in the segregated education system.[49] These South African connections would grow in importance in the second half of the century, but in the interwar period it was to the university colleges of South East Asia that Indian scholars mostly extended their reach. Academic vacancies in these colleges were advertised in India as well as locally and in Britain. However, Indian applicants were – as a 1927 letter from the principal of University College Ceylon to the Colonial Secretary reveals – only really considered 'in the event of no better applicant being found in the United Kingdom'.[50] Graduates from the settler world were also preferred, but pressures for 'nativisation', combined with economic downturn, meant that throughout the 1930s Indian graduates from British universities – cheaper than British candidates and less objectionable to the locally-run councils – frequently gained employment as lecturers and professors at university colleges in Rangoon, Ceylon and Singapore.[51] The territories of British rule around the Indian Ocean thus offered Indian scholars opportunities for employment and advancement, creating new regional alignments of intellectual and institutional power that ran parallel to those of the British academic world.

Black students found themselves more restricted. They suffered significantly under notions of racial hierarchy, and from the limited opportunities for university education in Africa and the West Indies. Aside from Fourah Bay College (1827), only Fort Hare in South Africa (1916), Makerere Technical College in East Africa (1922), the College of Tropical Agriculture in Trinidad (1924) and Achimota College on the Gold Coast (1927) offered higher education to Africans.[52] Moreover, before the 1920s, only a handful of government scholarships were available to take students to Britain. Church missions sent some African students to the Scottish universities, where students from the West Indies also found places, with others travelling to Canada, particularly for medical education. However, as the Great War drew to a close, even this latter route was closed off by Canadian institutions that claimed 'patients objected to being brought into contact with coloured students'.[53] Throughout the 1920s the number of black students in Britain remained relatively small, and many looked instead to the United States as well as Russia and Europe for higher education opportunities.[54]

But the 1930s witnessed the emergence of a new imperative toward welfare and development in the Colonial Office and a new co-operation between colonial administrators, social anthropologists, social scientists and British universities, which increasingly turned attention towards the tropical empire and to questions of colonial administration.[55] At the same time, increasing numbers of students from East and West Africa and the West Indies were coming to Britain to study (the 1935–36 *Yearbook* puts their number at 206), making British universities a more important site than ever before for black intellectual exchange.[56] This opened up some new opportunities. At the London School of Economics (LSE) Bronislaw Malinowski's emphasis on ethnography and functionalism was calling into question the notions of race difference and the premises behind indirect rule, while a new emphasis upon colonial studies led to the appointment in 1938 of Arthur Lewis as the School's first black faculty member.[57] Inspired by these ideas and openings, from the 1930s black intellectuals in Britain began organising their own journals and associations, from which they mounted increasingly stinging criticisms of the system that enabled British academics to monopolise knowledge of Africa. 'I am well aware', wrote Jomo Kenyatta in the preface to his 1938 book *Facing Mount Kenya*, 'that I could not do justice to the subject without offending those "professional friends of the African" who are prepared to maintain their friendship for eternity as a sacred duty, provided only that the African will continue to play the part of an ignorant savage so that they can monopolise the office of interpreting his mind and speaking for him.'[58] Worried about students who went 'back to their own country embittered', conscious of the need for colonial development, and concerned at 'the possibility of a reversion to the drift [of African students] towards French universities' as well as German and Russian institutions, in 1944 the Asquith Commission into Colonial Higher Education finally recommended the establishment of university colleges in the West Indies and West Africa, and universities in East Africa and Malaya.[59] This stimulated higher education in Africa, but it would not be until the 1950s that these institutions would offer real employment opportunities for black intellectuals.

For both Indian and black students, the LSE was a hub for this activity and two teachers in particular – Harold Laski and Bronislaw Malinowski – loomed large. They offered both intellectual and practical support. While Malinowski's functionalist approach undermined the notion of racial hierarchies, Laski's socialist analysis of imperialism and support for Indian independence provided an explanation for the oppression colonial students felt. In many ways both men acted as the kind of 'agents' to which settler students had long had access. Malinowski helped Kenyatta and Nathaniel Fadipe, among others, obtain grants to support their research, and he employed Africans as translators and sponsored their publications.[60] In 1925 Laski became close friends with Krishna Menon and lent him his active support, lecturing at events, writing articles, accepting students Menon sent him, and agitating with Indian nationalists for independence. They helped attract to the LSE a stream of students that made it what the American ambassador to the United Nations, Daniel Moynihan, in 1974 called 'the most important institution of higher education in Asia and Africa'.[61]

Yet it is important to note that both Laski and Malinowski were themselves shaped by British academic world connections and particularly by their own somewhat marginal place within them. Educated before the war in Krakow, Leipzig and London (at the LSE), Malinowski was among the German-speakers who had travelled to Australia for the 1914 British Association meeting. Unable to return to Europe because of the war, and already well connected to British anthropology thanks to his time at the LSE, in Australia he used these connections to make friends with a number of senior professors including Baldwin Spencer, and, according to his biographer, their 'combined patronage laid the very foundation of his future work'.[62] These Australian professors supported him with the hospitality, funds and introductions that enabled him to travel to Papua and Melanesia. He spent the war moving back and forth between his fieldwork and periods of study, writing in Australia works that were well received in London. He also courted the daughters of two of his Australian patrons, causing much controversy before marrying Elsie Masson in 1919, moving to the Canary Islands and then taking up the position of lecturer in social anthropology at the LSE in 1923.

If Malinowski was a Polish outsider, Laski was on the surface very much an English insider who shone at Manchester Grammar School and won a scholarship to New College, Oxford. Recommended by the college's warden, H. A. L. Fisher, as a replacement for the position of lecturer in modern history at McGill, he accepted the post and moved to Montreal in 1914. This was a welcome move, as Laski was Jewish and his parents had refused to acknowledge his marriage in 1911 to Frida Kerry. But in Canada Laski found more than just freedom from a suffocating family: he also found America. Unhappy at McGill, soon after his arrival he set about making contacts that would in 1917 enable him to move to a position at Harvard University. When he left England for Montreal Laski had one friend in America.[63] When he moved back to the LSE in 1920, he was infamous for boasting about his connections there. If Malinowski had used the networks of the British academic world to position himself within the emerging field of British anthropology, then Laski used them as a hinge to get out of Britain and into America, where he forged relationships and engaged in political activism that would shape the rest of his career. It is tempting to think that – Polish and Jewish – their existence on the edges of the greater British academic world fostered their sympathy for those who, because of the colour of their skin, were excluded from it.

Refugee scholars

While American encroachment opened up new vistas for British and settler academics, the challenges to the British dominance of knowledge mounted by anti-colonial activists unsettled the assumptions underpinning British rule in the dependent empire. But it was the arrival of refugee scholars from Germany and Eastern Europe in 1933 that most seriously disrupted the mechanisms on which the British academic world was based.

One of the early measures introduced by the Nazi party following its seizure of power in Germany in March 1933 was the passage on 7 April of the 'Law for the Reconstitution of the Professional Civil Service'. It forced the immediate dismissal of all civil servants – including teachers and academics – who were not of 'Aryan' descent, as well as those who were opponents of the regime. This led to the exodus from Germany of large numbers of Jewish and German scholars. These numbers swelled further in 1938 following the annexation of Austria and the exacerbation of anti-semitic violence in Germany. By 1938 it is estimated that over 2,120 European academics had migrated, about half of them to Britain.[64] Although the British government was not generally sympathetic to refugees, as early as 12 April 1933 it had made an exception for those 'prominent Jews ... who had achieved distinction whether in pure science, applied science, such as medicine or technical industry, music or art'.[65] Yet it also made it clear that no funds would be provided for their support. Instead, funding was provided by an organisation founded by William Beveridge – then director of the LSE – who, along with Ernest Rutherford, in May 1933 established the Academic Assistance Council (AAC) – later the Society for the Protection of Science and Learning (SPSL).[66] Aided by the *Notgemeinschaft Deutscher Wissenschaftler im Ausland* and by the American Emergency Committee for Displaced Scholars, from its foundation the AAC aimed to provide financial support for displaced scholars. It also acted as 'a centre of information', operating a register that held a curriculum vitae, a list of publications, and a selection of testimonials for each individual.[67] Supported by many of the most prominent academics in Britain, by 1939 it had raised about £90,000, much of which came from subscriptions and donations from relief organisations such as the Central British Fund for German Jewry.[68] By the end of the war the AAC/SPSL had generated records for 2,541 refugee scholars, of whom about 600 were in 1946 still living in Britain, in temporary or permanent capacities. Most of the others moved on to the United States, with smaller numbers placed in the British Commonwealth and other countries.[69]

The urgent need to find academic homes for this influx of refugee scholars both reorientated and circumvented the informal networks that had long been crucial to academic appointments in Britain and the settler universities. Initially, those German scholars with pre-existing connections to British universities mobilised these ties and, with their credentials vouched for by British professors, found places in British institutions.[70] They were then able to certify the experience of their hopeful former colleagues. The AAC register formalised and centralised this process. Virtually overnight, it brought into being a tangible, paper archive that recorded the kind of information that, for

British and settler scholars, had never needed to be written down. By organising temporary positions for these European scholars, the AAC also gave them the chance of acquiring the social capital that was so important in the British system. In doing so, it created a mechanism that facilitated the injection of individuals from the German and European systems into British universities.

But British universities were alien places for many of the new arrivals. Not only did they find the university sector to be small, with limited job prospects (in 1938–39 there were only 3,994 academics in the United Kingdom teaching 50,002 students in sixteen institutions), but they also found the educational system to be based on very different principles and practices from those they had known in Germany.[71] The Nobel Prize-winning Tübingen nuclear physicist Hans Albrecht Bethe – who in 1934 left a temporary position at the University of Bristol for a permanent position at Cornell – later alluded to his feeling of being an outsider: 'England', he recalled, 'had been used to having Englishmen and Commonwealth people in their universities and so we refugees were rather a foreign element'.[72] But if this sense of otherness proved an obstacle for some, it was also the basis of the significant intellectual influence that the émigrés exerted on British scholarship. From a foreign system, they brought new ideas, new methods and new connections that would energise and redirect many disciplines.[73]

This dislocation of the intimate social practices at the heart of the British academic world was also felt in the settler universities. They, however, were not overwhelmingly enthusiastic about its impact. The AAC, the *Notgemeinschaft* and the Emergency Committee sent their early circulars to the Dominion universities as well as to those in Britain, and much private correspondence passed between them. Yet little came of these initial overtures. While in India universities and industrial groups were eager to secure highly qualified European candidates, the settler universities were much more reluctant. On the one hand they found themselves in significant financial hardship. Hit by the Great Depression and largely dependent on government grants, university administrators and departmental heads found it hard to see how further numbers could be accommodated in universities where many of the staff had already taken pay cuts.[74] But settler universities also resisted the arrival of individuals who did not meet their traditional criteria or come via the usual routes. Here the reply of an Ottawa museum official to a request from the AAC is revealing: 'Appointment [of] Germans, not generally favoured, but good British men most acceptable.' Indeed, the Courtauld Institute's W. G. Constable had earlier worried that 'national feeling in Canada would be too strong to allow an opening for discharged Germans'.[75] Across the British academic world the crisis of the 1930s resulted in a renewed commitment to what was held up as the 'British' democratic tradition.[76] Yet there was undoubtedly also another aspect that, as elsewhere, underpinned the settler universities' reluctance to accept the refugee scholars, and that was anti-Jewish feeling. Although many settler academics were sympathetic – the University of Western Australia's professor of chemistry, N. T. M. Wilsmore, was sure that Jewish professors would 'prove an asset to the British empire' – others rejected out of hand the possibility of taking them even when, in late 1934, the Carnegie Corporation informed the AAC that it would fund thirty-six fellowships for displaced scholars to go to Commonwealth universities outside Britain for a period of three (later two) years.[77]

Yet for universities the Carnegie grants were attractive. They offered the possibility in financially desperate times of securing, at cut-price, scholars of international repute.[78] Also influential was the correspondence campaign inaugurated by the general secretary of the AAC, Walter Adams, following the Carnegie's announcement. He not only wrote to the vice-chancellors of every settler university but also mobilised the expansive networks of the British academic world, organising professors in Britain to write to their settler colleagues urging them to submit applications for one of the Carnegie fellowships.[79] Adams thus co-opted pre-existing networks of trust, appealing simultaneously to settler universities' sympathies as well as their balance sheets.[80] As centralised assistance organisations were for the most part not launched in the Dominions, this use of private networks was crucial. In fact, many settler placements arose as the result of already established connections, some of which were often desperately tenuous.[81] Displaced in Oxford, a Dr. H. Appel invoked a mutual connection with Leipzig's Professor Burckhardt Helferich when he wrote to Harold Hibbert at McGill in 1935; and Gerhard Herzberg used his ties with Canada's J. W. T Spinks (who had in the winter of 1933 spent some time in Herzberg's Darmstadt laboratory) to secure a Carnegie-funded position at the University of Saskatchewan.[82] Meanwhile, settler academics in Britain, including Ernest Rutherford and W.K. Hancock, used their networks to help get scholars admitted to the Dominions.[83] According to the records of the AAC, by the end of the war, the settler colonies had absorbed sixty-one refugee scholars. Not all settled permanently or in university posts, and many more went to Australia and Canada than to New Zealand or South Africa, yet their stay, whether permanent or temporary, revitalised teaching and stimulated research in these countries.[84] Bringing foreign accents, foreign manners and foreign connections, their presence in settler institutions embodied the changes that were shifting patterns of academic scholarship across the globe.

Towards the nation

Although penetrating the mechanism at the heart of the wider British academic system, the arrival of refugee scholars did not destroy the connective infrastructure or dismantle the deep ties that, since the late nineteenth century, had helped knit the British academic world together. The Second World War once again mobilised these networks, drawing settler scientists into Britain and into the war effort in large numbers. But the active collaboration with the United States that the war facilitated drew many settler scientists into new relationships, not only with American and international scholarship but also at home. And although the old ties persisted, the alternative institutional and intellectual alignments that in the interwar period had begun to supplement British networks, began in the late 1940s and 1950s to supplant them. Settler universities turned inwards and focused their energies on building locally the academic infrastructure they had previously thought about in more expansive terms.

When war was declared in September 1939, both the British armed forces and the government were acutely conscious of the value of universities and their personnel, and they were careful not to make the same mistakes that had blighted the initial stages of the conflict in 1914. Not only was recruitment regulated so as to maintain a flow of trained young scientists from the universities, but from late 1938 a central register of men holding scientific qualifications had been drawn up to best make use of their talents. University scientists were redeployed into government and industrial work, and across the United Kingdom commercial bodies moved into university laboratories, forging close relationships between the two sectors that would have long-term consequences for scientific and industrial research in Britain. As Michael Sanderson has pointed out, the 'university scientist totally penetrated those areas of government where science was involved', participating in a research effort that was much more co-ordinated than had been the case in 1914–18.[85]

Even in this more centralised scientific war, however, the informal connections that underpinned British academia remained important. Rutherford's physics network was again significant. Central to this network was the Australian Mark Oliphant, an 1851 Exhibitioner and former student of Rutherford's, who since 1937 had held the chair of physics at the University of Birmingham.[86] Supervising war work on radar and atomic research, in 1940 he had realised the feasibility of developing an atomic bomb, and in August 1941 was instrumental in communicating the urgency of the situation to the hitherto unresponsive Americans, providing information that instigated the Manhattan project and drew the United States and Britain into active collaboration. To secure uranium supplies, but also with the view to collaborating with the United States, the British government extended its atomic research scheme to Canada, where it built upon the work of two of Rutherford's former students (G. C. Laurence at the Canadian National Research Council, and B. W. Sargent at Queen's University).[87] Consolidating the informal relations that had developed following the 1940 arrival in Ottawa and Washington of A. V. Hill, R. H. Fowler (Rutherford's physicist son-in-law), and Henry Tizard (former reader at Oxford and chairman of the Aeronautical Research Committee), the British government established formal co-operation with the US in August 1943. Various groups of Cavendish physicists – including the Australians Oliphant and H. S. W. Massey, and a New Zealander, R. R. Nimmo – were subsequently admitted into the American project and, once in the United States, they drew in other Cambridge-educated Australians, including E. H. S. Burhop. Meanwhile, another Rutherford student, Ernest Marsden, who in 1926 had founded the DSIR in New Zealand, used his ties to the many Cambridge men involved in the project to secure the participation of several young New Zealand physicists. As the work of numerous historians has shown, this 'British' wartime atomic research was built upon the expansive and personal connections of physicists that extended far beyond the British Isles.[88] Neither was it just in physics that British academic world networks were marshalled to the cause of Allied scientific co-operation: Roy MacLeod has written of the contributions Dominion scientists made to various aspects of wartime science.[89] As Charles Stacey's attempt to account for the Canadian universities' role in the development of military technology in the Second World War shows, British and settler science were still deeply enmeshed. It is 'impossible to produce any definite quantitative assessment of the value of Canadian research and development as a contribution to Allied victory', he wrote:

> A major difficulty is simply the fact that it *was a contribution* – a joint effort. Many Canadian projects were closely related to British ones and were essentially adaptations or development of ideas or devices on which much British work had already been done. To arrive at a definitive evaluation of the relative importance of contributions in cases of this sort seems out of the question.[90]

After the war these expansive connections were again taken up by academics returning to their careers. Although detailed research remains to be done, there is some indication that in this period significant numbers of British graduates continued to find jobs in settler universities. John Hargreaves reports that in the post-1945 decade at least thirty Aberdeen graduates obtained academic or scientific posts in

Canada, with a further fifteen finding positions in Australia and New Zealand.[91] Similarly, an expanded number of travelling scholarships continued to take settler graduates to Britain. Despite the emergence of an Australian PhD in 1946, large numbers of graduates continued to travel to Britain for doctoral work. Between 1945 and 1965, in chemistry alone, 159 Australians made the overseas journey to pursue doctoral work in the UK. As Ian Rae suggests, 'Australian supervisors continued to "place" in suitable [British] laboratories graduates who were received by professors who had been the supervisors' supervisors, or were themselves Australians'.[92] It was only in 1959, with the expansion of the (Australian) Commonwealth Scholarship Scheme (introduced in 1951), that the balance tipped, and for the first time Australians undertook more science PhDs at home than abroad. Aided by the war, which once again served as a social as well as an intellectual crucible, a new generation of settler scholars assumed the mantle of agents in Britain, while a still restricted UK university sector carried another wave of British academics to settler universities.

It is also possible to see the decades after the war as a time of renewed academic imperialism in the colonies and dependencies that comprised the 'new' Commonwealth.[93] The universities established in East and West Africa were staffed by large numbers of British academics, and by smaller numbers of Dominion, American and European teachers. They were joined by British scholars on short-term placements and by a growing number of academics undertaking consultancy work, who constituted part of the internationally sponsored project of 'development' in which various forms of 'expertise' played a central role.[94] As Roy MacLeod has again demonstrated, the demands of imperial co-operation in science during the war helped weave 'a fabric of relationships that survived to influence Commonwealth and international science diplomacy' long after it.[95]

Yet the British and settler scholars treading the old routes of empire in the decades after the Second World War did so amidst altered Commonwealth relations. Not only had the Statute of Westminster (1931) laid the foundations for new relations with the Dominions, but Indian independence and the increasing importance of what came to be called the 'new Commonwealth' had significantly expanded the old club. Moreover, as the example of atomic physics shows, British political and diplomatic interests now presaged a new orientation – one based upon intellectual co-operation with the United States – and this emphasis upon collaboration and co-operation with American science provided the context for the refashioning of relations with the Dominions as well.

We can see this in the changing structures of scientific organisation during the war.[96] Desiring more effective communication between American scientists and the British and Canadians in Ottawa, in 1941 the War Cabinet sent formal scientific representation to Washington in the form of two Cavendish-trained men, the director of the National Physical Laboratory, Charles Darwin, and the Canadian, William Webster. The office they ran (the British Central Scientific Office or BCSO) served as 'a scientific clearing house', channelling most of the written and human traffic that flowed between America and Britain until 1943 when it was absorbed into the formal machinery of government that constituted 'Whitehall in Washington'. Meanwhile, early in the war, first Canada, then New Zealand, Australia, South Africa, and finally India, sent their own scientific representatives to London, leading to the establishment in 1942 of a UK-based Colonial Research Committee. But by 1943 the work being undertaken by Dominion research councils had expanded sufficiently for them, too, to have separate formal representation in Washington. It was therefore in America, in the process of developing *imperial* scientific 'co-operation', that these settler scientists first became independent representatives of their respective *national* scientific communities. Although all were products of the British academic world, in Washington they sought to build skills and institute national structures of knowledge that would foster post-war science in their respective homelands.

These objectives had been in sight since at least the 1920s, when the Great War had led governments in Britain and the settler colonies alike to establish their own institutions in the form of councils or departments of scientific and industrial research. From the 1920s the Australian and New Zealand bodies had sent unofficial and official scientific representatives to London with the aim of developing joint work in agriculture and mining, and although Canada was notably more reticent to join in this imperial effort, the passing of the Statute of Westminster saw more formal proposals for what was now called 'co-operation', culminating in the 1936 British Commonwealth Scientific Conference.[97] This new emphasis upon 'co-operation', which implied a degree of equality, reflected the increasingly self-conscious stance of the Dominions. It found expression not just in the growth of national scientific associations but also in the emergence of economic and historical studies and the production of art and literature. Until as late as the 1950s these articulations of intellectual self-sufficiency tended to be absorbed by, or framed within, a Dominion nationalism that understood the settler societies as independent members of a wider British polity. But the changing geo-political relations of the post-war period shifted the role of these institutional and cultural expressions and their meaning.

At the same time, in the United Kingdom new configurations of domestic and international relations were turning individuals, institutions and governments away from the settler world and towards the United States and Europe. Suez, decolonisation and the United Kingdom's 1961 application to join the European Economic Community signalled Britain's retreat from the 'British abroad' and forced the Dominions to reconsider their cultural, economic and political identities.[98] Shaped by the contingencies of local power and politics, this process was by no means uniform. While South Africa retreated into the isolation of Afrikaner nationalism and Canada was drawn closer into its wary but intimate dance with the United States, Australia reluctantly faced the change, and New Zealand clung on to old identities. The complex nature of these shifts, and their various local causes and manifestations for universities and academics, is properly the subject of other investigations, but the outlines of its consequences are clear enough in the histories of settler universities in the late 1950s and early 1960s. Coinciding with the wider swing towards area studies and with increasing measures to formalise academic practices, settler universities turned away from their reliance on the trans-oceanic personal networks that, since the 1880s, had connected them to Britain. Supported by national research grants and an emerging national apparatus of higher educational institutions, students increasingly undertook doctoral study at home, providing a pool of locally trained candidates to supplement those who qualified abroad. National disciplinary associations and national journals provided new vehicles for research, while sabbatical leave was just as often taken locally as in Britain. Increasingly, new international ties – with the United States, but also with regional neighbours – drew settler academics along alternative paths.

It was not that the old routes and practices disappeared. Throughout the second half of the century, appointments, travelling scholarships and personal networks continued to forge close relationships between academics in Britain and those in Canada, Australia, New Zealand and South Africa, and the legacies of these connections remain evident in the disciplinary and institutional ties that link workers in numerous disciplines across the globe today. In the same way, personalised systems of trust and informal long-distance connections continued to shape the ways universities and those who worked in them operated. But the relative importance of, the motivations behind, and the purposes imagined for such networks changed. Dominion and imperial frames and focuses were remade as national and international ones, even as the old reliance on diffuse, informal and personal connections was reshaped by centralised and professional systems of university governance and administration. This 'renationalisation of knowledge' in the Dominions – the origins of which can be traced back to the inter-war period – has often been cast as the beginnings of their scientific and scholarly independence. Yet it also represented a repurposing of the mechanisms that once linked settler universities to Britain, and an untying of the expansive British academic community that had once stretched across the world.

–◆–

At the first congress held after the Second World War, the Universities' Bureau of the British Empire changed its name to the 'Association of Universities of the British Commonwealth'. On the occasion of its fiftieth anniversary in 1963 it underwent a further reinvention, losing its designation as 'British' and becoming instead the 'Association of Commonwealth Universities' (ACU). With 133 member universities, only twenty-five of which were situated in the United Kingdom, the ACU of 1963 was dramatically different from the organisation that had come into existence in London fifty years earlier. The change in name reflected the reformulation of the Commonwealth as a multiracial community of independent nations. But it also represented a final departure from the expansive conception of the British nation that had underpinned the organisation's inception.[99]

Beginning in the interwar period, national and international forces appropriated and repurposed the various mechanisms that since the 1880s had de-territorialised aspects of settler universities and linked them into a wider British academic world. American philanthropy provided scholarships and travel grants to the United States; anti-colonial activists undermined euro-centric knowledge assumptions; refugee scholars disrupted appointment practices; and a new national-ism localised academic orientations. Additional forces pulled in other directions: the intellectual and cultural organisations associated first with the League of Nations, and then with the United Nations, created alternative structures for co-operation, and the Soviet Union provided a hub for many on the left.[100] These new ties and supplementary con-nections eroded the density and reach of the networks on which the British academic world had been based.

These shifts were part of a much wider process in which institutions of knowledge across the world were reterritorialised in the period after the Second World War. Seeing universities as powerful organs for the formation of identity and the projection of power, states nationalised the organisation of academia: they supported the foundation of new universities, increased funding for them, sponsored academic research, enlarged student numbers, provided state bursaries and developed new professional bodies. These measures created patterns of academic territoriality that linked universities to their national contexts in new ways. At the same time they also internationalised universities' engagement with their fellows abroad. When scholars travelled on academic exchanges, took up travelling scholarships or attended international conferences, they now did so not as members of the expansive British academic world, but rather as representatives of national scholarly communities. It would not be until the 1980s, when a new phase of government reform began to dismantle these national structures and replace them with another wave of de-territorialisation (this time in the form of marketised mechanisms) that the universities in what had once been the settler colonies would again see themselves in global terms – and then it would be as very different kinds of institutions.

Notes

1 USA, *J. T. Wilson Papers*, P162/3/7/Holme to Wilson, 22 Aug. 1944. Edgeworth David was professor of geology, Mungo MacCallum was professor of English and for a time served as vice-chancellor, and Frederick Augustus Todd was professor of Latin.

2 UMA, *Registrar's Correspondence*, UM312/1926/145/Copy of letter sent by Bainbridge to the Prime Minster's Department regarding American lecturers, 1926.

3 Pietsch, 'Wandering Scholars?'. See supplementary data.

4 UTA, *Office of the President*, A1967-0007, box 26/*Travelling Expenses.*

5 UTA, *Carnegie Foundation*, A68-007, box 158/03/Henry S. Pritchett (President, Carnegie Foundation) to Hutton (acting President) Nov. 23, 1906; box 158/04/01/Falconer to Prichett, 15 May 1908; box 158/04/01/Falconer to Pritchett, 9 Apr. 1908. For a history of the Foundation, see Ellen Condliffe Lagemann, *Private Power for the Public Good* (Middletown, CT: Wesleyan University Press, 1983).

6 UTA, *Office of the President*, A1967–0007/box 7/file 43/J. G. Schurman, President of Cornell University to Falconer, 21 Nov. 1908.

7 *Ibid.*, box 11/file 34/290, Falconer's form letter to American universities regarding sabbatical leave (Harvard, Princeton, Cornell, Columbia, Chicago, Missouri, Minnesota, Michigan, Wisconsin), 5 Jan. 1910; see also files 71 and 72, 16, box 26/files 47–52 for other matters.

8 UTA, *Carnegie Foundation*, box 158/04/05/Falconer to Pritchett, 5 Oct. 1911.

9 *Ibid.*, box 158/04/John G Bowman to Falconer, 29 Mar. 1910.

10 *Ibid.*, box 158/04/05, Pritchett to Falconer, 23 Apr. 1912.

11 *Ibid.*, box 49/Copy of letter from Henry S. Pritchett to W. Peterson [principal at McGill] forwarded to Falconer from Peterson, 4 July 1917.

12 See, for example, Robert S. Patterson, 'American Influences on Progressive Education in Canada', *The School*, 26 (1938): 472–7; R. S. Sommerville, 'Is Canada Becoming Americanized?' *The Empire Review*, 55 (1926): 537–40; Nancy M. Sheehan, 'Philosophy, Pedagogy and Practice: The Iode and the Schools in Canada, 1900–1945', *Historical Studies in Education*, 2 (1990): 307–22.

13 *Second Congress Proceedings, 1921*, p. 441.

14 *Ibid.*, p. 412.

15 *Ibid.*, p. 411.

16 *Ibid.*

17 MUA, *Office of Principal, Auckland Campbell Geddes*, RG2/c.40/232/American Assoc[iation] of Univ[ersity] Professors – Appointment service.

18 Charles Harvey *et al.*, 'Andrew Carnegie and the Foundations of Contemporary Entrepreneurial Philanthropy', *Business History*, 53, no. 3 (2011): 425–50, p. 434.

19 Andrew Carnegie, *The Gospel of Wealth* (New York: 1889).

20 Raymond Blaine Fosdick, *The Story of the Rockefeller Foundation* (New York: Harper and Row, 1952).

21 Although extensive research exists on the Carnegie Corporation and Rockefeller Foundation's involvements in the United States, Great Britain and South Africa, work on their activity in the rest of the British world is only just developing. See Richard Glotzer, 'A Long Shadow: Frederick P. Keppel, the Carnegie Corporation and the Dominions and Colonies Fund Area Experts 1923–1943', *History of Education*, 38, no. 5 (2009): 621–48; Mary Carroll, 'Republic of the Learned: The Role of Libraries in the Promotion of a U.S. Democratic Vision', *History of Education*, 38, no. 6 (2009): 809–23; Collins, 'Creating Women's Work in the Academy and Beyond'; Lambert and Lester, 'Geographies of Colonial Philanthropy'.

22 There are numerous others. For example, see Jeffrey David Brison, *Rockefeller, Carnegie, and Canada: American Philanthropy and the Arts and Letters in Canada* (Montreal: McGill-Queens University Press, 2005).

23 UTA, *Office of the President*, A1967-0007/box 62/635/Vincent to Dr C. K. Clarke, Dean of the Faculty of Medicine, Toronto, 24 Dec. 1919.

24 *Ibid.*, A1967-0007/box 62/656/Edwin R Embree, Secretary Rockefeller Foundation, to Falconer, 19 Nov. 1920.

25 Marianne Fedunkiw, *Rockefeller Foundation Funding and Medical Education in Toronto, Montreal, and Halifax* (Montreal: McGill-Queen's University Press, 2005), pp. 5, 45.

26 Julia Horne, 'What We Saw in Australia: Carnegie Men and Australian Universities Between the Wars', paper delivered at the Philanthropy and Public Culture Workshop, delivered at Melbourne, 2010.

27 Richard Glotzer, 'The Influence of Carnegie Corporation and Teachers College, Columbia, in the Interwar Dominions: The Case for Decentralized Education', *Historical Studies in Education*, 1, no. 1–2 (2000): 93–111.

28 Russell to Keppel, 2 Apr. 1928, quoted in Glotzer, 'A Long Shadow', p. 640.

29 Australia and New Zealand Report by Dr J. E. Russell, 1928; Russell to Keppel, 24 Apr. 1928, quoted in Horne, 'What We Saw in Australia'.

30 Glotzer, 'A Long Shadow', p. 621. The Library reports use the same language: 'Canada is a democracy,' read the report written in 1931, '[yet] there are thousands of people in Canada – yea, tens and hundreds of thousands – who have no access to such resources [as books].' Ridington, *Libraries in Canada*, p. 7. See also Carroll, 'Republic of the Learned'.

31 Russell to Keppel, 2 Apr. 1928, quoted in Glotzer, 'A Long Shadow', p. 640.

32 *Ibid.*, p. 621.

33 Horne, 'What We Saw in Australia'; Selleck, *The Shop*, p. 683.

34 NLA, MS 9258 Records of Harkness Fellowships of the Commonwealth Fund: Australian Division/Historical note. See *Fellowships and Scholarships Open to Foreign Students for Study in the United States* (New York: Institute of International Education, 1929); *The Yearbook of the Universities of the Empire, 1936*, Appendix XXIII, no. 33; *A List of International Fellowships for Research* (London: International Federation of University Women, 1934).

35 For a later example of American attempts to understand the British Commonwealth university sector, see Oliver Cromwell Carmichael, *Universities: Commonwealth and American, a Comparative Study* (New York: Harper, 1959).

36 Robert F. Arnove (ed.), *Philanthropy and Cultural Imperialism: The Foundations at Home and Abroad* (Indiana: Indiana University Press, 1982).

37 NAUK, *Department of Education and Science: Private Office Papers (Series 1)*, PRO/ED24/1994, 'Information on Dominion and Indian Students at British Universities'; *The Yearbook of the Universities of the Empire, 1936*, pp. 953–4. The 1936 *Yearbook* states that 1971 came from Asia; 311 from Egypt; 52 from Nigeria and West Africa; 154 from the West Indies; and, not included in the empire total, also 66 from South America. See also Sumita Mukherjee, *Nationalism, Education and Migrant Identities: The England Returned* (London: Routledge, 2009), p. 24; Alex T. Carey, *Colonial Students: A Study of Social Adaptation of Colonial Students* (London:

Secker and Warburg, 1956), pp. 28–9.

38 Susan D. Pennybacker, *From Scottsboro to Munich: Race and Political Culture in 1930s Britain* (Princeton, N.J.: Princeton University Press, 2009), p. 1.

39 The AHRC funded projected based at the University of Oxford, 'Making Britain: South Asian Visions of Home and Abroad', 2007–2010, examined some of these. Dadabhai Naoroji, Britain's first South Asian Member of Parliament, was a crucial figure for Indians. See Rozina Visram, *Asians in Britain: 400 years of history* (London: Pluto Press, 2002), pp. 137–9; Boehmer, *India Arrived*.

40 C. L. R. James, *Beyond a Boundary* (London: Stanley Paul, 1963), p. 18.

41 Robert Tignor, *W. Arthur Lewis* (Princeton, NJ: Princeton University Press, 2006), pp. 37–8. When in 1948 he was appointed to a chair at Manchester University, Lewis became the first black professor in Great Britain. In 1979 he won the Nobel Prize.

42 Marc Matera, 'Colonial Subjects: Black Intellectuals and the Development of Colonial Studies in Britain', *Journal of British Studies*, 49, no. 2 (2010): 388–418, pp. 404–5.

43 Cohn, *Colonialism and Its Forms of Knowledge*; David Livingstone and Charles W. J. Withers (eds), *Geographies of Nineteenth-Century Science* (Chicago, IL: University of Chicago Press, 2011); Sujit Sivasundaram, *Nature and the Godly Empire: Science and Evangelical Mission in the Pacific, 1795–1850* (Cambridge: Cambridge University Press, 2005); Harrison, *Medicine in an Age of Commerce and Empire*.

44 The first Indian to teach in Britain was probably Sheth Ghoolam Hyder, who was appointed as assistant professor in Persian at the East India Company's college at Haileybury in 1808. However, the Company terminated the appointment of Indians in its colleges in 1823. For Indians in Britain, see Michael H. Fisher, *Counterflows to Colonialism: Indian Travellers and Settlers in Britain, 1600–1857* (Delhi: Permanent Black, 2004).

45 Sanjay Seth, *Subject Lessons: The Western Education of Colonial India* (New Delhi: Duke University Press, 2007), p. 32. On Tagore and Gandhi, see also pp. 163–7.

46 Kathleen O'Connell, *'Siksar Herfer*: Education out of Whack', in Patrick Colm Hogan and Lalita Pandit (eds), *Rabindranath Tagore: Universality and Tradition* (Madison, NJ: Fairleigh Dickinson University Press, 2002), pp. 65–82.

47 Mukherjee, *Nationalism, Education and Migrant Identities*, pp. 113–37.

48 James R. Brennan, 'South Asian Nationalism in an East African Context: The Case of Tanganyika, 1914–1956', *Comparative Studies of South Asia, Africa and the Middle East*, 19, no. 2 (1999): 24–39; Herbert Luthy, 'India and East Africa: Imperial Partnership at the End of the First World War', *Journal of Contemporary History*, 6, no. 2 (1971): 55–85.

49 Six graduates from India were hired to staff the Sastri school established in Durban in 1930.

50 NAUK, *Ceylon University College*, CO 54/884/6: Lecturer in Economics 1927, Letter sent 9 Apr. 1927.

51 *Ibid.*, CO 54/884/6: Lecturer in Economics 1927, Letter sent 9 Apr. 1927. See also NAUK, *Ceylon University College*, CO 54/919/2: Vacancy of Professor of Physics 1933.

52 For a list of staff at Fort Hare, see Kerr, *Fort Hare 1915–48*, pp. 275–7.

53 In 1921 Canadian universities did petition the Colonial Office to be allowed to establish a medical school under their auspices in the West Indies, but this attempt to contain Caribbean students did not meet with approval. NAUK, *Barbados Despatches*, CO 28/293/65/Enclosure in confidential dispatch of 4 June 1918, petition from West Indian Club of Queen's University; UTA, *Office of the President*, box 71/103/Falconer to Hill, 18 Oct. 1921.

54 Jason C. Parker, '"Made-in-America Revolutions"? The "Black University" And the American Role in the Decolonization of the Black Atlantic', *Journal of American History*, 96 (2009): 727–50.

55 Douglas Rimmer and Anthony Kirk-Greene (eds), *The British Intellectual Engagement with Africa in the Twentieth Century* (London: Macmillan, 2000); Robert H. Bates, V. Y. Mudimbe, and Jean O'Barr (eds), *Africa and the Disciplines: The Contributions of Research in Africa to the Social Sciences and Humanities* (Chicago, IL: Chicago University Press, 1993); Jack Goody, *The Expansive Moment: Anthropology in*

Britain and Africa, 1918–1970 (Cambridge: Cambridge University Press, 1995).

56 *Yearbook of the Universities of the Empire, 1936*, p. 953; Philip S. Zachernuk, *Colonial Subjects: An African Intelligentsia and Atlantic Ideas* (Charlottesville, VA: University of Virginia Press, 2000), pp. 97–101.

57 Zachernuk, *Colonial Subjects*, p. 108; Matera, 'Colonial Subjects', p. 396.

58 Kenyatta, *Facing Mount Kenya*, p. xviii. Quoted in Matera, 'Colonial Subjects', p. 404.

59 NAUK, *Asquith Commission*, CO 958 CHEC serial no. 51, CHEC serial no. 136, Part IV: Summary of the Recommendations of the Commission.

60 Matera, 'Colonial Subjects', p. 396.

61 Daniel P. Moynihan, 'The United States in Opposition', *Commentary* (1975): 42–4.

62 Michael Young, *Malinowski: Odyssee of an Anthroplogist 1884–1920*, vol. 1 (New Haven, CT: Yale University Press, 2004), p. 297. His patrons were Orme Masson, Baldwin Spencer, Edward Charles Stirling and the secretary of the Department of External Affairs, Atlee Hunt.

63 Isaac Kramnick and Barry Sheerman, *Harold Laski: A Life on the Left* (London: Hamish Hamilton, 1993), p. 81.

64 Gerhard Hirschfeld, 'German Refugee Scholars in Great Britain, 1933–1945', in Anna Bramwell (ed.), *Refugees in the Age of Total War* (London: Unwin Hyman, 1988), p. 153. See also Jeremy Seabrook, *The Refuge and the Fortress: Britain and the Flight from Tyranny* (Basingstoke: Palgrave Macmillan, 2009).

65 Quoted in Hirschfeld, 'German Refugee Scholars in Great Britain, 1933–1945', p. 153. See also Louise London, *Whitehall and the Jews, 1933–1948* (Cambridge: Cambridge University Press, 2000).

66 William Beveridge, *A Defence of Free Learning* (Oxford: Oxford University Press, 1959); Walter Adams, 'The Refugee Scholars of the 1930s', *The Political Quarterly*, 39, no. 1 (1968): 7–14; Hirschfeld, 'German Refugee Scholars in Great Britain, 1933–1945'.

67 'The British Academic Assistance Council', *Science, New Series*, 77, no. 2009 (1933): 620–1.

68 Adams, 'The Refugee Scholars of the 1930s', p. 19.

69 Figures quoted in Hirschfeld, 'German Refugee Scholars in Great Britain, 1933–1945', p. 156.

70 London, *Whitehall and the Jews, 1933–1948*, p. 48.

71 Figures given in A. H. Halsey (ed.), *Trends in British Society since 1900: A Guide to the Changing Social Structure of Britain* (London: Macmillan, 1972), pp. 206, 211. See also Hirschfeld, 'German Refugee Scholars in Great Britain, 1933–1945', p. 156.

72 Hans Albrecht Berthe, 'Interview with Lillian Hoddeson' (Niels Bohr Library and Archives, American Institute of Physics, 29 April 1981), accessed 5 July 2011, www.aip.org/history/ohilist/4505.html.

73 This influence in a variety of disciplines has been widely noted. See, for example, Gustav V. R. Born, 'The Effect of the Scientific Environment in Britain on Refugee Scientists from Germany and Their Effects on Science in Britain', *Berichte zur Wissenschaftsgeschichte*, 7, no. 3 (1984): 129–43; Mitchell G. Ash and Alfons Söllner (eds), *Forced Migration and Scientific Change: Emigré German-Speaking Scientists and Scholars after 1933* (Cambridge: University of Cambridge, 1996).

74 Bodleian Libraries Special Collections (BLSC), *Society for the Protection of Science and Learning*, MS SPSL/142/1–2/British Empire. For an Indian example see MS SPSL/150/2/146/Benares Hindu University to General Secretary, 15 Mar. 1939. For responses from settler universities, see MS SPSL/142/1/Registrar (University of the Witwatersrand) to the AAC, 28 Aug. 1933; MS SPSL/142/1/A.G. Hatcher (Memorial University College, Newfoundland) to Walter Adams (AAC), 25 Sept. 1935; MS SPSL/142/1/Register (Auckland University College) to AAC, 4 Jan. 1934.

75 *Ibid.*, MS SPSL/128/3/W.G. Constable (Courtauld Institute of Art) to Walter Adams, 2 June 1934. Answering the SPSL's 1947 inquiry as to whether 'as a matter of principle' the Australian CSIR would be willing to consider applications from suitably qualified displaced persons, L. G. Dobbie replied: 'the Council is rather lukewarm towards the idea of offering employment to such persons unless they are outstandingly good

men and of well established repute. One of the big difficulties is that all their lives they have been used to ways very different from our own and it is a matter of major difficulty for many of them to become adjusted sufficiently to our methods to really give of their best.' MS SPSL/140/2/Dobbie (Australian Scientific Research Liaison) to J. Ursell (Secretary, SPSL), 2 Oct. 1947.

76 *University of Toronto President's Report for 1936*, (Toronto: University of Toronto, 1936), p. 24.

77 BLSC, *Society for the Protection of Science and Learning*, MS SPSL/140/2/ N. T. M. Wilsmore (University of Western Australia) to C. S. Gibson (Hon. Secretary, Academic Assistance Council), 2 Mar. 1935. For an account of anti-Semitism and refugee scholars in Canadian universities, see Zimmerman, 'Narrow-Minded People', pp. 291–315.

78 BLSC, *Society for the Protection of Science and Learning*, MS SPSL/157/1–4/ Correspondence concerning candidates for Carnegie Empire Scholarships.

79 *Ibid.*, MS SPSL/59/5/Letter re. Carnegie offer to Vice-Chancellors, South Africa; MS SPSL/24/W. Adams to Rutherford, 18 Dec. 1934; MS SPSL/29/C. S. Gibson to R. Waley Cohen, 2 Nov. 1934; MS SPSL/57/C.M. Skepper (Assistant Secretary, AAC) to Jon Phillips (Department of Botany, University of Witwatersrand), 22 Dec. 1934.

80 For example, in November 1938 the University of Tasmania's E. J. G Pitman noted that many of the teaching staff had received letters indicating that well qualified men would be to accept a temporary post and this had convinced them to make one available. *Ibid.*, MS SPSL/140/2/E.J.G. Pitman (University of Tasmania) to AAC Secretary, 17 Nov. 1938.

81 The Canadian Society for the Protection of Science and Learning was founded in 1939.

82 UTA, *Harold Hibbert Papers*, MS 3076 C2/69, Appel to Hibbert, 14 Aug. 1935; Lawrence D. Stokes, 'Canada and an Academic Refugee from Nazi Germany: The Case of Gerhard Herzberg', *Canadian Historical Review*, 57, no. 2 (1976): 150–70. The experience of Walter Boas, who went to Melbourne on a Carnegie scholarship, provides another example. See Clarebrough and Head, 'Walter Boas 1904–1982'; L. M. Clarebrough and A. K. Head, 'Walter Boas 1904–1982', *Historical Records of Australian Science*, 6, no. 4 (1987): 507–17.

83 Rutherford, who was President of the AAC, was particularly active; and in 1939, W. K. Hancock, serving the organisation's Birmingham branch, reported: 'my whole life is comforting refugees and getting people jobs'. Jim Davidson, *A Three-Cornered Life: The Historian W. K. Hancock* (Sydney: UNSW Press, 2010), p. 138.

84 The total number of refugee scholars taken by the British Dominions was thirty-two in Canada, twenty-three in Australia, five in New Zealand, and one in South Africa, with an additional eight in India. BLSC, *Society for the Protection of Science and Learning*, MS SPSL/1/5/Fifth Report, 1946.

85 Sanderson, *Universities and British Industry, 1850–1970*, pp. 339–41.

86 Brebis Bleaney, 'Sir Mark (Marcus Laurence Elwin) Oliphant, AC, KBE', *Biographical Memoirs of Fellows of the Royal Society*, 47 (2001): 383–93.

87 Margaret Gowing, *Britain and Atomic Energy, 1939–1945* (London: Macmillan, 1964), pp. 71–9, 187–8; Ross Galbreath, 'The Rutherford Connection: New Zealand Scientists and the Manhattan and Montreal Projects', *War in History*, 2, no. 3 (1995): 306–19.

88 Galbreath, 'The Rutherford Connection', pp. 311–13; Roy MacLeod, 'All for Each and Each for All: Reflections on Anglo-American and Commonwealth Scientific Cooperation, 1940–1945', *Albion*, 26, no. 1 (1994): 79–112; Ronald W. Clark, *Tizard* (London: Methuen and Co., 1965). There is an extensive literature on the development of atomic weapons in the Second World War, and the role of collaboration in it. For an excellent review article, see Robert Seidel, 'Books on the Bomb', *Isis*, 81, no. 308 (1990): 519–28.

89 For an account of the participation of the various Dominions in wartime scientific research see Roy MacLeod (ed.), *The Commonwealth of Scienc*; Roy MacLeod (ed.), *Science and the Pacific War: Science and Survival in the Pacific, 1939–1945* (Dordrecht: Kluwer, 2000); R. W. Home, 'Science on Service, 1939–1945', in R. W.

Home (ed.), *Australian Science in the Making* (Sydney: Cambridge University Press, 1988); David Zimmerman, *The Great Naval Battle of Ottawa* (Toronto: University of Toronto Press, 1989); Avery, *The Science of War*; Frank R. Callaghan, ed., *Science in New Zealand* (Wellington: A.H. and A.W Reed, 1957); Roy MacLeod, 'Allied Scientific Collaboration in the Second World War: Some Anniversary Reflections', *War in History*, 2, no. 3 (1995): 253–8.

90 Charles P. Stacey, *Arms, Men and Governments: The War Policies of Canada, 1939–1945* (Ottawa: Queen's Printer, 1970), p. 512.

91 John D. Hargreaves, *Academe and Empire: Some Overseas Connections of Aberdeen University, 1860–1970* (Aberdeen: Aberdeen University Press, 1994), pp. 55–60.

92 Ian D. Rae, 'They Had to Go: Australian Chemists Who Took Doctor of Philosophy Degrees in Britain, 1945–65', *Historical Records of Australian Science*, 12, no. 3 (1999): 331–61, p. 357.

93 Wm. Roger Louis and Ronald Robinson, 'The Imperialism of Decolonisation', *Journal of Imperial and Commonwealth History*, 22, no. 3 (1994): 462–511.

94 Heike Jöns, 'Academic Travel from Cambridge University and the Formation of Centres of Knowledge, 1885–1954', pp. 356, 358–9. Joseph Morgan Hodge, *Triumph of the Expert: Agrarian Doctrines of Development and the Legacies of British Colonialism* (Athens: Ohio University Press, 2007).

95 MacLeod, 'All for Each and Each for All', p. 80.

96 For a detailed examination of its complex history, see *Ibid*.

97 Donald J. C. Phillipson, 'The National Research Council of Canada: Its Historiography, Its Chronology, Its Bibliography', *Scientia Canadensis*, 15, no. 2 (1991): 177–93.

98 Stuart Ward, 'The End of Empire and the Fate of Britishness', in H. Brocklehurst and R. Phillips (eds), *History, Nationhood and the Question of Britain* (Basingstoke: Palgrave Macmillan, 2003); A. G. Hopkins, 'Rethinking Decolonization', *Past and Present*, 200 (2008): 211–47.

99 Ward, 'The End of Empire and the Fate of Britishness', pp. 251–2; Hugh W. Springer, *The Commonwealth of Universities* (London: The Association of Commonwealth Universities, 1988).

100 Laqua, 'Transnational Intellectual Cooperation, the League of Nations, and the Problem of Order'.

CONCLUSION

In 1909, three years into his appointment as professor of classics at the University of Adelaide, Henry Darnley Naylor published a book on Latin and English idiom with Cambridge University Press. In the preface, written in Adelaide in October 1908, Naylor thanked two men for their help in its production: his fellow Cambridge prizeman and former colleague T. G. Tucker, professor of classical philology at the University of Melbourne, and his friend and former teacher at Cambridge, Peter Giles. Separated by distance, but united by common institutional affiliations and bonds of affection, these men – in Adelaide, Cambridge and Melbourne – maintained their connections throughout their lives and careers. More than a century later, how are we to understand the academic world in which they lived?

First, Naylor's world was expansive. Settler universities like Adelaide saw themselves as members of the wider British academic community. From the 1880s until the Second World War they instituted mechanisms such as travelling scholarships, leave-of-absence programmes, and appointments practices that de-territorialised key aspects of academic life, enabling scholars to sustain connections and build careers that straddled the distances of empire. Universities in both Britain and the settler colonies accorded official recognition to the 'British academic world' these scholarly ties created: they enshrined it in statutes that gave preferential standing to each other's degrees, and they expressed it in imperial associations such as the 1903 Allied Colonial Universities Conference and the Congresses of the Universities of the British Empire. In part, this book has sought to write the settler universities back into the history of British academia.

Second, Naylor's world was one made by intimate and personal ties. As the preface to his 1909 book suggests, informal long-distance relationships underpinned most aspects of his and his contemporaries' academic practice, conditioning the way they accessed information, published their research and obtained appointments. These relationships were made in specific sites – in laboratories, in 'the field', and even on board ships – but they were not confined to these locations. Instead, scholars carried their friendships with them as they travelled. These personal connections were crucial to the way academics in settler universities made knowledge: they could bring those working at the geographic margins of empire close to the intellectual centres of 'British' scholarship. Moreover, informal ties were essential to the formal organisation and operation of the institutions in which academics worked. Private association and personal knowledge helped constitute the public institutional practices of universities across Britain and the settler world.

Yet the forms of familiarity that included Naylor simultaneously worked to marginalise and exclude many others. He benefited from an academic world made by social and institutional practices that at once reflected and helped sustain the raced and gendered as well as the geo-political hierarchies of the period. Individual partialities and prejudices, and the institutional practices that aided and exploited them, created highly uneven landscapes of scholarly access and exchange. Connected to its networks and advantaged by its cultures of sociability, Naylor and Laby and scholars like them moved along the broad highways of the British academic world. But personal ties that straddled oceans could frequently fail to cross the country, or even the road. Men like Brailsford Robertson or the Irish candidates for physics positions, who lacked the right connections, travelled much more difficult paths. Dadabhai Naoroji and Jomo Kenyatta found themselves virtually off the map. And all the time, working in the background, women like Margaret Hodgson and Helen Hogg, and the many wives and daughters whose contributions as correspondents and assistants have gone unrecorded, provided much of the hidden labour that made many of these journeys possible. It would not be until the last quarter of the twentieth century that they were able to undertake them in their own right. We need to recognise that, although it was expansive, Naylor's world was also exclusionary, shifting and unequal.

The congress that Naylor attended in London in 1912 temporarily made this world tangible. In the formal sessions, but more especially outside them, delegates from universities across Britain and the empire performed together the ordinarily diffuse exchanges that created the British academic world. When Rosebery delivered the speech with which this book opened, Naylor and his fellow delegates clapped and cheered because Rosebery's imperial rhetoric evoked this world. It summoned a geographically expansive community that was united by affection and by co-operation. But his words were also addressed to the 'gentleman' in the audience and invoked a 'family' that, although it stretched from St Andrews to Saskatchewan, did not reach Delhi. In their interactions at the congress, the delegates enacted these delineations and reinforced them. Just as Naylor's preface (like all our prefaces) reveals the topographies of his own individual scholarly universe, the proceedings of the 1912 Congress exposes those of the academic world he inhabited.

The categories of national history do not help us make sense of this world. Segmenting the story of universities in Britain and the Dominions was part of the post-war project of nationalising knowledge. It fragmented the long-distance connections that had shaped settler institutions and the lives of those who worked in them. But to cast these connections as 'transnational' is also misleading. It ignores the racial and imperial imperatives that, as late as the 1960s, still framed what R. B. Haldane in 1903 had called 'the great British nation in its different parts'.[1] Naylor's career points to our need for an at-once more capacious and more demarcated way of thinking about British and settler universities in this period.

Framed and facilitated by the structures of empire, the British academic world was one of the many limited worlds of late nineteenth- and early twentieth-century globalisation. Made by affections and connections that cut up the vast reaches of the globe, these worlds were not universal. Rather, they stretched in partial and particular directions, linking people who knew each other, and people who knew people who knew each other. In the midst of social, economic and geo-political changes that were often as frightening as they were exciting; in contexts in which information was imperfect and opportunities restricted, such limited worlds provided ways of making sense of globalising forces, and ways of making lives and careers within them. When Naylor travelled to England, wrote to his friends in Cambridge, or bumped into colleagues in the Adelaide University Common Room, he – and hundreds, if not thousands, of those like him – helped to inscribe the boundaries and mould the contours of an expansive but bounded academic community. The peculiarities of their intimate feelings, the reach of their personal ties and the routes of their repeated migrations created relative forms of proximity and distance that helped reshape the geographies of empire and fashion the circumscribed spaces of lived global connection.

Note

1 'Official Report of the Allied Colonial Universities Conference', p. 118.

Foundation dates of universities and colleges established in Britain and the Empire before the Second World War

Entries printed in italic face are colleges that prepared students to sit the examinations of other degree-granting bodies.

11th century	University of Oxford
c.1209	University of Cambridge
1410–13	University of St Andrews
1451	University of Glasgow
1495	University of Aberdeen
1583	University of Edinburgh
1592	Trinity College, Dublin
1663	Séminaire de Québec, Quebec City (became Université Laval in 1852)
1789	King's College, Windsor (Royal Charter, 1802)
1795	*St Patrick's College, Maynooth* (did not award degrees; became a constituent college of the Catholic University of Ireland from 1876 and the National University of Ireland from 1910)
1800	King's College, New Brunswick (became Academy of Arts and Science, Fredericton, in 1785; Royal Charter, 1828)
1818	Dalhousie, Nova Scotia
1821	McGill College, Montreal (active from 1829; named McGill University from 1885)

Abbreviations: NUI, National University of Ireland; QUI, Queen's University of Ireland; RUI, Royal University of Ireland; UCGH, University of the Cape of Good Hope; UNISA, University of South Africa; UNZ, University of New Zealand.

1822	St David's College, Lampeter (Royal Charter, 1928)
1826	*University College, London* (affiliated with the University of London from 1836)
1827	King's College, Toronto (opened in 1843; became Trinity College in 1852)
1827	*Fourah Bay College, Freetown, Sierra Leone* (affiliated with Durham University from 1876)
1828–29	*King's College, London* (affiliated with the University of London from 1836)
1832	Durham University (Royal Charter, 1837)
1836	*Upper Canada Academy, Ontario* (later Victoria College and affiliated to the University of Toronto from 1892)
1836	University of London
1838	Acadia College, Nova Scotia (degrees granted from 1840)
1840	St Mary's University, Halifax (degrees granted from 1841)
1841	Queen's University, Kingston
1843	Bishop's College, Quebec (Royal Charter 1852)
1843	Mount Allison College, New Brunswick (Royal Charter 1858)
1848	College of Bytown (University of Ottawa from 1866)
1849	*Queen's College, Cork* (opened in 1840 and chartered in 1845; constituent college of Queen's University of Ireland (QUI) from 1850; affiliated to the Royal University of Ireland (RUI) from 1879; renamed University College, Cork, and functioned as a constituent college of the National University of Ireland (NUI) from 1908)
1849	*Queen's College, Belfast* (chartered 1845; constituent college of QUI from 1850; affiliated to the RUI from 1879; awarded Royal Charter in 1908 and became Queen's University, Belfast)
1849	*Queen's College, Galway* (chartered in 1845; constituent college of QUI from 1850; affiliated to the RUI from 1879; renamed University College, Galway, and functioned as a constituent college of the NUI from 1908)
1849	*University College, Toronto* (became the University of Toronto in 1853)
1850	Queen's University of Ireland (dissolved in 1882; refounded as the Royal University of Ireland in 1879)
1850	University of Sydney

1851	*Owens College, Manchester* (initially affiliated to the University of London; became a constituent college of the federal Victoria University, Manchester, in 1880; in 1904, following the dissolution of the federal university, it became the Victoria University of Manchester)
1852	Trinity College, Toronto (constituent college of the University of Toronto from 1904)
1853	University of Melbourne
1853	St Francis Xavier College, Nova Scotia (Royal Charter 1866; degrees granted from 1868)
1853	University of Toronto
1854	*Catholic University of Ireland* (became University College, Dublin, in 1880 and affiliated to the RUI; constituent college of the NUI from 1908)
1857	University of Calcutta
1857	University of Bombay
1857	University of Madras
1857	*Assumption College, Windsor, Ontario* (affiliated to the University of Western Ontario from 1919)
1859	University of New Brunswick
1869	*University of Otago* (constituent college of the University of New Zealand from 1874; became independent University of Otago in 1961)
1870	University of New Zealand (UNZ) (degrees granted from 1874)
1871	*Saint-Boniface College, Manitoba* (affiliated to the University of Manitoba from 1877)
1871	*Manitoba College* (affiliated to the University of Manitoba from 1877 and the University of Winnipeg from 1967)
1872	*University College, Wales, Aberystwyth* (affiliated to the University of London and to the University of Wales from 1893)
1873	*Canterbury College, Christchurch* (constituent college of the UNZ from 1874)
1873	University of the Cape of Good Hope (UCGH)
1873	*Mount Saint Vincent College (for women), Nova Scotia* (degrees granted from 1914; Royal Charter, 1925)
1874	*South African College* (affiliated to the UCGH)

1874	University of Adelaide
1875	Aligarh Muslim University
1875	*Mason College, Birmingham* (affiliated to the University of London; became the University of Birmingham in 1900)
1876	*University College, Bristol* (affiliated to the University of London; became the University of Bristol in 1909)
1877	University of Manitoba
1878	Western University of London Ontario (degrees granted from 1883)
1878	Université de Laval à Montréal (affiliated to the Université Laval; became the Université de Montréal in 1919)
1878	*Rangoon College* (affiliated to the University of Calcutta; became Rangoon University in 1920)
1879	*Firth College* (became University College of Sheffield in 1897 and affiliated to the University of London; became the University of Sheffield in 1905)
1879	Royal University of Ireland (Royal Charter, 1880; dissolved in 1908)
1880	Victoria University, Manchester (federal university)
1880	*University College, Dublin* (affiliated to the RUI; constituent college of the NUI from 1908)
1881	*Dundee College* (affiliated to the University of St Andrews)
1881	*Stellenbosch College* (became Victoria College in 1887; affiliated to the UCGH)
1881	*University College, Liverpool* (constituent college of Victoria University, Manchester; became the University of Liverpool in 1903)
1881	*Nottingham University College* (affiliated to the University of London; became the University of Nottingham in 1948)
1882	University of the Punjab
1882	*Auckland University College* (constituent college of the UNZ)
1883	*University College of South Wales and Monmouthsire, Cardiff* (affiliated to the University of London until 1893 and then to the University of Wales)

1884	*University College of North Wales, Bangor* (affiliated to the University of London until 1893 and then to the University of Wales)
1886	*Royal Holloway College* (affiliated to the University of London from 1900)
1887	McMaster University, Ontario
1887	University of Allahabad
1887	*Yorkshire College, Leeds* (constituent college of Victoria University, Manchester; became the University of Leeds in 1904)
1889	*Brandon College, Manitoba* (affiliated to McMaster University; became Brandon University in 1967)
1890	University of Tasmania
1892	*University College Reading* (became the University of Reading in 1926)
1893	University of Wales
1895	*London School of Economics* (affiliated to the University of London from 1900)
1896	*South African School of Mines, Kimberley* (affiliated to the UCGH; moved to Johannesburg and became the Transvaal Technical Institute in 1904 and Transvaal University College in 1906; became the South African School of Mines and Technology in 1910 and University College Johannesburg in 1920; became the University of the Witwatersrand and received a Royal Charter in 1922)
1896	*Canterbury Agricultural College* (affiliated to the UNZ)
1897	*Victoria University College, Wellington* (affiliated to the UNZ)
1899	*London School of Hygiene and Tropical Medicine* (affiliated to the University of London)
1900	University of Birmingham
1902	*Hartley University College, Southampton* (affiliated to the University of London; became University of Southampton and received a Royal Charter in 1952)
1903	*Victoria College, British Columbia* (affiliated with McGill University until 1908 when it became the University of British Columbia)
1903	University of Liverpool

1904	*Rhodes University College, Grahamstown* (affiliated to the UCGH; affiliated to the University of South Africa (UNISA) from 1918; became Rhodes University in 1951)
1904	*Grey College, Bloemfontein* (affiliated to the UCGH; became Grey University College in 1906 and affiliated to the UNISA from 1918; became University College of the Orange Free State c.1940 and the University of the Orange Free State in 1950)
1904	*Goldsmiths College* (affiliated to the University of London)
1904	University of Leeds
1904	Victoria University of Manchester
1905	*Straits Government Medical School from 1905* (became King Edward VII College of Medicine, Singapore, in 1921 and affiliated to the University of London; became the University of Malaya in 1849)
1905	University of Sheffield
1907	University of Saskatchewan
1907	*Imperial College of Science and Technology* (affiliated to the University of London)
1907	*Birkbeck College* (affiliated to the University of London)
1908	University of Alberta
1908	University of British Columbia (opened 1915)
1908	Queen's University, Belfast
1908	*Transvaal University College, Pretoria campus* (affiliated to the UCGH and UNISA from 1918; became University of Pretoria in 1930)
1908	Cairo University
1908	University of Western Ontario
1909	University of Bristol
1909	National University of Ireland
1909	University of Queensland
1909	*Natal University College* (affiliated to the UCGH and then the UNISA from 1918)
1911	University of Western Australia
1911	University of Hong Kong
1915	*Queen Mary, University of London* (affiliated to the University of London)

1916	*South African Native College, Fort Hare* (affiliated to the University of South Africa)
1916	University of Mysore
1916	Banaras Hindu University
1917	Patna University
1918	University of Cape Town
1918	Stellenbosch University
1918	University of South Africa (UNISA)
1918	Osmania University, Hyderabad
1919	*Potchefstroom University College* (affiliated to the UNISA from 1921)
1920	*Ceylon University College* (affiliated to the University of London; became Ceylon University in 1942)
1920	*University College, Swansea* (affiliated to the University of Wales)
1921	University of Dhaka
1921	University of Lucknow
1922	University of the Witwatersrand
1922	*Makerere University College, Uganda* (affiliated to the University of London from 1949; became the University of East Africa in 1963, offering courses leading to University of London degrees, and then the independent Makerere University in 1970)
1922	*University College of the South West of England, Exeter* (affiliated to the University of London; became the University of Exeter in 1955)
1924	*Waterloo College of Arts, Ontario* (became Wilfrid Laurier University in 1973)
1924	*Imperial College of Tropical Agriculture, Trinidad* (became part of University of the West Indies from 1962)
1925	*Memorial University College, Newfoundland* (became Memorial University in 1949)
1925	*Mandalay College* (affiliated to Rangoon; became Mandalay University in 1958)
1926	*New Zealand Agricultural College* (constituent college of the UNZ; became Massey Agricultural College in 1927 and Massey University in 1961)
1926	*Indian School of Mines, Jharkhand* (gained university status in 1967)

1926	University of Reading
1927	*University College, Hull* (affiliated to the University of London; became Hull University in 1957)
1927	*University College, Leicester* (affiliated to the University of London; became University of Leicester in 1957)
1928	*Raffles College, Singapore* (affiliated to the University of London; became part of the University of Malaya in 1949, and the University of Singapore in 1962)
1928	Annamalai University, Tamil Nadu
1924	*Achimota College, Gold Coast* (opened in 1927 as a secondary school offering matriculation exams of the University of London; became University College of the Gold Coast in 1948, affiliated to the University of London, which became the University of Ghana in 1961)
1930	University of Pretoria
1930	*Canberra University College* (affiliated with the University of Melbourne; became part of the Australian National University from 1960)
1931	*Mount Royal College, Calgary* (offering transfer courses for the University of Alberta)
1938	*New England University College* (affiliated with the University of Sydney; became the University of New England in 1954)

APPENDIX B

Timeline of institutions granted 'affiliated' status at the University of Oxford

1888	27 November	University of the Cape of Good Hope
		University of Sydney
1889	21 May	University of Calcutta
	29 October	University of the Punjab
1890	4 November	University of Bombay
1891	3 February	University of Adelaide
1894	19 June	University of Madras
	30 October	University of Melbourne
	13 November	University of New Zealand
	20 November	University of Allahabad
1895	26 November	University of Toronto
1899	2 May	McGill University, Montreal
1901	22 January	University of New Brunswick
1903	3 February	University of Malta
	22 October	University of King's College (Windsor, Nova Scotia)
		Dalhousie University (Halifax, Nova Scotia)
1904	15 March	Mt Allison College (Sackville, New Brunswick)
	24 May	University of Durham
	14 June	University of St Andrews

Source: University of Oxford First Supplement to the Historical Register: 1900–1920 (Oxford, 1921), pp. 328–30.

1904	14 June	University of Glasgow
		University of Aberdeen
		University of Edinburgh
	1 November	Harvard University (Cambridge, Massachusetts)
		Acadia University (Wolfville, Nova Scotia)
1905	14 February	University of Manitoba
	14 March	University of Queen's College (Kingston, Ontario)
	16 May	Wisconsin University
	24 October	Princeton University
	21 November	Laval University (Quebec City, Quebec)
		McMaster University (Toronto, Ontario)
1906	17 May	University of St Joseph's College (St Joseph, New Brunswick)
	22 May	Michigan University
1907	4 June	Brown University (Providence, Rhode Island)
	22 October	Cornell University (Ithaca, New York)
		Yale University (New Haven, Connecticut)
		University of Bishop's College (Lennoxville, Quebec)
		University of Ottawa
	12 November	University of Virginia
		Universities of the German Empire; the Austro-Hungarian Empire; and Switzerland
1908	12 May	Columbia University (New York City)
1910	14 June	University of Saskatchewan
		Vanderbilt University (Nashville, Tennessee)
	1 November	Leland Stanford Junior University (California); The University of California
1911	24 October	Bowdoin College (Brunswick, Maine)
		Haverford College (Haverford, Pennsylvania)
1912	13 February	Universities of the French Republic
		University of London
		University of Liverpool

1912	13 February	University of Leeds
		University of Sheffield
		University of Wales
		University of Birmingham
		The Victoria University of Manchester
1913	22 October	Johns Hopkins University (Baltimore, Maryland); University of Chicago
1914	10 February	The University of Queensland
	19 May	National University of Ireland; Queen's University of Belfast
	16 June	Dartmouth College (Hanover, New Hampshire)
		Minnesota University
		Oberlin College (Oberlin, Ohio)
	3 November	University of Alberta
1915	16 January	University of Bristol
1916	18 February	University of St Francis Xavier's College (Antigonish, Nova Scotia)
	24 October	University of Illinois
1917	10 June	University of Western Australia
1919	10 June	University of Pennsylvania
1920	2 March	University of Hong Kong

BIBLIOGRAPHY

Primary Sources

Manuscripts

Adelaide: University of Adelaide Archives (UAA)
Registrar's Correspondence, S200.
Theodore George Bentley Osborn Records, MSS 0020.

Birmingham: University of Birmingham Archives (UBA)
Library Committee Minutes.
Library Accessions Register.

Cape Town: University of Cape Town Archives (UCTA)
Mandelbrote Papers, BC576.
Personal File of H. G. Galbraith, AA1–156.
Social Anthropology (1921), AA 157–330.
Chair of Physics, AA 1–156.
Personal File of J. K. Wylie, AA 1–156.
J. Brock Papers, BC1041.
South African College Reports.

Canberra: Australian Academy of Science, Basser Library (AAS)
Grafton Elliot Smith Papers, MS56.
C. J. Martin Papers, MS11.
J. P. V. Madsen Papers, MS72.

Kingston: Queen's University Archives (QUA)
Principal's Office.
Board of Trustees Minutes.
Personnel Files.

London:
Bodleian Libraries Special Collections (BLSC)
Society for the Protection of Science and Learning, MS SPSL.
British Library (BL)
Warren Dawson Papers, Add 56303.
India Office Records, IOR.
National Archives UK (NAUK)
Ceylon University College, CO 54.
Barbados Dispatches, CO 28.
Colonies, General: Original Correspondence, CO 323.
Asquith Commission, CO 958.
Department of Education and Science: Private Office Papers (Series 1),
PRO/ED 24/1994.

London (*continued*):
Science Museum Library, Swindon Archives (SMLA)
  Rutherford Correspondence.
University of London Archives (ULA)
  University of London Minutes of Senate and Appendices.

Melbourne: University of Melbourne Archives (UMA)
  Council Minute Books, UM174.
  Library Accessions Books.
  Registrar's Correspondence, UM312.
  T. H. Laby Papers, UM85.
  R. M. Crawford Papers, Series 6.

Montreal: McGill University Archives (MUA)
  Louis Vessot King, MG 3026.
  Office of the Principal, William Peterson, RG2.
  Office of Principals, Arthur Currie, Arthur Eustace Morgan, and
    Lewis Williams Douglas, RG2.
  John Watson Fonds, 1064.
  Office of Principal, Auckland Campbell Geddes, RG2.

Sydney: University of Sydney Archives (USA)
  Minutes of the Senate, G1/1.
  Accountant's Office, G18/13.
  J. T. Wilson Papers, P162.
  Registrar's General Subject Files, G3.

Toronto: University of Toronto Archives (UTA)
  Carnegie Foundation, A68-007.
  Office of the President, A1967-0007.
  G.M. Wrong Papers, B2004–2005.
  President's Annual Reports.
  Harold Hibbert Papers, MS 3076.
  Clara Cynthia Benson Fonds.

Wellington: Archives New Zealand (ANZ)
  University of New Zealand Archives, AAMJ Acc W3119.

Newspapers and journals

The Argus (Melbourne) 1914.
Manchester Guardian, 1914.
Nature, 1890–1917.
New York Times, 1911.
Proceedings and Transactions of the Royal Society of Canada, 1885.
The Register, 1913.
Science, New Series, 1933.
Sydney Morning Herald, 1906.
The Times, 1901–1945.

Other printed sources

Annual Calendar of McGill College and University (Montreal, 1885–90).

Auckland University College Calendar (Auckland, 1896).

Bibliographic Record of the University of Sydney, 1851–1913 (Sydney, 1914).

Calendar of the South African College (Cape Town, 1906).

Calendar of the University of Adelaide (Adelaide, 1888–1939).

Calendar of the University of the Cape of Good Hope (Cape Town, 1913).

Calendar of the University of Cape Town (Cape Town, 1939).

Calendar of the University of Melbourne (Melbourne, 1911–29).

Calendar of the University of Strathclyde (Glasgow, 1892).

Calendar of the University of Sydney (Sydney, 1885–1923).

Congress of the Universities of the Empire, 1912: Report of Proceedings (London, 1912).

Fellowships and Scholarships Open to Foreign Students for Study in the United States (New York, 1929).

Fifth Quinquennial Congress of the Universities of the British Empire, 1936: Report of Proceedings (London, 1936).

Fourth Congress of the Universities of the Empire, 1931: Report of Proceedings (London, 1931).

Handbook of Indian Universities (Bangalore, 1928).

Historical Register of the University of Oxford (Oxford, 1900).

History of the Ministry of Munitions (London, 1918–23).

Imperial Education Conference: Convened by the Chief of the Imperial General Staff, June 11–12, 1919 (London, 1919).

List of International Fellowships for Research (London, 1934).

McGill University Calendar (Montreal, 1922–35).

New Zealand University Calendar (Wellington, Christchurch and Dunedin, 1901).

'Official Report of the Allied Colonial Universities Conference', *The Empire Review*, 6 (1903), pp. 71–128.

Oxford University Calendar (Oxford, 1900).

Proceedings of the Institute of Chemistry of Great Britain and Ireland (1918).

Queen's University Calendar (Kingston, 1929–31).

Record of the Science Research Scholars of the Royal Commission for the Exhibition of 1851: 1891–1929 (London, 1930).

Report of the Eighty-Fourth Meeting of the British Association for the Advancement of Science, Australia 1914 (London, 1915).

Second Congress of the Universities of the Empire, 1921: Report of Proceedings (London, 1921).

Statuta Universitatis Oxoniensis (Oxford, 1914).

Statutes of Cambridge and Passages from Acts of Parliament Relating to the University (Cambridge, 1928).

Student's Handbook to the University and Colleges of Cambridge (Cambridge, 1902–9).

Student's Handbook to the University and Colleges of Oxford (Oxford, 1909).

'Testimonials in Favour of Mr Daniel Wilson (Candidate for the Chair of

History and English Literature in the University of Toronto)' (1851).

'Testimonials in Favour of T.P. Anderson Stuart (Candidate for the Chair of Anatomy and Physiology in Sydney University)' (1882).

Third Congress of the Universities of the Empire, 1926: Report of Proceedings (London, 1926).

University of Calcutta Calendar for the Year (Calcutta, 1907).

University of Oxford First Supplement to the Historical Register: 1900–1920 (Oxford, 1921).

University Reform in New Zealand (Wellington, NZ, 1911).

University Teachers Association of New Zealand, *Some Aspects of University Teaching in New Zealand* (Christchurch, 1925).

University of Toronto President's Report for 1936 (Toronto, 1936).

Victoria University Calendar (Manchester, 1880).

Yearbook of the Universities of the [British] Empire (London, 1915–36).

Secondary Sources

Books and articles

Adams, J. C., *Seated with the Mighty: A Biography of Sir Gilbert Parker* (Ottawa: John Coldwell Adams, 1979).

Adams, W., 'The Refugee Scholars of the 1930s', *The Political Quarterly*, 39 (1968), 7–14.

Addison, W. I., *The Snell Exhibitions* (Glasgow: James MacLehose and Sons, 1901).

Adler, P. S., 'Market, Hierarchy, and Trust: The Knowledge Economy and the Future of Capitalism', *Organization Science*, 12 (2001), 215–34.

Ainley, M. G., 'Marriage and Scientific Work in Twentieth Century Canada: The Berkeleys in Marine Biology and the Hoggs in Astronomy', in H. M. Pycior, N. G. Slack and P. G. Abir-Am (eds), *Creative Couples in the Sciences* (New Brunswick: Rutgers University Press, 1996), pp. 143–55.

—, 'Gendered Careers: Women Science Educators at Anglo-Canadian Universities, 1920–1980', in P. Stortz and E. L. Panayotidis (eds), *Historical Identities: The Professoriate in Canada* (Toronto: University of Toronto Press, 2006), pp. 248–70.

Allibone, T. E., *The Royal Society and Its Dining Clubs* (Oxford: Pergamon Press, 1976).

Alter, P., *The Reluctant Patron: Science and the State in Britain, 1850–1920* (Oxford: Berg, 1987).

Anderson, F., *An Historian's Life: Max Crawford and the Politics of Academic Freedom* (Melbourne: Melbourne University Press, 2005).

Anderson, R. D., *Universities and Elites in Britain since 1800* (London: Macmillan, 1992).

Annan, N., *The Dons: Mentors, Eccentrics and Geniuses* (Chicago, IL: University of Chicago Press, 2001).

Appadurai, A. (ed.), *Globalization* (Durham, NC: Duke University Press, 2001).

Arnove, R. F. (ed.), *Philanthropy and Cultural Imperialism: The Foundations at Home and Abroad* (Bloomington, IN: Indiana University Press, 1982).

Ash, M. G., and A. Söllner (eds), *Forced Migration and Scientific Change: Emigré German-Speaking Scientists and Scholars after 1933* (Cambridge: University of Cambridge, 1996).

Ashby, E., *Community of Universities* (Southampton: The Association of Commonwealth Universities, 1963).

—, *Universities: British, Indian, African: A Study in the Ecology of Higher Education* (London: Weidenfeld and Nicolson, 1966).

Attard, B., *The Australian High Commissioners* (London: Menzies Centre for Australian Studies, 1991).

Auchmuty, J. J., *The Idea of the University in Its Australian Setting: A Historical Survey* (Melbourne: 1963).

Avery, D., *The Science of War: Canadian Scientists and Allied Military Technology* (Toronto: University of Toronto Press, 1998).

Badash, L., 'The Origins of Big Science: Rutherford at McGill', in M. Bunge and W. R. Shea (eds), *Rutherford and Physics at the Turn of the Century* (Folkestone: Dawson, 1979), pp. 23–41.

—, 'British and American Views of the German Menace in World War I', *Notes and Records of the Royal Society of London*, 34 (1979–80), 91–121.

Barff, H. E., *A Short Historical Account of the University of Sydney* (Sydney: Angus and Robertson, 1902).

Barton, P., P. Doyle and J. Vandewalle, *Beneath Flanders Fields: The Tunnellers War 1914–1918* (Staplehurst: Spellmount, 2004).

Basalla, G., 'The Spread of Western Science', *Science*, 156 (1967), 611–22.

Bates, R. H., V. Y. Mudimbe and J. O'Barr (eds), *Africa and the Disciplines: The Contributions of Research in Africa to the Social Sciences and Humanities* (Chicago, IL: Chicago University Press, 1993).

Bathelt, H., 'Buzz-and-Pipeline Dynamics: Towards a Knowledge-Based Multiplier Model of Clusters', *Geography Compass*, 1 (2007), 1282–98.

Beaglehole, J. C., *The University of New Zealand: An Historical Study* (Auckland: Whitcomb and Tombs, 1937).

—, *Victoria University College: An Essay Towards a History* (Wellington: New Zealand University Press, 1949).

Belich, J., *Replenishing the Earth: The Settler Revolution and the Rise of the Anglo-World, 1783–1939* (Oxford: Oxford University Press, 2009).

Bell, D., *The Idea of Greater Britain: Empire and the Future of World Order, 1860–1900* (Princeton, NJ, and Woodstock: Princeton University Press, 2007).

Ben-David, J., *The Scientist's Role in Society: A Comparative Study* (Edgewood Cliffs, NJ: Prentice-Hall, 1971).

Berthe, H. A., 'Interview with Lillian Hoddeson' (Niels Bohr Library and Archives, American Institute of Physics, 29 Apr. 1981), accessed 5 July 2011, www.aip.org/history/ohilist/4505.html.

Beveridge, W., *A Defence of Free Learning* (Oxford: Oxford University Press, 1959).

Bigge, J. T., 'Report of the Commissioner of Inquiry into the State of the Colony of New South Wales', *Parliamentary Papers*, 20 (1822).

Blackburn, R., *Evolution of the Heart: A History of the University of Toronto Library up to 1981* (Toronto: University of Toronto Library, 1989).

Bleaney, B., 'Sir Mark (Marcus Laurence Elwin) Oliphant, A.C., K.B.E.', *Biographical Memoirs of Fellows of the Royal Society*, 47 (2001), 383–93.

Bliss, M., *Banting: A Biography* (Toronto: McClelland and Stewart, 1984).

Boehmer, E., *Empire, the National, and the Postcolonial, 1890–1920* (Oxford: Oxford University Press, 2005).

—, *India Arrived: South Asian networks in Britain, 1870–1914* (Oxford: Oxford University Press, forthcoming).

Born, G. V. R., 'The Effect of the Scientific Environment in Britain on Refugee Scientists from Germany and Their Effects on Science in Britain', *Berichte zur Wissenschaftsgeshicte*, 7 (1984), 129–43.

Boucher, M., 'The Gilchrist Scholarship and the University of London in the Early Development of Higher Education for the Cape Colony', *Historia*, 8 (1968), 249–55.

—, *The University of the Cape of Good Hope and the University of South Africa, 1873–1946: A Study in National and Imperial Perspective* (Pretoria: Government Printer, 1974).

Branagan, D., 'David, Sir (Tannatt William) Edgeworth (1858–1934)', *Oxford Dictionary of National Biography* (Oxford University Press, 2004), accessed 25 Mar. 2011, http://217.169.56.137/view/article/32725.

—, *T. W. Edgeworth David: A Life* (Canberra: National Library of Canberra, 2005).

Brennan, J. R., 'South Asian Nationalism in an East African Context: The Case of Tanganyika, 1914–1956', *Comparative Studies of South Asia, Africa and the Middle East*, 19 (1999), 24–39.

Bridge, C. and K. Fedorowich, 'Mapping the British World', *Journal of Imperial and Commonwealth History*, 31 (2003), 1–15.

— (eds), *The British World : Diaspora, Culture, and Identity* (London, and Portland, OR: F. Cass, 2003).

Brison, J. D., *Rockefeller, Carnegie, and Canada: American Philanthropy and the Arts and Letters in Canada* (Montreal: McGill-Queens University Press, 2005).

Brooke, C. N. L., V. Morgan, D. R. Leader and P. Searby, *A History of the University of Cambridge: Vol. 4 1870–1990* (Cambridge: Cambridge University Press, 1988).

Brooks, F. T., 'Buller, Arthur Henry Reginald (1874–1944), Rev. V. M. Quirke', *Oxford Dictionary of National Biography* (2004), accessed 3 Aug. 2011, www.oxforddnb.com/view/article/32164.

Broom, R., 'The Existence of a Sterno-Coracoidal Articulation in a Fœtal Marsupial', *Journal of Anatomy and Physiology*, 31 (1897), 513–15.

Burbank, J. and F. Cooper, *Empires in World History: Power and the Politics of Difference* (Princeton, NJ: Princeton University Press, 2010).

Burton, A., 'Introduction: On the Inadequacy and the Indispensability of the Nation', in A. Burton (ed.), *After the Imperial Turn: Thinking With and Through the Nation* (Durham, NC: Duke University Press, 2003), pp. 1–26.

Butcher, B., 'Science and the Imperial Vision: The Imperial Geophysical

Experimental Survey, 1928–1930', *Historical Records of Australian Science*, 6 (1984), 31–43.

Byledbal, A., 'New Zealand Tunnellers Website', (2009), accessed 25 Mar. 2011, www.nztunnellers.com.

Callaghan, F. R. (ed.), *Science in New Zealand* (Wellington: A. H. and A. W. Reed, 1957).

Campbell, J., *Rutherford: Scientist Supreme* (Christchurch, NZ: AAS Publications, 1999).

Campbell, R., 'The Modest Hospitality of a Scholar: Badham and the First Bursaries', *University of Sydney Archives Record* (2005), pp. 13–22.

Cannon, J., 'Namier, Sir Lewis Bernstein (1888–1960)', *Oxford Dictionary of National Biography* (Oxford University Press, 2004), accessed 4 Oct. 2011, www.oxforddnb.com/view/article/35183.

Carey, A. T., *Colonial Students: A Study of Social Adaptation of Colonial Students* (London: Secker and Warburg, 1956).

Carlyle, E. I., 'Woolley, John (1816–1866)', *Oxford Dictionary of National Biography*, (Oxford University Press, 2004), accessed 27 Feb. 2007, www.oxforddnb.com/view/article/29958.

Carmichael, O. C., *Universities: Commonwealth and American, a Comparative Study* (New York: Harper, 1959).

Carnegie, A., *The Gospel of Wealth* (New York: 1889).

Carnes, M. C., and C. Griffen (eds), *Meanings for Manhood: Constructions of Masculinity in Victorian America* (Chicago, IL: University of Chicago Press, 1990).

Carroll, M., 'Republic of the Learned: The Role of Libraries in the Promotion of a U.S. Democratic Vision', *History of Education*, 38 (2009), 809–23.

Carse, G. A., and T. H. Laby, 'On a Relation between the Velocity and the Volume of the Ions of Certain Organic Acids and Bases', *Proceedings Cambridge Philosophical Society*, 13 (1906), 288–95.

—, 'A Relation between the Velocity and Volume of Organic Ions in Aqueous Solutions', *Proceedings Cambridge Philosophical Society*, 14 (1906), 1–12.

Chamberlain, J., *Imperial Union and Tariff Reform: Speeches Delivered from May 15 to Nov. 4, 1903: With an Introduction* (London: G. Richards, 1903).

Chambers, D. W., 'Does Distance Tyrannize Science?', in R. W. Home and S. G. Kohlstedt (eds), *International Science and National Scientific Identity: Australia between Britain and America* (Dordrecht: Kluwer Academic, 1991), pp. 19–38.

Charle, C., J. Schriewer and P. Wagner, *Transnational Intellectual Networks: Forms of Academic Knowledge and the Search for Cultural Identities* (Frankfurt: Campus, 2004).

Clarebrough, L. M., and A. K. Head, 'Walter Boas 1904–1982', *Historical Records of Australian Science*, 6 (1987), 507–17.

Clark, R. W., *Tizard* (London: Methuen and Co., 1965).

Cohen, D., and M. O'Connor, 'Comparative History, Cross-National History, Transnational History: Definitions', in D. Cohen and M. O'Connor (eds), *Comparison and History* (London: Routledge, 2004), pp. ix–xxiv.

Cohn, B., *Colonialism and Its Forms of Knowledge: The British in India*

(Princeton, NJ: Princeton University Press, 1996).

Cole, D. L., "'The Crimson Thread of Kinship': Ethnic Ideas in Australia, 1870–1914', *Historical Studies*, 14 (1971), 511–21.

—, 'The Problem of 'Nationalism' and 'Imperialism' in British Settlement Colonies', *Journal of British Studies*, 10 (1971), 160–82.

Collini, S., 'The Idea of 'Character' in Victorian Political Thought', *Transactions of the Royal Historical Society*, 35 (1985), 29–50.

—, *Absent Minds: Intellectuals in Britain* (Oxford: Oxford University Press, 2006).

Collins, J., 'Creating Women's Work in the Academy and Beyond: Carnegie Connections, 1923–1942', *History of Education*, 38 (2009), 791–808.

Cook, T., 'From Destruction to Construction: The Khaki University of Canada, 1917–1919', *Journal of Canadian Studies*, 37 (2002), 109–43.

Cooke, S. B., *Imperial Affinities: Nineteenth-Century Analogies and Exchanges between India and Ireland* (New Delhi: Sage Publications, 1993).

Cooper, F., *Colonialism in Question: Theory, Knowledge, History* (Berkeley, CA: University of California Press, 2005).

Cooter, R., M. Harrison and S. Sturdy (eds), *War, Medicine and Modernity* (Phoenix Mill: Sutton Publishing, 1998).

Courtice, F. C., 'Research in the Medical Sciences: The Road to National Independence', in R. W. Home (ed.), *Australian Science in the Making* (Cambridge: Cambridge University Press, 1988), pp. 277–307.

Crocker, W. R., 'Naylor, Henry Darnley (1872–1945)', *Australian Dictionary of Biography*, 10 (1986).

Crowther, J. G., *The Cavendish Laboratory, 1874–1974* (London: Science History Publications, 1974).

Cunich, P., *A History of the University of Hong Kong, Vol. 1, 1911–1945* (Hong Kong: HKU Press, 2012).

Currie, G. A. and J. L. Graham, *The Origins of the C.S.I.R.O.: Science and the Commonwealth Government, 1901–1926* (Melbourne: CSIRO Publishing, 1966).

Dallen, R. A., *The University of Sydney, Its History and Progress* (Sydney: 1914).

Dalziel, R., *The Origins of New Zealand Diplomacy: The Agent-General in London, 1870–1905* (Wellington: Victoria University Press, 1975).

Darwin, J., 'A World University', in Brian Harrison (ed.), *The History of the University of Oxford, Vol. III: The Twentieth Century* (Oxford: Oxford University Press, 1994) .

—, 'Imperialism and the Victorians: The Dynamics of Territorial Expansion', *English Historical Review*, 112 (1997), 614–42.

—, *The Empire Project: The Rise and Fall of the British World-System, 1830–1970* (Cambridge: Cambridge University Press, 2009).

Davidson, J., *A Three-Cornered Life: The Historian W. K. Hancock* (Sydney: UNSW Press, 2010).

Dawson, W. H. (ed.), *The Yearbook of the Universities of the Empire, 1921* (London: 1921).

Deacon, D., *Managing Gender: The State, the New Middle Class and Women*

Workers, 1830–1930 (Oxford: Oxford University Press, 1989).

Dean, K., 'Inscribing Settler Science: Ernest Rutherford, Thomas Laby and the Making of Careers in Physics', *History of Science*, 41 (2003), 217–40.

—, 'Settler Physics in Australia and Cambridge, 1850–1950' (Cambridge, 2004).

—, 'Demonstrating the Melbourne University Respirator (Lessons Australia Learned from World War I)', *Australian Journal of Politics and History*, 53 (2007), 392–406.

Dent, D., 'Famous Men Remembered', *The Chemical Engineer* (1986), pp. 56–7.

Dilke, C., *Greater Britain, a Record of Travel in the English-Speaking Countries During 1866 and 1867* (London: Macmillan, 1868).

Dirks, N. B., *Castes of Mind: Colonialism and the Making of Modern India* (Princeton, NJ: Princeton University Press, 2001).

Dobbie, J. J., 'The Address of the Retiring President', *Proceedings of the Institute of Chemistry of Great Britain and Ireland* (1918), pp. 25–42.

Doyle, P., M. R. Bennett and F. M. Cocks, 'Geology and Warfare on the British Sector of the Western Front 1914–18', in. E. P. F. Rose and C. P. Nathanail (eds), *Geology and Warfare: Examples of the Influence of Terrain and Geologists on Military Operations* (Bath: Geological Society, 2000), pp. 179–291.

Drayton, R., 'Where Does the World Historian Write From? Objectivity, Moral Conscience and the Past and Present of Imperialism', *Journal of Contemporary History*, 46 (2011), 671–85.

Drower, M. S., *Flinders Petrie: A Life in Archaeology* (Madison, WI: University of Wisconsin Press, 1995).

Drummond, I. M., 'The Imperial Vision: Dream and Action in the Nineteen-Twenties', in *British Economic Policy and the Empire, 1919–1939* (London: Allen and Unwin, 1972), pp. 36–88.

—, *Political Economy at the University of Toronto: A History of the Department, 1888–1982* (Toronto: University of Toronto, 1983).

Dubow, S., *Scientific Racism in Modern South Africa* (Cambridge: Cambridge University Press, 1995).

—, 'Human Origins, Race Typology and the Other Raymond Dart', *African Studies*, 55 (1996), 1–30.

—, 'Opération Coup de Poing', *Archaeological Dialogues*, 10 (2003), pp. 26–32.

—, *A Commonwealth of Knowledge: Science, Sensibility, and White South Africa, 1820–2000* (Oxford: Oxford University Press, 2006).

Duncan, W. G. K., and R. A. Leonard, *The University of Adelaide, 1874–1974* (Adelaide: Rigby, 1973).

Dunlop, E. W., 'The Public High Schools of New South Wales, 1883–1912', *Journal of the Royal Australian Historical Society*, 51 (1965), 60–86.

Dyhouse, C., 'Social Darwinistic Ideas and the Development of Women's Education in England, 1880–1920', *History of Education*, 5 (1976), 41–58.

—, 'The British Federation of University Women and the Status of Women in Universities, 1907–1939', *Women's History Review*, 4 (1995), 465–85.

Eells, W. C., 'The Origin and Early History of Sabbatical Leave', *Association of American University Professors Bulletin*, 48 (1962), pp. 253–6.

Egglestone, W., *Scientists at War* (Toronto: Oxford University Press, 1950).

Ellis, H., 'Intercourse with Foreign Philosophers': Transnational Collaboration and the British Association for the Advancement of Science, 1870–1914' (paper presented at 'International values and global science' workshop, University of Exeter, Aug. 2012).

Endersby, J., *Imperial Nature: Joseph Hooker and the Practices of Victorian Science* (Chicago, IL: University of Chicago Press, 2008).

Falconer, R. A., 'The Gilchrist Scholarships: An Episode in the Higher Education of Canada', *Proceedings and Transactions of the Royal Society of Canada*, 27 (1933), 5–13.

Fedunkiw, M., *Rockefeller Foundation Funding and Medical Education in Toronto, Montreal, and Halifax* (Montreal: McGill-Queen's University Press, 2005).

Finnegan, D. A., 'The Spatial Turn: Geographical Approaches in the History of Science', *Journal of the History of Biology*, 41 (2008), 369–88.

Fisher, H. A. L., *The Place of the University in National Life* (Oxford: Oxford University Press, 1919).

— (ed.), *British Universities and the War: A Record and Its Meaning* (London: The Field and Queen, 1917).

Fisher, M. H., *Counterflows to Colonialism: Indian Travellers and Settlers in Britain, 1600–1857* (Delhi: Permanent Black, 2004).

Fleming, D., 'Science in Australia, Canada and the United States: Some Comparative Remarks', *Proceedings of the Tenth International Congress of the History of Science*, (1964), pp. 179–96.

Fleming, J. A., 'Science in the War and after the War', *Nature*, 96, no. 2398 (1915), 181–5.

Fletcher, J. M., 'The Universities in the Age of Western Expansion. The Colonial Factor in Research and Higher Education: Leiden, 27–29 September 1991', *History of Universities*, 11 (1992), 268–9.

Fosdick, R. B., *The Story of the Rockefeller Foundation* (New York: Harper and Row, 1952).

Foulkes, C. H., *Gas! The Story of the Special Brigade* (Edinburgh: W. Blackwood and Sons, 1934).

Friedland, M. L., *The University of Toronto: A History* (Toronto: University of Toronto Press, 2002).

Frost, S. B., *McGill University for the Advancement of Learning: Vol. 1, 1801–1895* (Montreal: McGill-Queen's University Press, 1980).

—, *McGill University for the Advancement of Learning: Vol. 2, 1895–1971* (Montreal: McGill-Queen's University Press, 1980).

Froude, J. A., *Oceana, or England and Her Colonies* (London: Longmans, Green and Co., 1886).

Füredi, F., *The Silent War: Imperialism and the Changing Perception of Race* (London: Pluto, 1998).

Galbreath, R., 'The Rutherford Connection: New Zealand Scientists and the Manhattan and Montreal Projects', *War in History*, 2 (1995), 306–19.

—, *D.S.I.R.: Making Science Work for New Zealand* (Wellington, NZ: Victoria University Press, 1998).

Gallagher, J., and R. Robinson, 'The Imperialism of Free Trade', *Economic History Review*, 6 (1953), 1–15.

Gandhi, L., *Affective Communities: Anticolonial Thought and the Politics of Friendship* (New Delhi: Permanent Black, 2006).

Gardner, W. J., *Colonial Cap and Gown: Studies in the Mid-Victorian Universities of Australasia* (Christchurch, NZ: University of Canterbury, 1979).

Gay, H., 'Invisible Resource: William Crookes and His Circle of Support, 1871–81', *British Journal for the History of Science*, 29 (1996), 311–36.

Gertler, M. S., *Manufacturing Culture: The Institutional Geography of Industrial Practice* (Oxford: Oxford University Press, 2004).

—, 'Buzz without Being There? Communities of Practice in Context', *Community, Economic Creativity, and Organization* (2008), 203–27.

Gibson, F., *Queen's University, Vol. 2, 1917–1961* (Kingston and Montreal: McGill-Queen's University Press, 1983).

Giddens, A., *The Consequences of Modernity* (Cambridge: Polity, 1991).

Gillet, M., *We Walked Very Warily: A History of Women at McGill* (Montreal: Eden Press Women's Publications, 1981).

Girard, M., *A Strange and Formidable Weapon: British Responses to World War I Poison Gas* (Lincoln, NE: University of Nebraska Press, 2008).

Glotzer, R., 'The Influence of Carnegie Corporation and Teachers College, Columbia, in the Interwar Dominions: The Case for Decentralized Education', *Historical Studies in Education*, 1 (2000), 93–111.

—, 'A Long Shadow: Frederick P. Keppel, the Carnegie Corporation and the Dominions and Colonies Fund Area Experts 1923–1943 ', *History of Education*, 38 (2009), 621–48.

Goldschmidt, B., 'Uranium's Scientific History, 1789–1939' (paper presented at the Fourteenth International Symposium, London, 1989), accessed 7 Dec. 2007, http://socrates.berkeley.edu/~rochlin/ushista.html.

Goodman, D., '"There Is No-One to Whom I Can Talk': Norman Harper and American History in Australia', *Australasian Journal of American Studies*, 23 (2004), 5–20.

Goodman, J., A. Jacobs, F. Kisby and H. Loader, 'Travelling Careers: Overseas Migration Patterns in the Professional Lives of Women Attending Girton and Newnham before 1939', *History of Education*, 40 (2011), 179–96.

Goodman, J., and J. Martin (eds), *Gender, Colonialism and Education: The Politics of Experience* (London: Woburn Press, 2002).

Goodman, J., G. McCulloch and W. Richardson, 'Introduction: 'Empires Overseas' and 'Empires at Home': Postcolonial and Transnational Perspectives on Social Change in the History of Education', *Paedagogica Historica*, 45 (2009), 695–706.

Goody, J., *The Expansive Moment: Anthropology in Britain and Africa, 1918–1970* (Cambridge: Cambridge University Press, 1995).

Gorman, D., *Imperial Citizenship: Empire and the Question of Belonging* (Manchester: Manchester University Press, 2006).

Gowing, M., *Britain and Atomic Energy, 1939–1945* (London: Macmillan, 1964).

Greenlee, J., 'The ABCs of Imperial Unity', *Canadian Journal of History*, 14 (1979), 49–64.

—, *Education and Imperial Unity* (New York: Garland, 1987).

Grieve, W. G., and B. Newman, *Tunnellers: The Story of the Tunnelling Companies, Royal Engineers During the World War* (London: H. Jenkins, 1936).

Grewal, I., *Home and Harem: Nation, Gender, Empire and the Cultures of Travel* (London: Leicester University Press, 1996).

Gusewelle, J. K., 'Science and the Admiralty During World War I: The Case of the B.I.R.', in G. Jordan (ed.), *Naval Warfare in the Twentieth Century, 1900–1945: Essays in Honour of Arthur Marder* (London: Croom Helm, 1977), pp. 105–17.

Haber, L. F., *The Poisonous Cloud: Chemical Warfare in the First World War* (Oxford: Clarendon Press, 1986).

Hackmann, W., 'Underwater Acoustics and the Royal Navy, 1893–1930', *Annals of Science*, 36 (1979), 255–78.

—, *Seek and Strike: Sonar, Anti-Submarine Warfare and the Royal Navy, 1914–1954* (London: Her Majesty's Stationary Office, 1984).

Hall, C., *White, Male and Middle Class: Explorations in Feminism and History* (London: Polity Press, 1992).

—, 'Introduction: Thinking the Postcolonial, Thinking the Empire', in C. Hall (ed.), *Cultures of Empire: A Reader* (Manchester: Manchester University Press, 2000).

—, and S. O. Rose (eds), *At Home with the Empire: Metropolitan Culture and the Imperial World* (New York: Cambridge University Press, 2006).

Halsey, A. H. (ed.), *Trends in British Society since 1900: A Guide to the Changing Social Structure of Britain* (London: Macmillan, 1972).

—, *Decline of Donnish Dominion: The British Academic Professions in the Twentieth Century* (Oxford: Clarendon Press, 1992).

—, 'Oxford and the British Universities', in B. Harrison (ed.), *The History of the University of Oxford: Vol. 8, the Twentieth Century* (Oxford: Oxford University Press, 1994), pp. 577–606.

Halsey, A. H., M. A. Trow and O. Fulton, *The British Academics* (London: Faber and Faber, 1971).

Hamersley, H., 'Cancer, Physic and Society: Interactions between the Wars', in R. W. Home (ed.), *Australian Science in the Making* (Cambridge: Cambridge University Press, 1988).

Hanaway, J., R. L. Cruess and J. Darragh, *McGill Medicine: 1885–1936* (Montreal: McGill University, 2006).

Hancock, W. K., 'The Moving Metropolis', in A. R. Lewis and T. F. McGann (eds), *The New World Looks at Its History* (Austin: University of Texas Press, 1963), pp. 140–1.

Hardt M., and Negri, A., *Multitude: War and Democracy in the Age of Empire* (New York: Penguin, 2004).

Hargreaves, J. D., *Academe and Empire: Some Overseas Connections of Aberdeen University, 1860–1970* (Aberdeen: Aberdeen University Press, 1994).

Harker, J. A., '(1) Tables of Physical and Chemical Constants, and Some Mathematical Functions (2) Smithsonian Miscellaneous Collections', *Nature*, 8 Feb. (1912), 477.

Harris, R. S., *A History of Higher Education in Canada, 1663–1960* (Toronto:

University of Toronto Press, 1976).

Harrison, M., *Medicine in an Age of Commerce and Empire* (Oxford: Oxford University Press, 2010).

—, *The Medical War: British Military Medicine in the First World War* (Oxford: Oxford University Press, 2010).

Hartcup, G., *The War of Invention: Scientific Developments, 1914–18* (London: Brassey's Defence Publishers, 1988).

Harvey, C., M. Maclean, G. Gordon and E. Shaw, 'Andrew Carnegie and the Foundations of Contemporary Entrepreneurial Philanthropy', *Business History*, 53 (2011), 425–50.

Harvie, D. I., *Deadly Sunshine: The History and Fatal Legacy of Radium* (Stroud: The History Press, 2005).

Headrick, D. R., *The Invisible Weapon: Telecommunications and International Politics, 1851–1945* (New York: Oxford University Press, 1991).

Heilbron, J., *Dilemmas of an Upright Man: Max Planck as Spokesman for German Science* (Berkeley, CA: University of California Press, 1986).

Henderson, G. C., *Reflections on the War* (Adelaide: G. Hassell and Son, 1916).

Hercus, E. O., and D. M. Sutherland, 'Thermal Conductivity of Air', *Proceedings of the Royal Society of London*, A145 (1934), 599–611.

Hight, J., and A. M. F. Candy, *A Short History of the Canterbury College* (Auckland: Whitcombe and Tombs, 1927).

Hirschfeld, G., 'German Refugee Scholars in Great Britain, 1933–1945', in A. Bramwell (ed.), *Refugees in the Age of Total War* (London: Unwin Hyman, 1988), pp. 152–63.

Hirst, E. L., 'John Read, 1884–1963', *Biographical Memoirs of Fellows of the Royal Society*, 9 (1963), 236–60.

Hobson, J. A., *Imperialism: A Study* (London: James Nisbet, 1902).

Hodge, J. M., *Triumph of the Expert: Agrarian Doctrines of Development and the Legacies of British Colonialism* (Athens: Ohio University Press, 2007).

— and B. M. Bennett (eds), *Science and Empire: Knowledge and Networks of Science in the British Empire, 1800–1970* (New York: Palgrave MacMillan, 2011).

Holgate, C. W., *An Account of the Chief Libraries of Australia and Tasmania* (London: Chiswick Press, 1886).

Home, R. W., 'Threlfall, Sir Richard (1861–1932)', *Australian Dictionary of Biography*, http://goo.gl/vCu8O.

—, 'First Physicist of Australia: Richard Threlfall at the University of Sydney, 1886–1898', *Historical Records of Australian Science*, 6 (1984), 333–57.

—, 'Science on Service, 1939–1945', in R. W. Home (ed.), *Australian Science in the Making* (Cambridge: Cambridge University Press, 1988), pp. 220–51.

—, (ed.), *Australian Science in the Making* (Cambridge: Cambridge University Press, 1988).

—, 'A World-Wide Scientific Network and Patronage System: Australian and Other Colonial Fellows of the Royal Society of London', in R. W. Home and S. G. Kohlstedt (eds), *International Science and National Scientific Identity* (Dordrecht: Kluwer Academic Publishers, 1991), pp. 157–79.

—, 'Introduction', *Physics in Australia to 1945* (1995), accessed 21 Oct. 2011, www.asap.unimelb.edu.au/bsparcs/physics/phys_int.htm.

—, 'The Royal Society and the Empire: The Colonial and Commonwealth Fellowship Part 1. 1731–1847', *Notes and Records of the Royal Society of London*, 56 (2002), 307–32.

—, 'The Royal Society and the Empire: The Colonial and Commonwealth Fellowship, Part 2: After 1847', *Notes and Records of the Royal Society of London*, 57, no. 1 (2003), 47–84.

— and S. G. Kohlstedt (eds), *International Science and National Scientific Identity* (Dordrecht: Kluwer Academic, 1991).

Hopkins, A. G., 'Rethinking Decolonization', *Past and Present*, 200 (2008), 211–47.

Horn, M., *Academic Freedom in Canada* (Toronto: University of Toronto Press, 1999).

Horne, J., 'What We Saw in Australia: Carnegie Men and Australian Universities between the Wars', paper delivered at the Philanthropy and Public Culture Workshop, Melbourne, 2010.

Horne, J., and G. Sherington, 'Extending the Educational Franchise: The Social Contract of Australia's Public Universities, 1850–1890', paper delivered at the International Standing Conference for the History of Education, 2008.

Hoskin, K., 'Examinations and the Schooling of Science', in R. MacLeod (ed.), *Days of Judgement: Science, Examinations, and the Organization of Knowledge in Victorian England* (Driffeld: Studies in Education, 1982), pp. 213–236.

Hyslop, R., 'Wheatley, Frederick William (1871–1955)', *Australian Dictionary of Biography* (Melbourne University Press, 1990), accessed 29 Mar. 2011, http://adbonline.anu.edu.au/biogs/A120507b.htm.

James, C. L. R., *Beyond a Boundary* (London: Stanley Paul, 1963).

Jebb, R., *Studies in Colonial Nationalism* (London: Edward Arnold, 1905).

Jenkin, J., 'The Appointment of W. H. Bragg, F.R.S., to the University of Adelaide', *Notes and Records of the Royal Society of London*, 40 (1985), 75–99.

—, 'Henry Herman Leopold Adolph Brose: Vagaries of an Extraordinary Australian Scientist', *Historical Records of Australian Science*, 3 (1999), 287–312.

—, 'William Henry Bragg in Adelaide', *Isis*, 95 (2004), 58–90.

—, *William and Lawrence Bragg, Father and Son* (Oxford: Oxford University Press, 2008).

Johns, W. H., *A History of the University of Alberta, 1908–1969* (Edmonton: University of Alberta Press, 1981).

Jöns, H., 'Academic Travel from Cambridge University and the Formation of Centres of Knowledge, 1885–1954', *Journal of Historical Geography*, 34 (2008), 338–62.

Kang, B., and M. Miller, 'An Overview of the Sabbatical Leave in Higher Education: A Synopsis of the Literature Base', *E.R.I.C. Document Reproductive Service*, no. ED 430 471 (1999).

Kannuluik, W. G., and L. H. Martin, 'The Thermal Conductivity of Some Gases at 0°C', *Proceedings of the Royal Society of London*, A144 (1934), 496–513.

Kay-Shuttleworth, U. J., and D. H. S. Cranage, *Gilchrist Educational Trust: Pioneering Work in Education* (Cambridge: Cambridge University Press, 1930).

Kaye, G. W. C., and T. H. Laby, 'Preface', in *Table of Physical and Chemical Constants and Some Mathematical Functions* (London: 1911).

Kenny, A., *The History of the Rhodes Trust* (Oxford: Oxford University Press, 2001).

Kerr, A., *Fort Hare 1915–48: The Evolution of an African College* (London: Hurst, 1968).

Ketchum, J. D., *Ruhleben: A Prison Camp Society* (Toronto: University of Toronto Press, 1965).

Kevles, D., 'Into Hostile Political Camps: The Reorganisation of International Science in World War One', *Isis*, 62 (1979), 47–60.

Kingwill, D. G., *The C.S.I.R.: The First 40 Years* (Pretoria: CSIR, 1990).

Knight, D., 'Review of N. Reingold and M. Rothernberg (Eds.), *Scientific Colonialism: A Cross-Cultural Comparison*', *Historical Records of Australian Science*, 7 (1987), 134–6.

Koch, T. W., *War Libraries and Allied Studies* (New York: G. E. Stechert and Co., 1918).

Kohn, M., *Trust: Self-Interest and the Common Good* (Oxford: Oxford University Press, 2008).

Kramnick, I., and B. Sheerman, *Harold Laski: A Life on the Left* (London: Hamish Hamilton, 1993).

Laby, T. H., 'Tables des constants de l'ionisation et de la radioactivité', *Le Radium*, 7 (1910), 189–96.

—, and G. E. Eddy, 'Quantitative Analysis by X-Ray Spectroscopy', *Proceedings of the Royal Society of London*, A127 (1930), 20–42.

—, and E. O. Hercus, 'The Mechanical Equivalent of Heat', *Philosophical Transactions of the Royal Society*, A227 (1927–28), 63–91.

— and G. W. C. Kaye, 'Gaseous Ionization and Pressure', *Philosophical Magazine, Series 6*, 16 (1908), 879–89.

Lagemann, E. C., *Private Power for the Public Good* (Middletown, CT: Wesleyan University Press, 1983).

Lake, M., and H. Reynolds, *Drawing the Global Colour Line: White Men's Countries and the International Challenge of Racial Equality* (Cambridge: Cambridge University Press, 2008).

Lambert, D., and A. Lester, 'Geographies of Colonial Philanthropy', *Progress in Human Geography*, 28 (2004), 320–41.

—, 'Introduction: Imperial Spaces, Imperial Subjects', in D. Lambert and A. Lester (eds), *Colonial Lives across the British Empire: Imperial Careering in the Long Nineteenth Century* (Cambridge: Cambridge University Press, 2006), pp. 1–31.

Laqua, D., 'Transnational Intellectual Cooperation, the League of Nations, and the Problem of Order', *Journal of Global History*, 6 (2011), 223–47.

Latour, B., *Science in Action: How to Follow Scientists and Engineers through Society* (Milton Keynes: Open University Press, 1987).

Laurence, P. M. (ed.), *Report of the University Commission* (Cape Town: Government Printers, 1914).

Legget, R. F., 'Chalmers Jack Mackenzie: 10 July 1888 – 26 February 1984', *Biographical Memoirs of Fellows of the Royal Society*, 31 (1985), 410–34.

Levine, P., *The Amateur and the Professional: Antiquarians, Historians and Archaeolgists in Victorian England, 1838–1886* (Cambridge: Cambridge University Press, 1986).

Liebhafsky, H. A., H. G. Pfeiffer, E. H. Winslow and P. D. Zemany, *X-Ray Absorption and Emission in Analytical Chemistry: Spectochemical Analysis with X-Rays* (New York: Wiley, 1960).

Livingstone, D. N., *Putting Science in Its Place: Geographies of Scientific Knowledge* (Chicago, IL: University of Chicago Press, 2003).

— and C. W. J. Withers (eds), *Geographies of Nineteenth-Century Science* (Chicago, IL: University of Chicago Press, 2011).

Lockyer, N., 'The War – and After', *Nature*, 64 (1914), 29–30.

London, L., *Whitehall and the Jews, 1933–1948* (Cambridge: Cambridge University Press, 2000).

Longley, R. S., *Acadia University* (Wolfville: Kentville Publishing, 1938).

Louis, W. R., and R. Robinson, 'The Imperialism of Decolonisation', *Journal of Imperial and Commonwealth History*, 22 (1994), 462–511.

Louw, J. A., 'A Brief History of the Medical Faculty, University of Cape Town', *South African Medical Journal* (Nov. 1979), 864–70.

Lowe, R., 'The Expansion of Higher Education in England', in K. H. Jarausch (ed.), *The Transformation of Higher Learning, 1860–1930* (Stuttgart: Klett-Cotta, 1982).

Luhmann, N., *Trust and Power: Two Works* (Chicester: Wiley, 1979).

—, 'Familiarity, Confidence, Trust: Problems and Alternatives', in D. Gambetta (ed.), *Trust: Making and Breaking Cooperative Relations* (New York: Basil Blackwell, 1988), pp. 94–107.

Luthy, H., 'India and East Africa: Imperial Partnership at the End of the First World War', *Journal of Contemporary History*, 6 (1971), pp. 55–85.

Macaulay, T. B., 'Minute of 2 February 1835 on Indian Education', in G. M. Young (ed.), *Macaulay, Prose and Poetry* (Cambridge, MA: Harvard University Press, 1957), pp. 721–4.

MacDonald, H., 'A Scandalous Act: Regulating Anatomy in a British Settler Colony, Tasmania 1869', *Social History of Medicine*, 20, no. 1 (2007): 39–56.

MacGregor, J. G., 'Letter Concerning the Gilchrist Educational Fund', (1895), accessed 31 Mar. 2011, http://www.archive.org/details/cihm_29095.

MacLeod, M., *A Bridge Built Halfway: A History of Memorial University College, 1925–1950* (Montreal: McGill-Queen's University Press, 1990).

MacLeod, R., 'Fathers and Daughters: Reflections on Women, Science and Victorian Cambridge', *History of Education*, 8 (1979), 321–33.

—, 'On Visiting the "Moving Metropolis": Reflections on the Architecture of Imperial Science', *Historical Records of Australian Science*, 5 (1982), 1–16.

—, 'Phantom Soldiers: Australian Tunnellers on the Western Front, 1916–17', *Journal of the Australian War Memorial*, 13 (1988), 31–43.

— (ed.), *The Commonwealth of Science: A.N.Z.A.A.S. and the Scientific*

Enterprise in Australasia, 1888–1988 (Melbourne: Oxford University Press, 1988).

—, 'The "Arsenal" in the Strand: Australian Chemists and the British Munitions Effort 1916–1919', *Annals of Science*, 46 (1989), 45–67.

—, 'The Chemists Go to War: The Mobilization of Civilian Chemists and the British War Effort, 1914–1918', *Annals of Science*, 50 (1993), 455–81.

—, 'All for Each and Each for All: Reflections on Anglo-American and Commonwealth Scientific Cooperation, 1940–1945', *Albion*, 26 (1994), 79–112.

—, 'Allied Scientific Collaboration in the Second World War: Some Anniversary Reflections', *War in History*, 2 (1995), 253–8.

—, '"Kriegsgeologen and Practical Men": Military Geology and Modern Memory, 1914–18', *British Journal for the History of Science*, 28 (1995), 427–50.

— (ed.), *Science and the Pacific War: Science and Survival in the Pacific, 1939–1945* (Dordrecht: Kluwer, 2000).

—, 'Sight and Sound on the Western Front: Surveyors, Scientists, and the Battlefield Laboratory: 1915–1918', *War and Society*, 18 (2000), 26–46.

—, 'Leverhulme Lectures', delivered at the University of Oxford, 2007.

—, 'The Scientists Go to War: Revisiting Precept and Practice, 1914–1919', *Journal of War and Culture Studies*, 2 (2009), 37–51.

—, *Archibald Liversidge, F.R.S.: Imperial Science under the Southern Cross* (Sydney: Sydney University Press, 2010).

—, 'The Royal Society and the Commonwealth: Old Friendships, New Frontiers', *Notes and Records of the Royal Society of London*, 64, Supplement 1 (2010), 137–149.

MacLeod, R., and E. K. Andrews, 'The Origins of the D.S.I.R.: Reflections on Ideas and Men, 1915–1916', *Public Administration*, 48 (1970), 23–48.

—, 'Scientific Advice in the War at Sea, 1915–1917: The Board of Invention and Research', *Journal of Contemporary History*, 6 (1971), pp. 3–40.

MacLeod, R., and P. Collins (eds), *The Parliament of Science: The British Association for the Advancement of Science, 1831–1981* (Northwood: Science Reviews, 1981).

Magee, G. B., and A. S. Thompson, *Empire and Globalisation: Networks of People, Goods and Capital in the British World, C.1850–1914* (Cambridge: Cambridge University Press, 2010).

Maier, C., 'Consigning the Twentieth Century to History: Alternative Narratives for the Modern Era', *American Historical Review*, 105 (2000), 807–31.

Mangan, J. A., *Athleticism in the Victorian and Edwardian Public School: The Emergence and Consolidation of an Educational Ideology* (London: Falmer Press, 1986).

— (ed.), *Making Imperial Mentalities: Socialisation and British Imperialism* (Manchester: Manchester University Press, 1990).

Martin, G., 'The Idea of Imperial Federation', in R. Hyam and G. Martin (eds), *Reappraisals in British Imperial History* (London: Macmillan, 1975), pp. 121–39.

Massey, D. B., *For Space* (London: Sage, 2005).

Massey, H. S. W., 'T. H. Laby, F.R.S.', *The Australian Physicist*, Dec. (1980).

Matera, M., 'Colonial Subjects: Black Intellectuals and the Development of Colonial Studies in Britain', *Journal of British Studies*, 49 (2010), 388–418.

McClintock, A., *Imperial Leather: Race, Gender, and Sexuality in the Colonial Contest* (New York: Routledge, 1995).

McCulloch, G., and R. Lowe, 'Introduction: Centre and Periphery – Networks, Space and Geography in the History of Education', *History of Education*, 32 (2003), 457–9.

McGibbon, I., and P. Goldstone (eds), *The Oxford Companion to New Zealand Military History* (Auckland: Oxford University Press, 2000).

McKillop, A. B., *Matters of Mind: The University in Ontario, 1791–1951* (Toronto: University of Toronto Press, 1994).

McNab, R., *The Story of South Africa House* (Johannesburg: Jonathan Bell, 1983).

McNally, P. F. (ed.), *Readings in Canadian Library History, Vol. 1.* (Ottawa: Canadian Library Association, 1986).

McNeish, J., *Dance of the Peacocks: New Zealanders in Excile in the Time of Hitler and Mao Tse-Tung* (Auckland: Vintage, 2003).

Michie, H., and R. Thomas (eds), *Nineteenth Century Geographies: The Transformation of Space from the Victorian Age to the American Century* (New Brunswick, NJ: Rutgers University Press, 2002).

Middell, M., and K. Naumann, 'Global History and the Spatial Turn: From the Impact of Area Studies to the Study of Critical Junctures of Globalization', *Journal of Global History*, 5 (2010), 149–70.

Millard, R., 'The Crusade for Science: Science and Technology on the Home Front, 1914–1918', in D. MacKenzie (ed.), *Canada and the First World War: Essays in Honour of Robert Craig Brown* (Toronto: University of Toronto Press, 2005), pp. 300–22.

Morantz-Sanchez, R. M., 'The Many Faces of Intimacy: Professional Choices among Nineteenth and Early Twentieth Century Women Physicians', in P. G. Abir-Am and D. Outram (eds), *Uneasy Careers and Intimate Lives: Women in Science, 1787–1979* (New Brunswick, NJ: Rutgers University Press, 1987), pp. 77–103.

Morell, J. B., 'Science and Scottish University Reform: Edinburgh in 1826', *British Journal for the History of Science*, 6 (1972), 39–56.

Morgan, J. R., 'A History of Pitchblade', *Atom*, 329 (1984), 63–8.

Morison, P., *J. T. Wilson and the Fraternity of Duckmaloi* (Amsterdam: Rodopi, 1997).

Morrell, W. P., *The University of Otago, a Centennial History* (Dunedin: University of Otago Press, 1969).

Morris, D., 'Mueller, Sir Ferdinand Jakob Heinrich Von (1825–1896)', *Australian Dictionary of Biography*, accessed 3 Aug. 2011, http://goo.gl/yfUCA.

Moynihan, D. P., 'The United States in Opposition', *Commentary* (1975), 42–4.

Muirhead, E., *A Man Ahead of His Times: T. H. Laby's Contributions to Australian Science* (Melbourne: Spectrum Publications, 1996).

Mukherjee, S., *Nationalism, Education and Migrant Identities: The England Returned* (London: Routledge, 2009).

Munn, R., and J. Barr, *New Zealand Libraries: A Survey of Conditions and Suggestions for Their Improvement* (Christchurch: New Zealand Library Association, 1934).

Munn, R., E. R. Pitt and Carnegie Corporation of New York., *Australian Libraries: A Survey of Conditions and Suggestions for Their Improvement* (Melbourne: Australian Council for Educational Research, 1935).

Murray, B. K., *Wits: The Early Years: A History of the University of the Witwatersrand Johannesburg and Its Precursors, 1896–1939* (Johannesburg: Witwatersrand University Press, 1982).

Neill, J. C. (ed.), *The New Zealand Tunnelling Company 1915–1919* (Auckland: Whitcombe and Tombs, 1922).

Newton, A. P., *The Universities and Educational Systems of the British Empire* (London: W. Collins, 1924).

O'Connell, K., '*Siksar Herfer*: Education out of Whack', in P. C. Hogan and L. Pandit (eds), *Rabindranath Tagore: Universality and Tradition* (Madison, NJ: Fairleigh Dickinson University Press, 2002), pp. 65–82.

O'Connor, J. J., and E. F. Robertson, 'George Alexander Carse', *The MacTutor History of Mathematics Archive* (University of St Andrews, 2008), accessed 1 May 2008, http://goo.gl/o3AV4.

O'Hara, G., *Britain and the Sea since 1600* (Basingstoke: Palgrave Macmillan, 2010).

Ophir, A., and S. Shapin, 'The Place of Knowledge: A Methodological Survey', *Science in Context*, 4 (1991), 3–21.

Osborne, W. A., 'Remembrance of Things Past: How Biochemistry Came to Melbourne', *Meanjin*, 20 (1961), 209–14.

Owen-Smith, J., and W. W. Powell, 'Knowledge Networks as Channels and Conduits: The Effects of Formal Structure in the Boston Biotechnology Community', *Organization Science*, 15 (2004), 5–21.

Parker, J. C., '"Made-in-America Revolutions"? The "Black University" And the American Role in the Decolonization of the Black Atlantic', *Journal of American History*, 96 (2009), 727–50.

Patterson, R. S., 'American Influences on Progressive Education in Canada', *The School*, 26 (1938), 472–7.

Pattison, M., *Suggestions on Academical Organisation* (Edinburgh: Edmonston and Douglas, 1868).

—, 'Review of the Situation', in M. Sanderson (ed.), *The Universities in the Nineteenth Century* (London, 1975), pp. 135–6.

Pennybacker, S. D., *From Scottsboro to Munich: Race and Political Culture in 1930s Britain* (Princeton, NJ, and Woodstock: Princeton University Press, 2009).

Penson, L. M., 'The Origin of the Crown Agency Office', *English Historical Review*, 40 (1925), 196–206.

Perkin, H. J., *The Rise of Professional Society: England since 1880* (London: Routledge, 1989).

Perraton, H. J., *Learning Abroad: A History of the Commonwealth Scholarship and Fellowship Plan* (Cambridge: Cambridge Scholars Publishing, 2009).

—, 'Overseas students in British universities 1900–2010: Practice without policy', paper delivered at the Institute of Historical Research, London (Mar. 2011).

Perrone, F., 'Women Academics in England, 1870–1930', *History of Universities*, 12 (1993), 339–67.

Phillips, A. A., *A. A. Phillips on the Cultural Cringe* (Melbourne: Melbourne University Press, 2006).

Phillips, H., and H. M. Robertson, *The University of Cape Town 1918–1948: The Formative Years* (Cape Town: UCT Press, 1993).

Phillipson, D. J. C., 'The National Research Council of Canada: Its Historiography, Its Chronology, Its Bibliography', *Scientia Canadensis*, 15 (1991), 177–93.

Picken, D. K., 'Thomas Howell Laby, 1880–1946', *Obituary Notices of Fellows of the Royal Society*, 5 (1948).

Pickles, K., 'Colonial Counterparts: The First Academic Women in Anglo-Canada, New Zealand and Australia', *Women's History*, 10 (2001), 273–98.

Pietsch, T., 'Wandering Scholars? Academic Mobility and the British World, 1850–1940', *Journal of Historical Geography*, 36 (2010), 377–87.

—, 'Between the Nation and the World: J. T. Wilson and Scientific Networks in the Early Twentieth Century', in B. M. Bennett and J. M. Hodge (eds), *Science and Empire: Knowledge and Networks of Science across the British Empire, 1800–1970* (New York: Palgrave Macmillan, 2011), pp. 140–60.

—, 'Many Rhodes: Travelling Scholarships and Imperial Citizenship in the British Academic World, 1880–1940', *History of Education*, 40 (2011), 1–17.

—, '"Mending a Broken World": The Universities and the Nation, 1918–36', in L. Beers and G. Thomas (eds), *Brave New World: Imperial and Democratic Nation-Building in Britain between the Wars* (London: Institute of Historical Research, 2012), pp. 161–80.

—, 'Rethinking the British World', *Journal of British Studies*, 52 (2013).

Pitt, S. A., *Memorandum: Libraries of South Africa, Rhodesia and Kenya Colony* (New York: Carnegie Corporation of New York, 1929).

Potter, S. J., *News and the British World: The Emergence of an Imperial Press System 1876–1922* (Oxford: Clarendon Press, 2003).

—, 'Empire, Cultures and Identities in Nineteenth- and Twentieth-Century Britain', *History Compass*, 5 (2007), 51–71.

—, 'Webs, Networks and Systems: Globalization and the Mass Media in the Nineteenth- and Twentieth- Century British Empire', *Journal of British Studies*, 46 (2007), 621–46.

Prentice, A., 'Boosting Husbands and Building Community: The Work of Twentieth-Century Faculty Wives', in P. Stortz and E. L. Panayotidis (eds), *Historical Identities: The Professoriate in Canada* (Toronto: University of Toronto Press), pp. 271–98.

Prest, J., 'The Asquith Commission', in B. H. Harriso (ed.), *The History of the University of Oxford: Vol. 8, the Twentieth Century* (Oxford: Clarendon, 1994), pp. 27–44.

Pycior, H. M., N. G. Slack and P. G. Abir-Am (eds), *Creative Couples in the Sciences* (New Brunswick, NJ: Rutgers University Press, 1996).

Rae, I. D., 'They Had to Go: Australian Chemists Who Took Doctor of

Philosophy Degrees in Britain, 1945–65', *Historical Records of Australian Science*, 12 (1999), 331–61.

Raj, K., *Relocating Modern Science: Circulation and the Construction of Knowledge in South Asia and Europe, 1650–1900* (Basingstoke: Palgrave Macmillan, 2007).

—, 'Introduction: Circulation and Locality in Early Modern Science', *British Journal for the History of Science*, 43 (2010), pp. 513–17.

Ridington, J., *Libraries in Canada: A Study of Library Conditions and Needs* (Toronto: Ryerson Press, 1933).

Rimmer, D., and A. Kirk-Greene (eds), *The British Intellectual Engagement with Africa in the Twentieth Century* (London: Macmillan, 2000).

Ritchie, W. (ed.), *The History of the South African College, 1829–1918* (Cape Town: T. M. Miller, 1918).

Roberts, J. K., 'The Design of an Induction Motor with Large Air Gap and Rotating Field Magnets', *Proceedings of the Royal Society of Victoria*, 32 (1919–20), 156–63.

Roberts, J. K. and A. R. Miller, *Heat and Thermodynamics* (London: 1960).

Robinson, C. S., 'Kenneth Bingham Quinan', *The Chemical Engineer* (1966), 290–7.

Robinson, R., *Africa and the Victorians: The Official Mind of Imperialism* (London: MacMillan, 1961).

Rogers, G. E., 'Robertson, Thorburn Brailsford (1884–1930)', *Australian Dictionary of Biography*, (2006), accessed 18 Nov. 2007, http://goo.gl/k9NnV.

Rose, E. P. F., and M. S. Rosenbaum, 'British Military Geologists: The Formative Years to the End of the First World War', *Proceedings of the Geologists' Association*, 104 (1993).

Rostow, E. V., J. Harney, A. Côté and E. Sirluck (eds), *Nationalism and the University* (Toronto: University of Toronto Press, 1973).

Rothblatt, S., *The Revolution of the Dons: Cambridge and Society in Victorian England* (London: Faber and Faber, 1968).

—, *The Modern University and Its Discontents the Fate of Newman's Legacies in Britain and America* (Cambridge: Cambridge University Press, 1997).

Rothschild, E., 'Arcs of Ideas: International History and Intellectual History', in Gunilla Budde, Sebastian Conrad and Oliver Janz (eds), *Transnationale Geschichte: Themen, Tendenzen Und Theorien* (Göttingen: Vandenhoeck and Ruprecht, 2006), pp. 217–26.

Roy, P., *Indian Traffic: Identities in Question in Colonial and Postcolonial India* (Berkeley, CA: University of California Press, 1998).

Rutherford, E., 'Henry Gwyn Jeffreys Moseley', *Nature*, 96 (1915), 33–4.

Ryan, J. R., 'Visualising Imperial Geography: Halford Mackinder and the Colonial Office Visual Instruction Committee, 1902–1911', *Ecumene: A Journal of Environment, Culture, Meaning*, 1 (1994), 157–76.

—, *Picturing Empire: Photography and the Visualization of the British Empire* (Chicago, IL: University of Chicago Press, 1997).

Sack, R. D., 'Human Territoriality: A Theory', *Annals of the Association of American Geographers*, 73 (1983), 55–74.

Sanderson, M., *Universities and British Industry, 1850–1970* (London:

Routledge and Kegan Paul, 1972).

Sanderson, M. J., 'Introduction', in M. Sanderson (ed.), *The Universities in the Nineteenth Century* (London: Routledge and Kegan Paul, 1975), pp. 1–25.

Schaffer, S., L. Roberts, K. Raj and J. Delbourgo (eds), *The Brokered World: Go-Betweens and Global Intelligence, 1770–1820* (Sagamore Beach, MA: Science History Publications, 2009).

Schroeder-Gudehus, 'Challenge to Transnational Loyalties: International Scientific Organisation after the First World War', *Science Studies*, 3 (1973), 93–118.

Schück, H., and R. Sohlman, *The Life of Alfred Nobel* (London: W. Heinemann, 1929).

Seabrook, J., *The Refuge and the Fortress: Britain and the Flight from Tyranny* (Basingstoke: Palgrave Macmillan, 2009).

Seidel, R., 'Books on the Bomb', *Isis*, 81 (1990), 519–28.

Selleck, R. J. W., *The Shop: The University of Melbourne, 1850–1939* (Melbourne: Melbourne University Press, 2003).

Serle, G., 'Monash, Sir John (1865–1937)', *Australian Dictionary of Biography* (Melbourne University Press, 1986), accessed 29 Mar. 2011, http://goo.gl/pYxKh.

Seth, S., *Subject Lessons: The Western Education of Colonial India* (New Delhi: Duke University Press, 2007).

Shapin, S., *A Social History of Truth: Civility and Science in Seventeenth-Century England* (Chicago, IL: University of Chicago Press, 1994).

—, 'Placing the View from Nowhere: Historical and Sociological Problems in the Location of Science', *Transactions of the Institute of British Geographers*, 23 (1998), 5–12.

Sheehan, N. M., 'Philosophy, Pedagogy and Practice: The Iode and the Schools in Canada, 1900–1945', *Historical Studies in Education*, 2 (1990), 307–22.

Sherington, G., 'Athleticism in the Antipodes: The A.A.G.P.S. of New South Wales', *History of Education Review*, 12 (1983), 16–28.

Sherington, G., and J. Horne, 'Modes of Engagement: Universities and Schools in Australia, 1850–1914', in P. Cunningham, S. Oosthuizen and R. Taylor (eds), *Beyond the Lecture Hall: Universities and Community Engagement from the Middle Ages to the Present Day* (Cambridge: University of Cambridge, Faculty of Education, 2009), pp. 133–50.

Shotton, F. W., 'William Bernard Robinson King', *Biographical Memoirs of Fellows of the Royal Society*, 9 (1963), 171–82.

Silver, H., "Things Change but Names Remain the Same': Higher Education Historiography 1975–2000', *History of Education*, 35 (2006), 121–40.

Simpson, R., *How the Phd Came to Britain* (Guildford: Society for Research into Higher Education, 1983).

Sinclair, K., *A History of the University of Auckland, 1883–1983* (Auckland: 1983).

Sinha, M., *Colonial Masculinity: The 'Manly Englishman' and the 'Effeminate Bengali' in the Late Nineteenth Century* (Manchester: Manchester University Press, 1995).

Sivasundaram, S., *Nature and the Godly Empire: Science and Evangelical*

Mission in the Pacific, 1795–1850 (Cambridge: Cambridge University Press, 2005).

Skilling, H. G., *Canadian Representation Abroad* (Toronto: Ryerson Press, 1945).

Sommerville, R. S., 'Is Canada Becoming Americanized?' *The Empire Review*, 55 (1926), 537–40.

Springer, H. W., *The Commonwealth of Universities* (London: The Association of Commonwealth Universities, 1988).

Squier, S., 'Conflicting Scientific Feminisms: Charlotte Haldane and Naomi Mitchinson', in B. T. Gates and A. B. Shteir (eds), *Natural Eloquence: Women Re-inscribe Science* (Wisconsin, WI: University of Wisconsin Press, 1997), pp. 179–95.

Stacey, C. P., *Arms, Men and Governments: The War Policies of Canada, 1939–1945* (Ottawa: Queen's Printer, 1970).

Stallybrass, W. T. S., 'Oxford in 1914–18', *Oxford Magazine* (Winter 1939), p. 41.

Stephen, D. M., '"Brothers of the Empire?": India and the British Empire Exhibition of 1924–25', *Twentieth Century British History*, 22 (2011), pp. 164–88.

Stokes, L. D., 'Canada and an Academic Refugee from Nazi Germany: The Case of Gerhard Herzberg', *Canadian Historical Review*, 57 (1976), 150–70.

Stoler, A. L., and F. Cooper, 'Between Metropole and Colony: Rethinking a Research Agenda', in A. L. Stoler and F. Cooper (eds), *Tensions of Empire: Colonial Cultures in a Bourgeois World* (Berkeley, CA: University of California Press, 1997), pp. 1–56.

Stone, L., 'The Size and Composition of the Oxford Student Body, 1580–1910', in L. Stone (ed.), *The University in Society, Vol. 1* (Oxford and Princeton, NJ: Oxford University Press, 1975), pp. 3–111.

Stray, C., 'Flying at Dusk: The 1906 Praelections', in C. Stray (ed.), *The Owl of Minerva: The Cambridge Praelections of 1906* (Cambridge: Proceedings of the Cambridge Philological Society, 2005), 1–12.

—, 'From Oral to Written Examinations: Cambridge, Oxford and Dublin, 1700–1914', *History of Universities*, 20 (2005), 76–130.

Sturdy, S., 'War as Experiment: Physiology, Innovation and Administration in Britain, 1914–1918: The Case of Chemical Warfare', in R. Cooter, M. Harrison and S. Sturdy (eds), *War, Medicine and Modernity* (Phoenix Mill: Sutton Publishing, 1998), pp. 65–80.

Symonds, R., '"The Foundations of All Good and Noble Principles": Oxonians and the Australian Universities in the Nineteenth Century', in H. Morphy and E. Edwards (eds), *Australia in Oxford* (Oxford: Oxford University Press, 1998), pp. 77–89.

—, *Oxford and the Empire* (Oxford: Clarendon Press, 2000).

Tabili, L., *We Ask for British Justice: Workers and Racial Difference in Late Imperial Britain* (Ithaca, NY: Cornell University Press, 1994).

Terraine, J., *Business in Great Waters: The U-Boat Wars, 1916–1945* (London: Cooper, 1989).

Theobald, M. R., *Knowing Women: Origins of Women's Education in Nineteenth-Century Australia* (Cambridge: Cambridge University Press,

1996).

Thompson, A. S., *Imperial Britain: The Empire in British Politics, C.1880–1932* (Harlow: Longman, 2000).

Thompson, G. E., *A History of the University of Otago, 1869–1919* (Dunedin: J. Wilke, 1919).

Thomson, A. D., 'Some Pioneer Women Graduates in Botany from Canterbury University College' (Centre for Studies in New Zealand Science History, date unknown), accessed 30 Sept. 2011, http://goo.gl/3wqZP

Thomson, J. J., 'Sir Richard Threlfall: 1861–1932', *Obituary Notices of Fellows of the Royal Society*, 1 (1932), 45–53.

Tignor, R., *W. Arthur Lewis* (Princeton, NJ: Princeton University Press, 2006).

Todd, A., 'James Kenner, 1885–1974', *Biographical Memoirs of Fellows of the Royal Society*, 25 (1979), 389–405.

Turner, A. Logan, *Sir William Turner, KCB, FRS: A Chapter in Medical History* (Edinburgh: Blackwood, 1919).

Turney, C., U. M. L. Bygott and P. R. Chippendale, *Australia's First: A History of the University of Sydney* (Sydney: University of Sydney in association with Hale and Iremonger, 1991).

Tyrrell, I. R., *Transnational Nation: United States History in Global Perspective since 1789* (Basingstoke: Palgrave Macmillan, 2007).

—, 'Reflections on the Transnational Turn in United States History: Theory and Practice', *Journal of Global History*, 4 (2009), 453–74.

Vincent, E. W., and P. Hinton, *The University of Birmingham: Its History and Significance* (Birmingham: Cornish brothers, 1947).

Visram, R., *Asians in Britain: 400 years of history* (London: Pluto Press, 2002).

Vroom, F. W., *King's College: A Chronicle, 1789–1939* (Halifax, NS: Imperial Publishing Company, 1941).

W. H. G., '[Short Notices]', *Nature*, 25 April 1942.

Wagoner, P. B., 'Precolonial Intellectuals the the Production of Colonial Knowledge', *Comparative Studies in Society and History*, 45 (2003), pp. 783–814.

Waite, P. B., *The Lives of Dalhousie University* (Montreal: McGill-Queen's University Press, 1994).

Wang, Z., 'The First World War, Academic Science, and The "Two Cultures": Educational Reforms at the University of Cambridge', *Minerva*, 33 (1995), 107–27.

Ward, S., 'The End of Empire and the Fate of Britishness', in H. Brocklehurst and R. Phillips (eds), *History, Nationhood and the Question of Britain* (Basingstoke: Palgrave Macmillan, 2003).

Watts, R., 'Gendering the Story: Change in the History of Education', *History of Education*, 34 (2005), 224–41.

—, *Women in Science: A Social and Cultural History* (Abingdon: Routledge, 2007).

Webb, B., *Our Partnership* (London: Longmans Green, 1948).

Weickhardt, L. W., 'Leighton, Arthur Edgar (1873–1961)', *Australian Dictionary of Biography* (Melbourne: Melbourne University Press, 1986), accessed 2 Apr. 2012, http://goo.gl/bpyCA.

Whitehead, C., *Colonial Educators: The British Indian and Colonial Education Service 1858–1983* (London: I. B. Tauris, 2003).

—, 'The Historiography of British Imperial Education Policy, Part I: India', *History of Education*, 34 (2005), 315–29.

—, 'The Historiography of British Imperial Education Policy, Part II: Africa and the Rest of the Colonial Empire', *History of Education*, 34 (2005), 441–54.

Whitehead, K., 'From Youth to "Greatest Pedagogue": William Cawthorne and the Construction of a Teaching Profession in Mid-Nineteenth Century South Australia', *History of Education*, 28 (1999), 395–412.

Williams, B. R., and D. R. V. Wood, *Academic Status and Leadership in the University of Sydney, 1852–1987* (Sydney: University of Sydney, 2006).

Williams, E. T., 'The Rhodes Scholars', in M. G. Brock and M. C. Curthoys (eds), *The History of the University of Oxford: Vol. 7, Part 2, the Nineteenth Century* (Oxford: 2000), pp. 717–28.

Williams, T., *The Chemical Industry in the First World War* (London: Penguin, 1953).

Wilson, J., 'Post-Colonial Relocations: Australia, New Zealand and the Study of the Early European Past', *British Review of New Zealand Studies*, 16 (2006–7), 179–206.

Winter, J. M., 'Oxford and the First World War', in T. H. Aston and B. Harrison (eds), *The History of the University of Oxford: Vol. 8, the Twentieth Century* (Oxford: Oxford University Press, 1994), pp. 3–26.

Withers, C. W. J., 'Reporting, Mapping, Trusting: Making Geographical Knowledge in the Late Seventeenth Century', *Isis*, 90 (1999), 497–521.

—, 'Place and the 'Spatial Turn', in Geography and in History', *Journal of the History of Ideas*, 70 (2009), 637–58.

—, and D. Livingstone, 'Thinking Geographically About Nineteenth Century Science', in D. Livingstone and C. W. J. Withers (eds), *Geographies of Nineteenth Century Science* (Chicago, IL: University of Chicago Press, 2011), pp. 1–20.

Yaffe, L., *History of the Department of Chemistry McGill University* (Montreal: McGill University, 1978).

Young, M., *Malinowski: Odyssee of an Anthropologist 1884–1920* (New Haven, CT: Yale University Press, 2004).

Zachernuk, P. S., *Colonial Subjects: An African Intelligentsia and Atlantic Ideas* (Charlottesville, VA: University of Virginia Press, 2000).

Zeigler, P., *Legacy: Cecil Rhodes, the Rhodes Trust, and the Rhodes Scholarships* (New Haven, CT: Yale, 2008).

Zimmerman, D., *The Great Naval Battle of Ottawa* (Toronto: University of Toronto Press, 1989).

—, '"Narrow-Minded People": Canadian Universities and the Academic Refugee Crises, 1933–1941', *Canadian Historical Review*, 88 (2007), 291–315.

Zuckerman, H., J. R. Cole and J. T. Bruer (eds), *The Outer Circle: Women in the Scientific Community* (New York: W.W. Norton, 1991).

Other published sources

'Conditions of Scholarships Instituted by the Gilchrist Educational Trust for the Benefit of Youth Residing in the Dominion of Canada' (Gilchrist Educational Trust, 1880), accessed 31 Mar. 2011, www.archive.org/details/cihm_01464.

'Holmes, Walter Morrell (1883–1955)', *Encyclopedia of Australian Science*, accessed 21 Oct. 2011, www.eoas.info/biogs/P001694b.htm.

'Incorporation at Oxford' (Oxford University Archives), accessed 10 October 2011, www.oua.ox.ac.uk/enquiries/incorporation.html.

'The British Academic Assistance Council', *Science, New Series*, 77, no. 2009 (1933), pp. 620–1.

'The Elder Overseas Scholarship', accessed 30 Dec. 2010, www.hss.adelaide.edu.au/scholarships/elder_overseas_scholarship.html.

Unpublished dissertations

Boggs, A. M. 'Ontario's Royal Commission on the University of Toronto, 1905–06: Political and Historical Factors that Influenced the Final Report of the Flavelle Commission.' (MA thesis, Ontario Institute for Studies in Education–University of Toronto, 2007).

Dean, K., 'Settler Physics in Australia and Cambridge, 1850–1950' (PhD thesis, University of Cambridge, 2004).

Laidlaw, Z., 'Networks, Patronage and Information in Colonial Governance: Britain, New South Wales and the Cape Colony, 1826–1843' (DPhil thesis, University of Oxford, 2001).

INDEX

Lightning Source UK Ltd.
Milton Keynes UK
UKOW04f1107130316

270071UK00003B/72/P